CHURCH
ADMINISTRATION
HAND-
BOOK

BRUCE P. POWERS, EDITOR

CHURCH ADMINISTRATION HANDBOOK

A REVISED AND COMPLETELY UPDATED EDITION

BROADMAN
&HOLMAN
PUBLISHERS

Nashville, Tennessee

Published by Broadman & Holman Publishers, Nashville, Tennessee
Acquisitions & Development Editor: John Landers
Page Design and Typography: TF Designs, Mt. Juliet, Tennessee

4210-61
0-8054-1061-9

Dewey Decimal Classification: 254
Subject Heading: CHURCH ADMINISTRATION
Library of Congress Card Catalog Number: 96-26334

Scripture quotations are marked KJV, the King James Version of the Bible; NASB, the New American Standard Bible, © the Lockman Foundation, 1960, 1962, 1963, 1968, 1971, 1972, 1973, 1975, 1977, used by permission; NEB, The New English Bible, © The Delegates of the Oxford University Press and the Syndics of the Cambridge University Press, 1961, 1970, reprinted with permission; Phillips, reprinted with permission of Macmillan Publishing Co., Inc., from J. B. Phillips: The New Testament in Modern English, revised edition, © J. B. Phillips 1958, 1960, 1972; and the RSV, Revised Standard Version of the Bible, copyrighted 1946, 1952, © 1971, 1973.

Library of Congress Cataloging-in-Publication Data

Church administration handbook / Bruce P. Powers, editor.
    — Rev. and enlarged ed.
        p.   cm.
    Includes bibliographical references.
    ISBN 0-8054-1061-9
    1. Church management—Handbooks, manuals, etc. I. Powers, Bruce P.
BV652.C49   1996
254—dc20

96-26334
CIP

03 04 05 06 17 16 15

*To the Founding Class of the
Campbell University Divinity School,
pioneer students in a new school and
servant leaders in the twenty-first century*

Meet the Authors

William G. Caldwell
Dr. Caldwell is Professor of Administration, Southwestern Baptist Theological Seminary, Ft. Worth, Texas, and trainer for the National Association of Church Business Administrators.

Robert D. Dale
Dr. Dale is Assistant Executive Director and Director of the Leadership Center, Baptist General Association of Virginia, Richmond, Virginia.

Bob I. Johnson
Dr. Johnson is Dean and Professor of Church Administration, Boyce Bible School, Louisville, Kentucky.

Bruce P. Powers
Dr. Powers is Associate Dean and Langston Professor of Christian Education, Campbell University Divinity School, Buies Creek, North Carolina.

Judy J. Stamey
Dr. Stamey is Minister of Education and Administration, Ridglea West Baptist Church, Fort Worth, Texas, and trainer for the National Association of Church Business Administrators.

Contents

Section One:
How a Minister Relates to Organizations and People

Section Two:
How a Minister Performs Administrative Responsibilities

**Section Three:
How a Minister Develops Leadership and Ministry Skills**

List of Figures

Preface

This completely updated and enlarged edition of the widely-used *Church Administration Handbook*, with more than 40 percent new material, will now be more useful than ever. Church leaders, ministerial students, and professors have expressed thanks for having a comprehensive resource that provides basic principles and guidelines for church administration and leadership. More specifically, readers have appreciated having a guidebook that brings together theology and the practice of ministry within a framework of:

- concern for a church being alive and on mission for Christ;

- concern for church growth and discipleship development;

- concern for the work being done and for those doing it;

- concern for ministers as servant leaders; and

- concern for effective, goal-oriented administration.

This book is designed for two target groups: (1) ministers and staff members who are responsible for guiding their churches in the areas of planning, organizing, staffing, budgeting, and coordinating; and (2) ministerial students who are studying the life and work of a minister in a local church.

The content moves sequentially through three broad categories crucial to administrative leadership: (1) how a minister relates to organizations and to people; (2) how a minister performs administrative functions; and (3) how a minister develops leadership and ministry skills.

Each chapter provides basic information, then gives guidelines and procedures related to the topic. At the end of the book there is a list of resources for further information.

You can study the material systematically from beginning to end, or you can consult chapters topically as in a reference book. You will find a survey of foundational information and procedures in all major areas. The contents are not intended to be exhaustive, but to give sufficient guidance for administrators who then, if specialized assistance is necessary, can go or refer others to the resources listed.

The authors of this volume are well-suited to prepare a basic handbook and textbook for church administration. They have served in local churches, in denominational administrative positions, and as teachers. They are highly respected writers, speakers, and practitioners who believe that administration must support the church through positive, servant leadership among God's people.

This book is companion to the *Christian Education Handbook*, Bruce P. Powers, editor (Nashville: Broadman and Holman Publishers, 1996), one of the primary references and textbooks in educational administration. Together, these two handbooks provide the basic information and guidelines for administration and leadership in a local church.

Response to the first edition from church leaders, ministerial students, and teachers clearly demonstrates the need for resources in administration that give a clear and practical approach to leadership tasks. Many church leaders and theological students have told me, "If I could have just two books for use in the church, give me the *Church Administration* and *Christian Education Handbooks*!"

I would like to express appreciation to the authors, especially for their common vision of a biblically-based, servant-oriented style of leadership that they are sharing at every opportunity; to our colleagues and students who have helped us refine the concepts, values, and skills presented; and to the many denominational and church leaders who reacted to outlines, previewed this material in conferences, and encouraged the publication of this material for others.

I would like to express personal gratitude to John Landers of Broadman & Holman Publishers, who shepherded this project; to my wife, Jean Clark Powers, who assisted with the technical preparation of the manuscript; and to my colleagues and students who have supported, encouraged, and assisted me during the preparation of the manuscript.

Bruce P. Powers
Campbell University Divinity School
Buies Creek, North Carolina

SECTION ONE:

How a Minister Relates to Organizations and People

CHAPTER 1

Managing Christian Churches and Not-for-Profit Organizations

Robert D. Dale

Church administration is ministry, not methods. It's people, not paperwork. It's human processes, not inhumane policies. It's management, not manipulation.

Administration and management refer to an organization's "people processes" and help institutions use their resources well. In the church and other Christian organizations, administration is growing people, not simply doing things. Administration is vital if a church is to reach its mission. But "administrivia" is to be avoided if morale for the mission is to remain high.

ADMINISTRATION: SCIENCE, ART, GIFT

Church administration or management is a science, an art, and a gift. As a science, church management involves procedures and techniques that can be learned by study and by practice. As an art, administration calls for relational sensitivity, intuition, and timing. These artistic "people skills" are largely natural talents, but they can be enhanced by experience and training.

Additionally, the apostle Paul names administration as a spiritual gift (1 Cor. 12:28). Different translations of the New Testament refer to this gift by using a variety of terms such as "governments" (KJV), "administrators" (RSV), "workers of spiritual power" (Phillips), and the "power to guide" (NEB). The Greek term for administration in this passage translates as "helmsman." In the same manner that pilots steer their ships through the rocks and shallows safely to their destinations, ministers help to guide their congregations in the pursuit of their missions. Two important observations about steersmen apply also to Christian managers. First, helmsmen are members of the ship's larger crew. Steering is only one vital function in the operation of a ship or an organization. Likewise, ministers serve a congregation's overall needs. Second, helmsmen take orders from the captain. No minister stands above Christ in the management of Christian ministry.

OVERVIEW: CHOOSING, CREATING, CATALYZING, COORDINATING

Secular business management has become a highly sophisticated, technical field. Since congregations are volunteer, not-for-profit organizations and since ministers generally see themselves as paraprofessional managers, the model that follows is simplified to deal with only four initiative areas. Using this model, four actions—one personal and three congregational—describe church administration.

Fundamentally, church management calls for choosing, creating, catalyzing, and coordinating personal and organizational resources. The model describes basic processes in congregational management and specifies "what" (a definition of the process), "why" (a theological perspective), "who" (initiators of the processes), and "how" (the applications of the process).

CHOOSING: SELF-MANAGEMENT ACTIONS

Ministers who manage congregations or other Christian organizations make three crucial choices: they choose ad-ministry styles, start-up strategies, and a closure approach. These choices reflect the minister's freedom to select options or alternatives in the performance of ministry and management.

YOU CAN CHOOSE YOUR AD-MINISTRY STYLE

What? Ad-ministry style describes the process of selecting and using a management pattern consistently. Choosing a personal approach or a pattern of managing a congregation's or other Christian organization's resources boils down finally to how ministers structure their time. Self-management is, after all, largely the stewardship of time and life.

Why? Theologically, administrators can affirm several statements about style and the stewardship of time. (1) God is the God of time and history. God has done redemptive work through persons and amid history, through the Exodus, the Exile, the incarnation, and the empty tomb. God's use of time for redemption makes the use of our personal time precious. (2) The Bible speaks of two kinds of time: *chronos* and *kairos*. Chronos is the measured, durative time typical of clocks and calendars. All chronos belongs to God. Kairos smacks of timing and refers to time becoming ripe, full, and overflowing with opportunity (Mark 1:15; Luke 4:21; Matt. 16:3;

Luke 12:56). Ministers must use chronos well in order to be ready to use kairos at all. (3) Jesus had time enough to do God's will. Think of the scope of Jesus' task and the relatively short time he had to accomplish it in. Yet he seemed to manage both the task and the time frame without apparent frustration. Jesus knew that persons are given adequate time to accomplish God's purpose in their lives. (4) Grace frees Christians from yesterday's sin and guilt as well as tomorrow's fears and frustrations.

Who? Ministers have numerous resources for selecting a consistent administry style. Friends and advisors offer feedback. Studying the great biblical leaders provides behavioral models of effective ministry. Biographies of Luther, Wesley, famous evangelists and missionaries, and other organizational heroes and heroines yield insights into management styles. Taking into account that past leaders and current mentors minister in settings that differ from our personal circumstances, only we can make the final choice about our personal styles.

How? The basic management challenge for ministers today is self-management. Ministers set their own schedules and do eternal work that's always difficult to measure and evaluate. Time use, then, provides the proof of effective-style stewardship. Some principles guide ministers in time management:

- Find out how you're using your time now. Keep a time diary of your actual work activities for a week. What do you notice about your stewardship of your professional energies?

- Plan to use your time on priorities. Most effective ministers work from a prioritized "To Do" list of daily tasks. We also use a "quiet hour," an uninterrupted time for concentrating on crucial projects. We reserve the times when (thanks to our built-in biological clocks) we are at our best for working on our most challenging tasks. We plan before we attempt to complete our work.

- Work on a weekly and daily schedule. Regular structure improves productivity.

- Handle a piece of work once. Use a three-step cycle of action: start, work, stop.

- Delegate to team members. Free yourself for crucial tasks and give others a chance to participate and grow.

- Pace yourself. Move from intense involvement to "Sabbath" refreshment.

- Group similar tasks together. For example, think "communication" as a category and write a thank-you note while you're waiting for someone to come to the phone for another communication opportunity.

- Plan to grow personally and professionally.

- Live one day at a time.

- When uncertain or frustrated, ask yourself the basic time management question: "What's the best use of my time right now?"

YOU CAN CHOOSE YOUR MINISTRY START-UP STRATEGY

What? Ministry start-up generally refers to the first twelve to eighteen months of establishing ministry in a new post. Given average tenures, from thirty to fifty percent of a minister's total professional life is spent in the management of start-up transitions.

Why? Theologically speaking, the Christian view of history provides a foundation for ministry start-up work. (1) Christianity is a historical religion. The Bible is a book of history. For Christians, history really is His-story. (2) Christians believe history has a purpose. History has beginnings, middles, and ends—just like ministry has personal and organizational chapters. In God's plan, history's theme is redemption. (3) Christ is the apex or pivot point of history. Christ stands at the center of all history. Ministers must guard against an attitude of self-importance, especially at the beginning of a ministry when members often tend to overestimate a new minister's abilities.

Who? Personnel committees and pastor selection committees are increasingly serving temporarily as support groups for ministers. They, or another support network, provide encouragement, information about congregational or organizational reactions, advise on relationships and the progress of programs, give feedback, and help evaluate ministries.

How? Start-up is usually conceived as a three-step process: understanding and using the dynamics of the interim period, knowing what to expect in a new ministry setting, and developing a general strategy for establishing yourself in ministry relationships in a new post.[1] Here are some management ideas for each of the four areas.

Understanding and using the dynamics of the interim period. The interim period actually blends into the next minister's work. How the time between the former minister's resignation, firing, or death has been used determines the beginning point and shapes the climate of ministry start-up. Ordinarily, four issues arise during interim periods.

- The emotions of grief—loss, anger, and guilt—should be recognized and resolved.

- The period creates a management vacuum, shifting the internal leadership circle as old leaders pull back and new leaders emerge.

- Relationships to denominational resources are examined.

- Most important, the interim period allows the basic mission and identity of the church or organization to be evaluated and, if needed, redefined.

Knowing what to expect in a new ministry setting. Checklists of "things to be alert to" during start-up are an important tool. In random order, here are several predictable issues surrounding start-up:

- Most congregations tend to feel the minister is settled in after the moving van is gone and several casseroles have been delivered. More attention is usually paid to physical concerns than to emotional or spiritual issues.

- Generally, the denominational structures expect the new minister "to make things happen."

- The history of a congregation includes more than the statistical and sociological information ordinarily given a new or prospective minister. The congregation's beginnings, heroes, "golden years," conflicts, building programs, and sense of vision shape its present and its future.

- When the self-confidence of the minister or the congregation has eroded during the interim, two perils may develop. The congregation may become overly dependent on the minister as a rescuer. Or, the minister may feel the pressure for a "quick win" and fall back on programs that were successful elsewhere, whether or not these programs fit the needs of the new congregation.

- First impressions of you are built on intuitive responses to *Are you genuine?* and *Do you care?*

- Watch what surprises you during start-up, and take note of those events. Surprises indicate a difference between what you expected and what happened. If a pattern of surprises emerges, new ministers should examine that pattern carefully for expectations that are out-of-kilter.

- The "honeymoon" is a time when the new minister is given extra leeway. This momentum is precious and should be patiently invested in priority ministries.

- Early in start-up, change strategically what is needed, wanted, and supported.

- It's easier to follow effective ministers and build on the trust they've accumulated than to inherit the ill will assigned to ministers who have been disappointments.

- Expect to be tested.

- The end to the honeymoon is frightening and calls for clarifying and renegotiating expectations.

- Members with views like the new minister's will tend to move into the centers of power in the church or organization.

- The first conflict in a new ministry helps "set the rules" for future disagreements.

- When the new minister's leadership style exerts more initiative than the congregation expects, overlaps in responsibility occur, and conflict is apt to surface. When the new minister's leadership style takes less initiative than the congregation expects, vacuums in responsibility develop, and frustration results. The new minister is usually more able to sense the differences and adjust levels of leader initiative appropriately than the congregation-at-large.

Developing a general strategy for establishing yourself in ministry relationships in a new post. Broad strategy for start-up lends a structure for establishing ministry.[2] While numerous approaches are available, some guidelines clarify ministry priorities:

1. Begin with people and build bridging relationships for ministry and for personal encouragement.
2. Help the congregation or organization define its basic purpose, vision, or dream.
3. Build ministry on mainstream needs.
4. Cultivate healthy organizational habits that will facilitate Christian growth.

YOU CAN CHOOSE HOW TO CLOSE OUT A MINISTRY

What? Closure means saying good-bye to a church or organization at the conclusion of a tenure of ministry. Official documents like a constitution and bylaws may specify the mechanics of how the minister terminates, but the minister decides the *manner* of exiting. Closure flavors ministry and tends to make the minister's impact and reputation either better or worse.

Why? Eschatology provides a theological perspective for closure. (1) Christians believe that God will draw history to a close in a purposeful, redemptive, and decisive manner. (2) Human history, like all processes, has an end, and that conclusion is in God's hands.

Who? The minister works with appropriate committees, councils, and task forces to ensure an orderly and productive transition. Official documents may spell out formal procedures for an interim period or tradition may suggest informal approaches.

How? The good-bye process is largely a relational one. While proclamation (evangelism, preaching, teaching, and worship) and pastoral care (counseling, family ministry, grief work, and officiating special events) enter into closure strategies, management is the focus here. Closure involves several attitudes and actions:

- After resigning, ministers immediately become lame ducks and lose their change agent's influence quickly.

- How a congregation's or institution's members react to the minister's resignation is an indication of the minister's overall ad-ministry style. If ministers have encouraged or allowed the congregation to become dependent, the members may feel betrayed and panic. If ministers have developed and expanded the leadership base of the church and if administrative processes have been clearly identified and consistently used, the congregation will face interims with less anxiety and more confidence.

- Lame duck leaders should wrap up unfinished projects rather than attempt to launch new ministries.

- An exit interview may be offered by the minister. The experience of working with an overall responsibility for a church's ministry can lend insights into the potentials, problems, and characteristics of the congregation. This information would be helpful in the search for a new minister.

- A transition packet containing administrative documents and listings of community and denominational resources is a thoughtful gesture. These materials may assist the next minister's start-up.

CREATING: INNOVATIVE CONGREGATIONAL ACTIONS

Some management actions are administratively creative: *dreaming*, *evaluating*, and *planning*. These administrative initiatives focus on originating and producing new ministries and programs.

YOU CAN HELP YOUR CONGREGATION DEFINE ITS DREAM

What? Dreaming is the process of clarifying, taking ownership of, and communicating forcefully the congregation or organization's redemptive vision.[3]

Why? Jesus' vision of the kingdom of God formed his core teaching. (1) Over eighty times in the Gospels, Jesus spoke of the kingdom he came to introduce and embody. He mentioned the "kingdom of God" or the "kingdom of heaven" more than any other theme. (2) Most of Jesus' parables, the center of his teachings, describe what the kingdom is like. (3) The kingdom of God calls persons and their organizations to submit to God's rule and provides Christians with clues to Jesus' dream.

Who? Since every congregation has its own personality and since the Kingdom has a virtually endless variety of local embodiments, the membership at large should shape the congregation's dream of ministry. All leaders in the ministries of the church serve as guides for the process of dreaming.

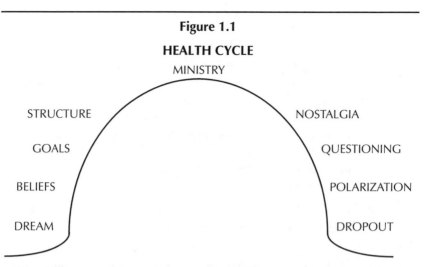

Figure 1.1

HEALTH CYCLE

How? Numerous steps can be used in guiding a congregation or institution to focus on its dream.

- Congregations move through a "health cycle" from vigor to disease (see figure 1.1). The Health Cycle model can be used to "read" the church, to discover the organization's stage of vitality or illness, and to find ways to renew the congregation.

- Broadly stated, healthy congregations build on and are renewed by their dreams, plan proactively, and minister to others. Unhealthy churches doubt themselves into decline (and, occasionally, death), reactively solve problems, and demand to be ministered to themselves.

- Preaching and teaching Jesus' parables can provide a consciousness-raising experience for a congregation to use when beginning to dream together about what God wants from them here and now.

- One important clue to a congregation's current vision is the dream of the founding group. Not all dreams are of equal value, of course. Negative and narrow visions tend to yield more rigid and ideological congregations. Mission-centered and service-oriented beginnings provide a more positive launch pad for the churches they birth.

- A balance between leader vision and broad congregational consensus yields two crucial elements for the dreaming process: *sharp focus* and *general ownership* of the vision.

YOU CAN HELP YOUR CONGREGATION EVALUATE ITS MINISTRY PROGRAMS

What? Evaluating is the process of discovering and duplicating the congregation or organization's successes while discovering and eliminating its failures. Evaluation provides an appraisal, feedback, and a control mechanism.

Why? Theologically, judgment provides a doctrinal framework for the administrative process of evaluation. Several affirmations apply: (1) While judgment is built into the fabric of human experience, God is the final judge. Both the New Testament and the creeds of Christian history declare that at the end of history Christ will return to judge. (2) Mere humans lack the objectivity to make valid judgments on others' lives. Christ pointed out our limited perspectives when he observed that we may be critical of the specks in others' eyes while we overlook the logs in our own eyes (Matt. 7:3–4). (3) Self-evaluation is, however, an ongoing discipline for every Christian (1 Cor. 9:24–27; 11:28). (4) In congregational settings, we measure a volunteer worker's service by the goals set earlier by the congregation-at-large. This approach is a type of self-evaluation, too. If the original goal-setting process involved the total congregation, then this volunteer has made two commitments to goals—one during the development of the congregation's original goals and another when he or she agreed to serve in the ministry programs of the church. Actions taken toward these goals can be observed and evaluated.

Who? Every group in a congregation with responsibility for ministry actions or for resource management should evaluate its work regularly. Many congregations use a representative church council to appraise the total program of the congregation. The evaluation process of monitoring, reviewing, and correcting intends to turn trial-and-error into trial-and-success (figure 1.2).

Figure 1.2

EVALUATION CYCLE

How? Evaluation involves five critical elements:

- Evaluating calls us to measure performance against purpose. Good evaluation demands that standards of effectiveness or success be established beforehand. Goals always precede evaluation.

- Evaluating uses both quantitative and qualitative information. *Objective* information—like statistics, attendance reports, and budget summaries—need to be considered. Additionally, *subjective* materials—opinions and other clues to the level of morale in the congregation—need to be included to balance perspectives and blend feelings into the factual picture.

- Evaluating uses a range of persons and a variety of methods. Both planners and implementers, along with persons involved in a program and those not involved, should be included in the evaluative process. Statistical records, interviews, questionnaires, and pretests and posttests provide a variety of data. Involve as many members as possible and gather only information that will be used. When information is requested, members assume it will be used and are disillusioned if it isn't. Expect persons with negative perspectives to speak up early and loudly; take their opinions seriously without overreacting.

Figure 1.3

EVALUATION MODEL

PAST **Positive (+)** *"In the past, I am proud* *that our church has . . ."*	**PAST** **Negative (-)** *"In the past, I am disappointed* *that our church has . . ."*
FUTURE **Positive (+)** *"In the future, I hope* *that our church will . . ."*	**FUTURE** **Negative (-)** *"In the future, I fear* *that our church will . . ."*

- Evaluation is a continuing cycle. Pre-evaluation provides status checks before a ministry is launched. Mid-evaluation double-checks progress either to assure that the project is on course or to make mid-course corrections. Post-evaluation combines an immediate debriefing after a project is completed as well as more seasoned reflections later on.

A model for evaluation should invite both positive and negative perspectives, and consider both past and future time frames (see figure 1.3).

YOU CAN HELP YOUR CONGREGATION PLAN EFFECTIVE MINISTRY PROGRAMS

What? Planning is the process of creating your organizational future before it happens. Planning attempts to write history in advance.

Why? Hope provides a theological foundation for planning. (1) God modeled orderliness and planning in creation and redemption. (2) The future is God's possession. Only God knows the future; only God holds the future. Planning, then, becomes an act of faith that the God who gave us today will also provide a meaningful tomorrow. (3) Ultimately, the Christian's hope is Christ. (4) Christians live between the times. Our planning efforts strive to move our organizations from where we are to where God wants us to be.

Who? The leader team for church planning includes the pastor and other church staff ministers as facilitators and resource persons as well as a specific planning group, like a church council. Remember that people support what they help plan. The participation guideline for planning, then, is: *Everyone who will be expected to implement the plan should be involved in planning.*

How? Planning provides congregations and organizations with reasonable targets for fulfilling their dream. Planning processes usually involve several considerations:

- Project planning, involving concrete acts of ministry, is the least abstract and simplest type of planning. Project planning appeals to smaller organizations and members with more concrete styles of thinking.

- In general, churches practice two types of planning: *operational* and *directional*. Operational planning is usually referred to as annual planning and implements the shorter-range operations of the dream. Directional planning, or long-range planning, forecasts the future needs and wants of your congregation, sets directions, and usually builds on a multi-year framework. A variety of computerized planning models are available for church use.

Figure 1.4

PLANNING SEQUENCE

- Ordinarily, planning begins with the dream or purpose of the congregation or with the needs of the church and community and, using that beginning point, develops goals. Budgeting, then, builds on the goals. New or different organizational structures extend out of budgeted goals. Ministry events and, finally, detailed actions are projected (see figure 1.4).

- Plan from ends to means and implement your plans from means to ends.

- Set congregational goals that are high but possible.

CATALYZING: RESPONSIVE CONGREGATIONAL ACTIONS

Catalysts in chemistry cause reactions and speed changes; they are change agents. Budgeting, motivating, and advertising are catalytic management activities for churches.

YOU CAN CHANGE YOUR CONGREGATION
THROUGH YOUR CHURCH BUDGET

What? Budgeting is the process of allocating resources toward goals by expressing the church's dream in dollars. An organization's budget is a theological document because it's an expression of its redemptive dream.

Why? Stewardship to the individual Christian and budgeting to the congregation reflect our response to God as Creator. (1) God calls believers to be partners and trustees in creation. Jesus followed this pattern when he made the good steward a key figure in the parables. (2) Our response to God's order of creation demands that Christians use things responsibly, love persons responsibly, and worship God responsibly. (3) The challenge of Christian stewardship is to *use* things, *love* persons, and *worship* God without mixing the verbs and objects. To mismatch the verbs and objects, such as using people, is to sin.

Who? In some smaller churches, an informal group may suggest a budget structure. But most congregations elect a committee (variously called stewardship, budget, or finance) to examine ministry plans, gather information on giving and spending, propose a basic budget structure, and implement an ongoing program of stewardship education.

How? Budgeting is resource management. The budget of an organization provides for the coordinated use of the church's four primary resources: money—through an adopted, unified budget; time—via the church's calendar; facilities—by way of the development and maintenance of buildings and properties; and, most importantly, people—through a plan of evangelism, member development, and leader enlistment and training.

The steps in budgeting vary with the philosophy being used. Ministry-action budgeting is the approach outlined here.[4]

- Analyze the congregation's current ministries.

- Request ministry groups to propose actions for the coming year.

- Evaluate the proposals.

- Prepare a budget for congregational discussion.

- Present the revised budget for congregational adoption.

- Fully educate the congregation about the budget and attempt to subscribe it completely.

- Keep the congregation informed throughout the church year about progress toward the ministry actions and the funds involved.

- Begin the review and evaluation process for the next year's budgeting procedures.

YOU CAN HELP YOUR CONGREGATION IMPROVE ITS MOTIVATIONAL CLIMATE

What? Motivating is the process of helping members discover, take ownership of, and use their reservoirs of spiritual energy.

Why? Theologically, the Holy Spirit is the Christian's motivator. (1) The Holy Spirit lives within the Christian (John 14:17). This biblical insight favors the internal theories of motivation ("Persons are motivated on their own to do something.") over the external approaches ("I cause others to act."). Manipulative "carrot-on-a-stick" approaches to motivating others are inconsistent with a reliance on the Spirit of Christ. Motivation in congregational settings, then, becomes largely a matter of setting a motivational climate and helping members channel their energies. (2) The Holy Spirit energizes Christians by encouraging and guiding us (John 14:18; Matt. 28:20). (3) The Holy Spirit ministers actively to our needs (John 14:25–31). The Spirit's internal ministry to our personal concerns is the model of motivational leadership for us to follow.

Who? The leader team for improving the motivational climate includes all organizational directors and leaders. Persons who have other members under their supervision must work to uplift the morale level of their portion of the overall organization.

How? Setting a motivational climate and helping members channel their energies toward the congregation's dream is the challenge of church leaders. Several management actions yield big dividends:

- Create a motivational climate by helping members meet their legitimate needs. People enjoy participating in an organization they can both give to and get from. Legitimate personal needs include our desire for recognition, structure, and intimacy. Legitimate interpersonal needs involve belonging with others in a meaningful group, influencing our group's life, and being loved by important others.

- Create a motivational climate by building a ministry team. Administrators know that churches thrive on an atmosphere of "We did it!" teamwork rather than a self-glorifying "I did it!" attitude. Once, I heard a pastor brag, "I raised three million dollars in a week. I deserve to tell them what to do!" Who does that pastor think contributed the three million? A "we" atmosphere builds a team for long-term, constructive ministry.

- Create a motivational climate by reaching clear agreements with your ministry team. People are motivated by knowing what's expected of them, by negotiating some issues, and by agreeing on their privileges and responsibilities. Groups are held together by promises their members make to one another. These promises or contracts keep us from the demotivating tyranny of undefined expectations. Leaders must build and maintain their credibility if they are to create a motivational climate.

YOU CAN HELP YOUR CHURCH ADVERTISE ITS MINISTRIES

What? Advertising is the process of communicating Christ's message and the congregation's image to its community by means of people, print, and other media.

Why? The concept of revelation provides a theological foundation for advertising the congregation's vision. (1) A revelation is an unveiling. For Christians, revelation refers almost exclusively to God and to God's redemptive actions. (2) God takes the initiative to establish a personal relationship with us. Then, believers become a basic channel for revealing God's kingdom and work. (3) God's revelation is concrete, direct, intense, and awesome. Christ's incarnation is the highest and most concrete revelation of God's nature and intent. (4) Revelation is dialogic. God is revealed to us; we praise and witness to God's mighty acts.

Who? The pastor and church staff usually coordinate communications about the congregation's ministry. Some churches elect a public relations committee to assist the overall congregation and its program groups in telling the stories of their ministry processes and events.

How? Just as a variety of approaches were used to communicate God's mighty acts (Heb. 1:1–2), congregations must work strategically to publicize their work. The management of an advertising process incorporates several steps:

- Advertising requires focus. That is, the answers to some questions keep advertising efforts on target. Which message? To whom? For what response? When? Through which media?

- Advertising means understanding the other person's circumstances and telling others how your ministry benefits them.

- Advertising uses "power" words to trigger a positive emotional response to your church and its ministries. Power words are graphic communication tools that make your church attractive and credible.

- Advertising uses images as well as words. A logo and pictures identify your church and its work.

- Advertising uses all available media. Desktop publishing, letterheads, bulletin boards, newsletters, and the print and electronic media help your church impact its members and its prospects.

- Advertising shows quality. Attractive material has impact. It sets moods, creates images, and builds expectations.

- Advertising conveys a clear message. One theme is presented to one audience. The action you hope your reader/hearer will take is specified.

COORDINATING:
BALANCING CONGREGATIONAL ACTIONS

Coordination calls on the church manager to relate the varied elements and activities properly so that ministry happens harmoniously: coordinating by organizing, staffing, and team building. These processes draw the people and administrative processes together for ministry.

YOU CAN ORGANIZE YOUR CONGREGATION'S MINISTRY

What? Organizing is the process of developing a structure and work plan that helps persons become meaningfully involved in the goals of the congregation.

Why? God's creation provides a theological perspective for the organizing process. (1) God is ultimately responsible for the being of the world. Creation depends on God to sustain it. (2) God's creation is good. This view argues against religious leaders who claim any organization is bad. (3) People are to be responsible stewards of God's creation. Organizational structuring is one congregational application of creation.

Who? The pastor, church staff, church council, program organizational leaders, and finally the entire congregation are responsible for creating new ministry units and pruning away old ones.

How? Organizing the congregation for action is a basic management practice.

- How much organization is necessary? A congregation is under-organized if portions of its dream have no structured work units to implement them. A congregation is over-organized if structured work units exist but have no direct connection to the dream. The implicit warning in these two statements is simple: Don't create unnecessary organizational units since new units have to be maintained after they are set up.

- Form follows function: That's the master principle of organization. The product you want determines the organization you need.

- Most organizing efforts move through a fairly predictable cycle.

  1. Define the congregation's dream.

  2. Define the ministry program you need to organize.

  3. Divide the ministry into manageable units.

  4. Relate the units of ministry into a workable arrangement.

  5. Enlist workers.

6. Clarify workers' tasks and train them to do the job.

7. Empower the workers to do their ministries by delegating authority to them that is equal to their responsibility.

8. Evaluate the program of ministry in case some reorganization is needed.

YOU CAN COORDINATE STAFFING YOUR CONGREGATION'S ORGANIZATIONS

What? Staffing is the process of finding, enlisting, training, and encouraging the congregation's volunteer and paid leaders.

Why? Spiritual gifts provide the basis for staffing the church's organization. (1) Every Christian is gifted for service. More than thirty different spiritual gifts are mentioned in the five New Testament listings (1 Cor. 12:4–10; 1 Cor. 12:28–30; Eph. 4:11; Rom. 12:6–8; 1 Pet. 4:10–11). All of these gifts are God-given and are closely tied to the Christian virtue of love (1 Cor. 13). (2) All of the spiritual gifts are significant and are designed to advance the gospel. (3) God provides every congregation with the human resources to implement its Kingdom dream. Members are the most valuable resource in any congregation.

Who? Most churches use a nominating committee to find, enlist, and offer preservice training to workers. Computerized talent searches simplify this committee's work.

How? Several issues are crucial to staffing church organizations:

- The ideal staffing system relates three persons to each job—one person training for the future, one doing the job now, and one experienced worker coaching the other two.

- Persons who are responsible for enlisting workers need to be clear about the motivations, rewards, and morale levels of volunteer workers (and how these factors differ from those of employees).

- Forecast the church's leadership needs.

- Identify future leaders.

- Enlist needed leaders. Link their personal gifts with organizational goals.

- Provide a listing of tasks and expectations and agree on what work will be done.

- Provide training opportunities for the new volunteer leaders.

- Provide supervisory-skills training for directors who will guide the volunteer staff.[5]

YOU CAN BUILD YOUR CHURCH'S MINISTRY TEAM

What? Team building is the process of turning diversity toward unity. Team building efforts are needed anytime two or more persons depend on each other and work together.

Why? Paul's "body of Christ" image of the church (Rom. 12 and 1 Cor. 12) lends theological substance to the management challenge of team building. (1) The body of Christ has diverse parts. Leadership in team building and coordination is required if congregations are to remain robust (Rom. 12:4,6). (2) All of the diversity is necessary for Christ's body to function well (1 Cor. 12:14–26). (3) Christ is the unifier of the diversity (1 Cor. 12:12–13).

Who? The pastor, church staff, and church council provide the primary resources for team building.

How? Team building holds two congregational concerns in balanced tension: creating a family atmosphere and getting ministry done. (See chapter 3, "Working with People.")

IMPLICATIONS: ACT NOW

The administrative model of choosing, creating, catalyzing, and coordinating provides church leaders several advantages. First, a framework for conceptualizing and examining your management tasks provides a platform for confident actions. Second, practice and theology are naturally and mutually related in this model. Third, this model helps ministers discover the broad administrative area(s) and/or specific skills they need to develop by further research and education.

These three advantages call for simple actions: think, believe, grow. The helm of the ship is in your hands. Act now as a Christian administrator.

CHAPTER 2

Church Organization

Bruce P. Powers

Organization in a church is *structure* designed to enable a congregation to make disciples, help members grow, and develop spiritual power in their lives. Organization is a way to help people find a place and direction in their spiritual journey; it is the design for relating to each other effectively in order to do the Lord's work.

Organization begins with the nature and mission of the church, for it is biblical foundations that should always determine programs and ministries. There are five distinguishing characteristics of the New Testament church: *worship, proclamation, education, ministry,* and *fellowship.* It is these traits that we define as the primary functions of a local church and around which all organization develops.

To support these five functions, we add a sixth that is implicit in Scripture and very much needed in today's church—*leadership.* Administrative leadership is the glue, or support, that enables the five primary functions to operate together—as the *body* of Christ. Thus, when a congregation is organized and functioning correctly, all efforts are focused on fulfilling the purpose of the church under the lordship of Jesus Christ. (See Eph. 4:1–16 and Rom. 12.)

Based on the functions of a church, programs and organizations are developed. These are *means,* or *ways,* for achieving the mission or purpose of the church; they are not *ends* in themselves. Each program or organization exists to achieve a specific purpose or portion of a church's ministry. And each, theoretically, should be the most effective structure to achieve the purpose for which it exists.

ORGANIZATIONAL DISTINCTIVES

Because of common objectives among evangelical churches—making disciples, enabling members to grow and mature, and developing spiritual awareness and power in the lives of believers—similar structures have evolved among denominations to enable churches to do their work. For example, most churches have various types of worship and fellowship opportunities as well as organizations to facilitate Bible study, discipleship development, mission activities, and Christian living. Although names of these may vary, such as Sunday school, Bible school, and church school, the functions and general organizational principles are remarkably similar from denomination to denomination.

BASIC CHURCH PROGRAMS

These structures or organizations are the primary channels for the ongoing ministries provided by a congregation. Activities are usually designed according to the ability and/or need level of participants. Basic church programs are designed to help a church achieve its objectives and, also, to meet the general needs of people in the congregation.[1]

The *basic* programs, or organizations, that exist in some form in most evangelical and Protestant churches will be covered in this chapter. Each program has a cluster of tasks that are essential, continuing, and important to the work of a church (see figure 2.1).

Figure 2.1

BASIC CHURCH PROGRAMS

There are six established church programs, each with a cluster of tasks that are basic, continuing, and of primary importance to the life of a church. Each program develops organization and seeks to involve the congregation in its work. These organizations form the foundation of church structure, and thus are called basic church programs. Listed below are the tasks that each program assumes in the life of the church.

BIBLE TEACHING

1. Reach persons for Bible study.
2. Teach the Bible.
3. Witness to persons about Christ and lead them into church membership.
4. Minister to persons in need.
5. Lead members to worship.

DISCIPLESHIP TRAINING

1. Reach persons for discipleship training.
2. Orient new church members for discipleship and personal ministry.
3. Equip church members for discipleship and personal ministry.

4. Teach theology, doctrine, ethics, history, and church polity.

5. Train church leaders for their tasks.

MUSIC MINISTRY

1. Provide musical experiences in congregational services.

2. Provide church music education.

3. Lead the church to witness and minister through music.

4. Assist the church programs in use of and training related to music.

BROTHERHOOD/MEN'S MISSION PROGRAM

1. Engage in missions activities.

2. Teach missions.

3. Pray for and give to missions.

4. Develop personal ministry.

WOMAN'S MISSIONARY UNION/WOMEN'S MISSION PROGRAM

1. Teach missions.

2. Engage in mission action and personal witnessing.

3. Support missions.

PASTORAL MINISTRIES

1. Lead the church in accomplishing its mission.

2. Proclaim the gospel to believers and nonbelievers.

3. Care for the church's members and other persons in the community.

All programs interpret and undergird the work of the local church and the denominational groups with which the congregation cooperates in mission and ministry efforts.

Other organizations are necessary to provide effective ministry in a church, but are not considered basic programs for all the congregation. These are primarily service-oriented (like media or recreation ministries) or specialized programs for subgroups in the congregation (like a club for senior adults).[2]

DETERMINING ORGANIZATIONAL STRUCTURE

The essential elements in deciding how to organize include:

1. Identifying the specific purpose of the organization.

Ask questions such as: Why does (should) it exist? What is its unique contribution to the church? What would happen if we did not have this organization?

2. Finding the best way to achieve the stated purpose.

Ask questions such as: What resources (leaders, facilities, denominational assistance, financial support, and such) are available? What are the priorities within and among the various organizations? What structures will provide efficient and effective team work among leaders and also contribute toward fulfilling the church's objectives?

3. Defining clear areas of responsibility and decision-making in the overall administration of the church, and in each component.

Ask questions such as: What is the distinct responsibility for each position? What decisions should the person in each position be able to make without consultation? What are the positions that link each level (or unit) with the larger body for purposes of planning, evaluation, communication, and such? Do all leaders have someone to whom they are responsible?

GENERAL COORDINATION

An effective organizational structure includes a church council or other administrative group which would be charged with planning, coordinating, and evaluating the church's programs and ministries. (Information about a church council is given in figure 2.2.)

Figure 2.2

CHURCH COUNCIL

The church council serves as a forum for a church's leaders to guide planning, coordination, conducting, and evaluation of the total work of the church. The council depends on the various church organizations to implement the church's program according to their assigned tasks. As chair of the church council, the pastor is able to lead in the development of a unified program that gives major attention to priority needs.

PRINCIPLE FUNCTION: to assist the church to determine its course, and to coordinate and evaluate its work.

METHOD OF ELECTION: church leaders become members of the church council as a result of election to designated church leadership positions.

TERM OF OFFICE: corresponds to term of office in church-elected position.

MEMBERS: pastor (chair), church staff members, program directors, deacon chair, stewardship committee chair, missions committee chair, and other committee chairs as needed.

DUTIES:

- Help the church understand its mission and define its priorities.
- Coordinate studies of church and community needs.
- Recommend to the church coordinated plans for evangelism, missions, Christian development, worship, stewardship, and ministry.
- Coordinate the church's schedule of activities, special events, and use of facilities.
- Evaluate progress and the priority use of church resources. In most churches, this group would be chaired by the pastor and would include:
- church staff members,
- leaders of all church programs and ministry organizations,
- leader of the deacons (or church board), and

- chairpersons of key committees (those closely related to the work of church programs and ministries, such as missions, stewardship, and nominating committees).

In larger churches with several full-time ministers, activities might need to be planned, coordinated, and evaluated through a separate, specialized council or committee in each major area of work. Members would include church staff personnel who have an assignment for that program or ministry, leaders representing the various components, and age-group coordinators (if used) as illustrated for educational ministry in figure 2.3.

Figure 2.3

ORGANIZATION FOR EDUCATIONAL ADMINISTRATION

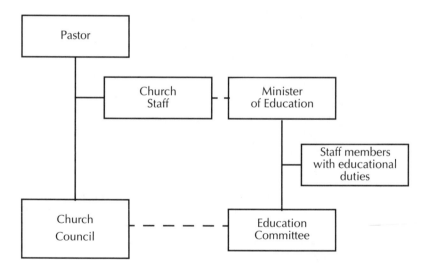

Similarly, each program organization would have an administrative council or staff to guide the work for which it is responsible, as shown in figure 2.4. (Information about a program council/staff is given in figure 2.5.)

Figure 2.4

ORGANIZATION FOR CHURCH PROGRAM ADMINISTRATION

Figure 2.5

PROGRAM COUNCIL AND/OR STAFF

PRINCIPAL FUNCTIONS: To assist the program to determine its course, to coordinate program efforts, and to relate to the church council for overall coordination.

MEMBERSHIP AND METHOD OF ELECTION: Directors of major units/age divisions in the program become members of the program council as a result of election by the church to program leadership positions. If there are no age division directors, the leader of each department represents his or her group.

TERM OF OFFICE: Corresponds to term of office in church-elected position.

REPORT: As a program, to the church; director serves on church council, or other general coordinating body.

DUTIES:
- Help the program understand its mission and define its priorities in the light of church priorities.
- Conduct studies of church and community needs related to program tasks.
- Coordinate the program's activities and schedules.
- Evaluate progress, effectiveness, and the priority use of church resources.

AGE-DIVISION COORDINATION

Whereas most administration is handled *within* programs, those who work with similar age groups in different organizations often need to link up to coordinate work and support each other. This can be achieved through age-level coordination.

The simplest approach is for leaders of a particular age division to meet periodically to coordinate their work and the use of space, equipment, and supplies. This is most effective for small churches and age divisions with few workers.

Another approach is to schedule periodic conferences for age-division coordination, the purpose being to deal with issues of common concern among leaders within each age group. Persons in each group could elect a convener to facilitate meetings and channel messages.

In large churches, age-group coordinators often will be necessary (some churches use directors or ministers in this role). Their principle function is to facilitate the work of all programs within the age division throughout the church. Coordinators should serve on the education committee, or church council. (Descriptive information concerning age-division coordination is given in figure 2.6.)

Figure 2.6

AGE-DIVISION COORDINATION

Age-division coordination may be accomplished in three ways: self-coordination, age-division conferences, or age-division coordinators/directors. The approach used by a church is determined by the complexity of the organization within the age division.

SELF-COORDINATION

Self-coordination exists when organization leaders of an age division voluntarily coordinate their work and the use of space, equipment, and supplies. It is the simplest and most effective. It is particularly suited for small churches and age divisions with few workers.

AGE-DIVISION COORDINATION CONFERENCES

Principal function: to serve as a counseling, advisory, and coordinating group when self-coordination is not adequate.

Members: leaders of departments, choirs, and other organizational units of a particular age division.

Convener: one of the members of the group elected by the group.

AGE-DIVISION COORDINATORS/DIRECTORS

Principal function: to counsel age-division leaders and coordinate the work of units within the age division as assigned.

Age-division coordinators are elected by the church and responsible to the pastor or minister of education as designated by the church. The pastor leads in developing procedures for providing consultative and advisory services to the minister of music and other staff members as needed.

DUTIES:

- Consult with department leaders to resolve philosophical, procedural, and scheduling problems.
- Give assistance in classifying and enrolling new members.
- Consult with department leaders to coordinate the use of program materials, supplies, equipment, and space.
- Give individual guidance to department directors and workers.
- Work with church program leaders to provide training opportunities for department leaders and workers.

- Work with director of recreation to provide appropriate services.
- Give assistance as needed to department directors in discovering and enlisting department workers.
- Coordinate age-division visitation.
- Encourage and provide assistance to leaders in planning and evaluating their work.
- Serve as ex officio members of program council.

GROUPING PEOPLE

There are three general approaches to dividing congregations into manageable groups for educational or other purposes: *age, compatibility,* and *interest*. To a lesser extent, some churches choose to create additional subgroupings by using distinctives such as gender and marital status.

AGE

Age grouping, or grading, is used most often when trying to match developmental needs of individuals with the educational experiences provided. This is the approach usually recommended by denominational program leaders to facilitate an ongoing, systematic study of curriculum materials by all ages.

Under this plan, organizational groupings follow a general pattern, but often are adjusted when subgrouping to allow for compatibility and/or interest groups. For example, the "Organization Planning Chart," figure 2.7, lists the major divisions, suggested maximum enrollment per unit, and worker-pupil ratio for preschool and children's departments. By completing the chart, you can figure out the number of classes/groups/departments needed and the approximate number of workers.

In a small church, try to have a nursery plus at least two departments for preschoolers (up through age two and ages three-five) and two for children (grades one-three and four-six). Only if space is not available should all preschoolers, or grades one through six, be together.

If space and leaders are available, set up three groups for preschoolers (up to age one; ages two and three; and ages four and five). Also, provide three groups for children (grades one and two; grades three and four; and grades five and six).

Provide at least two classes for youth if space and leadership are available and there are sufficient participants for each group (six or more enrolled). Divide older and younger youth, possibly using the same grading system as your local public school—junior high/middle school and high school.

If possible, provide a class for each group of twenty-five adults enrolled. Begin by dividing younger and older (using some midpoint age) or by having a class for women and a class for men. Additional classes might be graded as shown in the "Organization Planning Chart," or formed according to compatibility or interest.

Larger churches would add more classes/groups/departments for each of the age groups according to enrollment and the availability of leaders and space.

COMPATIBILITY

Grouping according to compatibility is used in many churches—particularly among adults—to allow persons who have the most in common to be together. People congregate due to factors such as preferred learning style or fellowship needs, and these preferences are established as a regular part of the organizational structure.

This grouping approach typically is used in combination with age grading and may be seen, for example, in a "Fellowship Bible Class." Sometimes the compatibility groupings develop informally, such as in a class of persons who have chosen to remain together despite suggestions that they promote to another age-group class.

INTEREST

Interest grouping is used when persons are free to select the most appealing study or activity. These groups exist as long as the particular study or activity is provided; consequently, this approach is used primarily with *short-term* educational activities and special emphases.

In some churches, all three approaches will be used; however, age-group divisions remain the foundation. Additional groups can be organized as necessary or appropriate to meet the needs of participants and to fulfill the purpose of the organization.

CHURCH OFFICERS AND COMMITTEES

In addition to basic programs, ministries, and councils, churches also are heavily dependent on elected church officials—*officers*—and *committees*.

Officers usually include moderator, clerk, treasurer, financial secretary, and trustees. These leaders fulfill not only needed duties for the congregation, but also serve in a legal capacity on behalf of the church. Persons who serve in these positions usually are recommended by a nominating committee and elected by the congregation to serve for a specified time. Information and guidelines are included at the end of the chapter, in the section on "Church Officers."

Committees exist to plan, coordinate, implement, and evaluate the work assigned to them by the church. With a small group of members who have specialized skills, a church committee can study and complete an assignment much more efficiently than can the congregation in business sessions. Materials about the work of church committees, duties of members, and sample descriptions for several committees are at the end of the

Figure 2.7
ORGANIZATION PLANNING CHART

		1 Member Classification Age (Grade)	2 Enrollment M	F	3 Prospects M	F	4 Total Possibilities M	F	5 Suggested Maximum Enrollment	6 Departments Needed	7 Suggested Maximum Enrollment	8 Classes Needed	9 Suggested Worker/ Member Ratio	10 Approximate No. of Workers Needed
									(5)	(6)	(7)	(8)	(9)	(10)
DIVISION		Pupil Possibilities							Department		Classes		Workers	
PRESCHOOL	Birth–1	Cradle Roll							35		x	x	1/6	
		Babies							9		x	x	1/3	
		Ones							9		x	x	1/3	
	2								12		x	x	1/4	
	3								16		x	x	1/4	
	4								16		x	x	1/4	
	5								16		x	x	1/4	
CHILDREN	Special Education								20		x	x	1/4	
	6 (Grade 1)								30		x	x	1/6	
	7 (Grade 2)								30		x	x	1/6	
	8 (Grade 3)								30		x	x	1/6	
	9 (Grade 4)								30		x	x	1/6	
	10 (Grade 5)								30		x	x	1/6	
	11 (Grade 6)								30		x	x	1/6	

ORGANIZATION PLANNING CHART (CONTINUED)

Group	Category									
YOUTH	12 (Grade 7)					60		12		1/8
	13 (Grade 8)					60		12		1/8
	14 (Grade 9)					60		12		1/8
	15 (Grade 10)					60		12		1/8
	16 (Grade 11)					60		12		1/8
	17 (Grade 12)					60		12		1/8
ADULT	18–24 (College)					125		25		1/5
	18–24 (Single)					125		25		1/5
	25–34 (Married)					125		25		1/5
	25–34 (Single)					125		25		1/5
	35–44 (Married)					125		25		1/5
	35–44 (Single)					125		25		1/5
	45–64 (Married)					125		25		1/5
	45–64 (Single)					125		25		1/5
	65–up					125		25		1/5
	Weekday S. S. Classes					X	x	25		1/5
	Adults Away					75	x	5	x	1/5
	Homebound					75	x	5	x	1/5
	Outreach Bible Study Group				x	x	x			x
	New Sunday Schools					x	x			x
	Pastor/Staff/Gen. Officers	x	x	x	x	x	x			x
	Total					x	x			x

a. Adult ratio in Column 9 includes care group leaders in the classes chapter, in the section on Resources for Use with Church Officers and Church Committees.[3]

CHOOSING A PATTERN

The amount of organizational structure needed by a church must be determined by each local congregation, depending on its size, needs, and resources. Ultimately, every church is responsible for finding how best to organize and administer its work. The guidelines and options that have been described will help you assess possibilities; but, in consultation with other church leaders, you must choose the most appropriate arrangement.

The variety and extent of church structure will vary greatly, depending on a church's size and resources. There is no standard organization, only the principle that there must be a balanced ministry in congregational life, focusing on worship, proclamation, education, ministry, and fellowship.

For possible patterns and assistance in evaluating church organization, see figure 2.8. By studying these options you can clarify how best to proceed with any adjustments needed in your church.

Figure 2.8a

CHURCH ORGANIZATION

Organization is grouping persons in a way that enables individuals and groups to accomplish their goals. In organization:

- Activities and responsibilities are assigned to individuals and groups.
- Working relationships are established.
- Responsibility and authority are delegated to enable individuals and groups to use initiative in their work.

ORGANIZATIONAL PATTERNS

Possible Organization Components. There are many organizational components a church can design to perform its work. Components commonly found include staff, deacons, church officers, church committees, coordinating units (councils), Sunday school, discipleship training, music ministry, mission organizations, media center/library, and recreation.

Effective Organization. Effective organization grows out of an understanding of the church's mission, resources, and traditions. No pattern is best, even for churches of a similar size. Each must develop its own organization. Objectives, priorities, tradition, availability of leaders, needs and numbers of people, space and equipment, and time considerations will influence decisions about organizational patterns in a church.

EVALUATING OPTIONS

Figure 2.8b gives suggestions and describes alternatives for organization. By studying these options you could determine how best to proceed with any adjustments needed in your situation.

GUIDELINES FOR THE ADMINISTRATOR

Here are guidelines that will enable you to give effective and strong leadership to church organizations:

1. *Determine the purpose and organizational structure for each program.* Prepare a chart listing every position and unit, and the name of every officer and teacher. Place this information at the front of a reference notebook/folder devoted to educational administration.

2. *Use, or establish, a church council or committee of key leaders to plan, coordinate, and evaluate the church's total ministry.* Meet at least monthly. (Suggestions for forming such a group are included in chapter seven, "Planning and Budgeting.")

3. *Prepare job descriptions for all positions.* Be sure to include duties, decision-making authority, and the person to whom the worker is responsible.

4. *Make annual plans for each organization.* Following the enlistment of officers for a new church year, schedule a *planning workshop* to develop goals and make plans for the next twelve months. Before the meeting, distribute the appropriate purpose and organizational statements to each leader along with suggested areas for evaluation and goal setting. Ask each organizational leader to consult with his or her coordinating group for orientation and evaluation, and to develop proposed goals and plans to be considered at the planning workshop. (See figures 2.9 and 2.10, p. 38.)

5. *Budget for regular expenses such as curriculum materials, and for all special items in the annual plan.* Delegate to organizational leaders as appropriate.

6. *Maintain a master calendar listing all plans, person(s) responsible, and budget provisions, if any.* Use this to monitor activities, record progress toward goals, as a diary of your reactions concerning various events, and as a guide in planning with the church staff.

7. *Maintain a complete record system for each organization listing persons involved, contact information, officers, and attendance records.* This information is needed for communication purposes and for planning.

8. *Use information to keep work focused.* Information gathered and the materials developed will be especially helpful when enlisting and orienting new leaders, planning for enlargement, determining organizational problems, and other similar administrative duties.

Figure 2.8b

Possibilities for Church Organization

Type of Unit Position	Churches with Fewer than 150 Members*	Churches with 150 to 399 Members	Churches with 400 to 699 Members	Churches with 700 to 1499 Members	Churches with 1500 or more Members
Staff	Pastor Music Director[1]	Pastor Music Director[1] Secretary[2] Custodian[2] Pianist/Organist[1]	Pastor Minister of Music and Education Secretary Custodian Organist[1] Pianist[1]	Pastor Minister of Music Minister of Education Secretaries[3] Custodians[3] Organist[1] Pianist[1] Age-Division Ministers[3]	Pastor Associate Pastor Minister of Education Minister of Music Business Administrator Minister of Recreation Evangelism/Outreach Minister Age-division Ministers Organist-Music Assistant Family Life Minister Secretaries[3] Custodians[3] Hostess Food service personnel[3]
Deacons	Deacons (1 deacon per 15 family units; minimum of 2 deacons)	Deacons (1 deacon per 15 family units)	Deacons (1 deacon per 15 family units)	Deacons (1 deacon per 15 family units)	Deacons (1 deacon per 15 family units)

Possibilities for Church Organization (Continued)

Type of Unit Position	Churches with Fewer than 150 Members*	Churches with 150 to 399 Members	Churches with 400 to 699 Members	Churches with 700 to 1499 Members	Churches with 1500 or more Members
Church Officers	Moderator (Pastor) Trustees Clerk Treasurer	Moderator Trustees Clerk Treasurer	Moderator Trustees Clerk Treasurer	Moderator Trustees Clerk Treasurer	Moderator Trustees Clerk Treasurer
Church Committees	Nominating Stewardship Missions Evangelism	Nominating Property and Space Stewardship Ushers Missions Preschool[4] Evangelism	Nominating Property and Space Stewardship Personnel Missions Preschool History Ushers Weekday Education[4] Public Relations Evangelism	Nominating Property and Space Stewardship Personnel Missions Preschool Food Service History Ushers Weekday Education[4] Public Relations Evangelism	Nominating Property and Space Stewardship Personnel Missions Preschool Food Service History Ushers Weekday Education[4] Public Relations Evangelism Other committees as needed
Service Programs	Media Services Director	Media Services Director (up to 3 workers) Recreation Director	Media Staff Recreation Staff	Media Staff Recreation Staff	Media Staff Recreation Staff
Special Ministries		Senior Adult Ministry	Senior Adult Ministry Singles Ministry	Senior Adult Ministry Singles Ministry	Senior Adult Ministry Singles Ministry Intergenerational Activities

Possibilities for Church Organization (Continued)

Type of Unit Position	Churches with Fewer than 150 Members*	Churches with 150 to 399 Members	Churches with 400 to 699 Members	Churches with 700 to 1499 Members	Churches with 1500 or more Members
Coordination	Church Council	Church Council WMU Council S. S. Council Brotherhood Council	Church Council S. S. Council C. T. Council Music Council WMU Council Brotherhood Council Division Coordination Conferences	Church Council S. S. Council C. T. Council Music Council WMU Council Brotherhood Council Division Coordination Conferences	Church Council S. S. Council C. T. Council Music Council WMU Council Brotherhood Council Media Services Council Division Coordination Conferences
Bible Teaching	General officers and organization for each age division	Departments of each age division	Multiple departments as needed	Multiple departments as needed	Multiple departments as needed
Church Training	Church Training Director Age-group leaders[4]	Member training groups and departments for each age division Equipping Centers New Church Member Training	Member training groups and departments for each age division Equipping Centers New Church Member Training	Member training groups and departments for each age division Equipping Centers New Church Member Training	Member training groups and departments for each age division Equipping Centers New Church Member Training
WMU	WMU Director Age level organizations as needed	Age level organizations as needed	Age level organizations as needed	Age level organizations as needed	Age level organizations as needed

Possibilities for Church Organization (Continued)

Type of Unit Position	Churches with Fewer than 150 Members*	Churches with 150 to 399 Members	Churches with 400 to 699 Members	Churches with 700 to 1499 Members	Churches with 1500 or more Members
Brotherhood	Brotherhood Director	Baptist Men Royal Ambassador groups as needed	Baptist Men Royal Ambassador groups as needed	Baptist Men Royal Ambassador groups as needed	Baptist Men Royal Ambassador groups as needed
Music Ministry	Music Director[5] Pianist Choir	Music Director[5] Organist Church Choir or Ensemble Age-division choirs when possible	Age-division choirs Instrumental groups as needed	Fully developed Music Ministry	Fully developed Music Ministry

[1] Volunteer or part-time

[2] Part-time

[3] As needed

[4] If needed

[5] Person serves as program leader and staff member

*NOTE: It is important to encourage, in any way possible, churches of 150 members or less to have choir, recreation, and other needed ministries even though directors or other leaders for that activity might not be listed in column one of this chart.

Figure 2.9

GOAL PLANNING WORK SHEET

Use the following when exploring and planning goals for your committee/workgroup/church.

1. Proposed goal:
2. What we hope to accomplish by this goal is to . . .
3. This goal is related to the following objective(s):
4. What is already being done related to this goal?
5. Specific age or interest group(s) to which goal is related.
6. We will feel we have made progress toward this goal when:
7. Major obstacles we see in implementing this goal:
8. Major resources needed to begin:
9. Decision regarding proposed goal:
    - Approved.
    - No decision at this time.
    - Hold for further discussion/development.
    - Develop action plan(s).
    - Secure input from . . .
    - Other.

Figure 2.10

SAMPLE FORMAT FOR PLANNING REPORT

Page ___ of ___
Program, Organization, or Officer _____ Date Prepared:_____
Objective:
Goal:
Action Plan #____:

Action	Person Responsible	Completion Date	Estimated Budget

9. *Evaluate programs and organizations periodically and annually.* Spend time before each church council or program committee meeting assessing the effectiveness of recent work. Look at records, review your master calendar, and check any information you have received or gained from your contact with the various programs, departments, or committees. Discuss current needs with other leaders and adjust the annual plan as necessary. Prepare annually an extensive evaluation to present to the congregation and to the planning workshop; use these in developing future goals and plans.

10. *Follow the basic principles of working with, for, and through people in administering church organizations.* The three I's will guide you:

Inform. Tell specifically what is happening and why. Seek a clear understanding of all plans and procedures, providing opportunities for open discussion of pertinent issues. Keep in touch with key leaders in all organizations.

Inspire. Minister to and support the persons with whom you work. Whatever you are as a leader will be the most powerful influence on those through whom you must work. Administration is not doing the work yourself, but *eliciting, combining,* and *guiding the resources of the congregation.* Your leadership will be multiplied through others.

Involve. Share leadership duties widely among responsible people. This requires giving major attention to:

- equipping leaders to do their tasks,
- delegating to them responsibility,
- supporting and encouraging them as they do their jobs, and
- involving workers in making decisions that will affect them or the duties for which they are responsible.

HOW TO RELATE TO ORGANIZATIONAL LEADERS

Administration, as described throughout this book, focuses on working with and through people. It does not mean that you make all the decisions, attend all the meetings, or do all the work yourself. Remember that your job is to coordinate and guide many areas of work rather than to immerse yourself in the details of one or two organizations. This requires serving as a *primary leader in a few groups* and as an advisor to many others.

The pastor, or other designated person responsible for the church's organizational life, is the chair of the general body that plans, directs, and evaluates all activities sponsored by the congregation. All program leaders participate with the minister(s) in this central leadership council, and then provide direct leadership in their respective organizations. The pastor and other staff ministers, then, would serve as advisors to the subgroups without having direct leadership responsibility.[4]

Thus the pastor or other designated person would have direct, administrative responsibility for one group, and would serve as advisor to the members of that body as they, in turn, lead their respective organizations. This organizational arrangement is illustrated in figure 2.11.

Figure 2.11

LINE AND STAFF RELATIONSHIPS

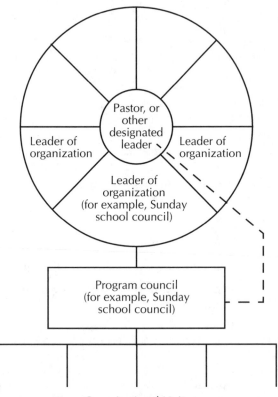

Organizational Units
(for example, age divisions, departments, and classes)

ORGANIZATIONAL RECORDS AND REPORTS

Each group, class, department, division, and program should keep records of its activities, and report regularly to the next larger unit. All basic programs and organizations, such as Sunday school, discipleship training, music ministry, and missions, should report regularly to the church. Provide an update of activities in monthly or quarterly business meetings, and a summary report at the end of the church year.

RECORDS

Program and ministry leaders should determine what information they and others need to keep informed and to give adequate guidance to the work of each organization. A record system usually is in place that can be adjusted as needs for information change. Religious book stores and publishers have a variety of record-keeping and report forms that can be used as-is or adapted for your situation.

Some have found it feasible to use computer systems to serve the records needs in a church. Individuals and companies are in business to help congregations with their use of computers not only with educational records, but also with financial and church membership records. Instead of taking several hours to prepare and type a report for the monthly business meeting, it can be processed in a few minutes using a computer.

Once leaders select an appropriate record system and secure the essential supplies for its operation, there should be training to assure proper use of the system. An annual training session for those who "do" the records can be a great help in getting accurate and complete information. For example, training would be useful for Sunday school group leaders, class secretaries, department secretaries, division secretaries, the general secretary, and hosts who work at welcome desks (including those who receive guests, get information from them, and help them find the appropriate group according to the church's grouping and grading plan).

Good records enable leaders to discover needs and opportunities so that appropriate and timely responses can be made. A secondary benefit concerns their historical value. Not only are records necessary when studying your heritage or dealing with legal issues, but data over the years can be studied for trends and needs that can be of significant use in determining leadership actions and planning strategy.

REPORTS

Each unit in an organization should report essential information to the leaders of the next larger unit of which it is a part. General leaders of a church organization need accurate and complete information about the effectiveness of the major units within the organization. Report forms that summarize the key items of information should be prepared by designated persons within each unit and sent to the general secretary.

It is important that organizations of the church periodically report on their work. This can be done in a monthly or quarterly business meeting, through a church newsletter, or by using promotional displays in major traffic areas. A summary report should also be presented at the end of the church year.

Use church publications to feature programs and ministries. Highlight special events, and include regular items such as a weekly or monthly report, schedule of activities, and pertinent information needed to keep the congregation informed. Use bulletin or information boards to report key items of information, such as attendance, number of visitors, and offerings. And, of course, make good use of the announcement period in regular services.

RESOURCES FOR USE WITH CHURCH OFFICERS AND COMMITTEES

On the following pages you will find additional information regarding the work of church officers and committees. This material is not intended to be exhaustive nor to substitute for guidebooks published specifically for church officers and committees. Rather, you will find helpful reference and administrative materials that you can easily use in providing leadership for your church.[5]

Figures 2.12 and 2.13 provide agenda outlines for church council and church business meetings. Information and job descriptions for church officers are in figures 2.14 through 2.18. Orientation materials and guidelines to train church committees are provided in figures 2.19 through 2.22. Sample committee guidelines (such as might be used to develop a church committee manual) for four key committees are in figures 2.23 through 2.26.

Figure 2.12

CHURCH COUNCIL AGENDA

1. Call to order by chairperson.
2. Scripture/prayer/devotional by person enlisted in advance.
3. Approval of/additions to agenda (distribute tentative agenda in advance).
4. Approval of minutes of last meeting.
5. Follow-up reports from last meeting, if scheduled.
6. Review and evaluate church program events and activities conducted since the last meeting. As appropriate, receive reports from program and ministry leaders, staff ministers, and committee chairs.
7. Preview and coordinate events and activities planned for the next three months.
8. Plan and/or overview future events and activities that are more than three months away.
9. Summary of meeting and decisions by chairperson.
10. Preparation of any recommendations.
11. Assignments for follow-up by next meeting (for example, special projects and reports).
12. Brief evaluation of meeting.
13. Adjourn.

Figure 2.13

CHURCH BUSINESS MEETING AGENDA

1. Call to order by moderator
2. Prayer/devotional
3. Approval of minutes from previous meeting(s)
4. Church clerk's report
    *   Request for letters
    *   Letters received (for new members)
    *   Deletions
    *   Membership statistics
5. Church treasurer's report
6. Old business
7. Reports from committees
    *   Standing committees
    *   Special committees
8. Reports from directors of programs and ministries
9. Report from church council
10. Report from deacons or other councils
11. Reports from ministerial staff
12. New business (from floor)
13. Adjourn with prayer

Figure 2.14

MODERATOR

PRINCIPAL FUNCTION: The chief responsibility of the moderator is to prepare for and preside at church business meetings; that is, to coordinate and facilitate productive business meetings in an orderly, efficient manner. (Many churches require that the pastor serve as moderator.)

DUTIES

1. Develop church business meeting agenda in cooperation with appropriate persons. Copies should be shared with church staff members, chairperson of deacons, and others included on the agenda prior to each session, if possible. (See the sample Church Business Meeting Agenda.)
2. Help members stay informed and involved in church business by promoting attendance and participation in business meetings.
3. Preside over all church business meetings.
4. Clarify matters voted on; determine action and follow up as appropriate.
5. Evaluate each business session and its activities.

RELATIONSHIPS

1. Work with the church clerk in preparation of agenda *before* business meetings and in preparation of minutes *after* meetings.
2. Consult with church staff members, committee chairpersons, program directors, and other responsible persons in preparation of the business meeting agenda and in evaluation of each business session and its activities.

3. Follow up after each business meeting with responsible committees, officers, individuals, and others to ensure that decisions are executed.
4. Be in touch with as many members as possible to know the spirit and mood of the congregation.
5. Serve as requested on the church council.

TIPS FOR MODERATORS

1. Maintain the spirit of Christian love and fellowship while presiding by conducting meetings in an orderly manner. (The moderator must maintain a neutral position while presiding. If it is necessary to become personally involved in debate on a question under consideration, ask an assistant to preside.)
2. Be familiar with prescribed parliamentary procedure. Help members to understand parliamentary procedure without embarrassing them.
3. Insist that motions be stated and seconded before they are discussed.
4. Suggest that a member make a motion by stating: "If a motion is in order, I move . . . ."
5. Call on the person who makes a motion to discuss it first.
6. Encourage full and free debate. Lead members to talk through their disagreements.
7. Execute business with dispatch, making certain that all matters are clear and concise. Avoid wasting time on trivialities. Bring people with differing views and perspectives together in the bond of love.
8. Alternate discussions so as to bring out both sides of a question. A member who has not spoken should be given preference over one who has. Be fair and courteous with all.
9. Respect the minority. The minority has a right to be heard even though the majority must prevail.
10. Always take the affirmative vote first. Take the negative vote next; and always take it.

Figure 2.15

CHURCH CLERK

PRINCIPAL FUNCTION: The church clerk is responsible for recording, processing, and maintaining accurate records of all church business meeting transactions. The clerk also is responsible for all official church membership records and communications. (Some responsibilities may be assigned to church staff members.)

DUTIES

1. Assist in preparation of the agenda for church business meeting(s).
2. Keep an accurate record (in the form of minutes) of all business transactions made and approved in church business meetings.
3. Present the minutes of the prior meeting(s) at each business meeting for official church approval.
4. Provide clerical assistance during the invitation period of the worship services for new members, rededications, and other decisions.
5. Maintain accurate member records. This includes: (a) adding new names and pertinent information to the chronological membership roll and dropping other names as necessary through transfer, inactivity, or death; (b) correcting records

for change of address or phone number; and (c) sending a memo as needed to all church personnel keeping separate records to avoid incorrect information.

6. Request letters by transfer from other churches for new members, forward letters to other churches requested by members, and notify persons when their names are removed from the church roll for any reason other than transfer of membership by letter.
7. Prepare and mail all official church correspondence.
8. Preserve records for present and future use.
9. Prepare the annual reports, submit for church approval, and send to appropriate offices.

RELATIONSHIPS

1. Work with the moderator in preparation of agenda before meetings and in preparation of minutes after meetings. (It may be necessary at times to consult with appropriate church staff members, program leaders, committee chairpersons, deacons, and others to be sure that the wording in the minutes is correct as given in the business meetings to avoid confusion either in the next business meeting or at later dates.)
2. Work with the church secretary in getting the minutes prepared for distribution to the members in the next business meeting. (A typed copy of the business meeting minutes should be sent to the church staff members and moderator no later than one week following a business session.)
3. Serve as resource person to the church historian and/or History Committee as requested. (If the church does not have a History Committee, the church clerk should be the church's designated historian.)
4. Provide statistical information on the church membership as requested.
5. Work with appropriate church staff members in handling official correspondence with other organizations/churches.
6. Work with the trustees in preparation of legal documents.
7. Work with various staff members, church program leaders, and committee chairpersons in preparing the annual church report.
8. Give necessary information about new members to the church office, to the person in charge of new member orientation, and to program leaders so the new members can be enlisted in appropriate programs.

Figure 2.16

TREASURER

PRINCIPAL FUNCTION: The church treasurer is responsible for the proper receipt, accounting, and disbursement of church funds within policies established by the church for adequate financial control. The treasurer's work focuses primarily on financial records and payment procedures rather than the handling of cash. (In larger churches, this duty is sometimes assigned to a staff member who works with all church financial matters.)

DUTIES

1. Keep accurate records in appropriate financial journals of all monies received and disbursed.
2. Reconcile monthly bank statements and correct ledgers as needed.

3. Sign checks in accordance with church policies and procedures, always veri-
    fying supporting data for each check request.
4. Make monthly and annual reports to the Finance Committee and the church.
5. Provide for records of individual contributions to be maintained.
6. Suggest possible investment opportunities; advise about bond purchasing.
7. Keep church staff informed of any trends or changes in fiscal matters.
8. Instill and preserve high financial morale throughout the congregation.
9. Submit accurate financial records for annual audit according to church policy.

RELATIONSHIPS

1. Serve as ex officio member of the Finance Committee. Confer with this com-
    mittee in:
    *   recommending and establishing policies related to receiving, accounting,
        and disbursing of church money.
    *   developing the annual church budget and coordinating the annual steward-
        ship campaign.
    *   preparing and presenting a monthly financial report in the church business
        meeting. (Also confer with moderator about presentation of report.)
    *   providing a continuing program of stewardship education for the church.
2. Receive copy of deposit slip and summary of receipts record from the Counting
    Committee after each deposit.
3. Work closely with the financial secretary in maintaining records of individual
    contributions.
4. Confer with the church staff members and deacons to maintain communication
    in financial matters of the church.
5. Work with staff members, officers, and organizations in administering financial
    details of church projects.
6. At the request of the Finance Committee, serve as advisor to various requesting
    committees in preparing and maintaining their budgets.
7. Be available to help individual church members plan the personal and family
    budget.
8. Serve as requested on the church council. Advise the council and various com-
    mittee chairpersons about available funds and budgeted funds.

Figure 2.17

FINANCIAL SECRETARY

PRINCIPAL FUNCTION: The financial secretary is responsible for maintaining accurate records of individual member contributions.

DUTIES

1. Post offerings weekly to individual accounts.
2. Mail a quarterly and annual statement of contributions to each contributor.
3. Provide statistical financial data as requested by treasurer, Finance Committee,
    and/or the church staff.

RELATIONSHIPS

1. Receive copy of deposit slip, summary of receipts record, and individual offer-
    ing envelopes from the Counting Committee after each deposit.
2. Work with the treasurer in the posting and reporting of member contributions.

3. Work with the church secretary in mailing member contribution reports.
4. Serve as resource person to the church staff, church program leaders, officers, and committees to provide needed statistical information about patterns of giving.
5. Maintain confidentiality about specific member contributions, except with approved persons.
6. Serve as requested on the church council.

Figure 2.18

TRUSTEES

PRINCIPAL FUNCTION: The trustees serve as legal representatives in all transactions related to the church. They hold legal title to the church property and they sign all documents related to the purchase, sale, mortgaging, or rental of church property after approval by the church in regular business session.

DUTIES

1. Hold legal title to all church property (as required by state law) and act only as directed by the church in regular business session.
2. Sign all legal documents involving church property, upon direction by the church in regular business session.
3. Maintain an up-to-date inventory of all church property, mortgage loans, and insurance on church property. (Such information should be kept in a safety deposit box with copies filed in the church office for ready reference.)

RELATIONSHIPS

1. Relate to appropriate civil officials in all legal matters involving the church.
2. Keep abreast of latest insurance and legal changes (innovations, programs, etc.), report such changes to the appropriate church leaders, and advise the church staff and any committees concerning legal matters.
3. Counsel with appropriate church officers and committees in matters related to church properties.
4. Maintain all church legal documents in conjunction with the church clerk.
5. If qualified, serve as resource personnel to the church staff and church families in legal matters.
6. Report on legal issues related to the church as necessary and/or requested.
7. Serve as requested on the church council.

Figure 2.19

THE WORK OF CHURCH COMMITTEES

BENEFITS:

1. The use of committees spreads the administrative load among members of the congregation and broadens participation. This provides church staff members and deacons more freedom for ministry to the people. Through committees responsibility is delegated, and the church is helped to perform its tasks.
2. The use of committees utilizes skills and talents of members of the congregation and makes the church a more efficient and effective ministering body.

3. The use of committees gives opportunity for differing points of view to be presented and reconciled, thereby producing more harmony among church members.

TYPES OF COMMITTEES:

There are two kinds of work done by committees in a church. The first type of work relates to the long-term, ongoing ministries and programs that are basic to the church's life, such as the financial program. For this type of work, the church needs to have committees that are permanent. Such a committee is called a *standing* (or regular) committee. The Stewardship Committee and the Property Committee are examples of standing committees. The members should serve on a rotating basis, with a portion of the committee being replaced each year.

Rotation assures that there are experienced members on a committee and, also, that there are always new people with fresh ideas being involved in church life. Committee members usually serve a three-year term, with one third of the group rotating off each year. After a year off, persons may be reelected to the same committee if the church desires.

The second type of committee work in a church relates to short-term or temporary needs, such as planning for a homecoming or conducting a fund-raising drive. For this type of work, a church uses committees that operate only long enough to accomplish their assigned task. This kind of committee is called a *special,* or *ad hoc,* committee. A Building Committee and Pastor Selection Committee are examples. The members of a special committee do not rotate, but serve as long as the committee exists.

Standing committees carry out very different functions from special committees. The work of standing committees usually revolves primarily around the needs of the church to maintain the best of what it now has. Standing committees give attention to maintaining, operating, and stabilizing already-existing ministries and programs that are ongoing.

Special committees, in contrast, usually focus their work on the needs of the church that are short term, such as for constitutional revision or adding an addition to a building. They give attention to creating something new or to revising something old. Special committees are formed and disbanded as needed; they should not continue beyond the time needed to perform their church-assigned task.

In planning an effective committee structure for a church, balanced attention should be given to meeting the need that a church has to maintain both long-term and short-term ministries and programs. Long-term ministries and programs require standing committees. Short-term ministries and programs need special committees.

The work of all church committees should be coordinated by a central coordinating unit such as the church council. Thus, the chairpersons of all church committees should serve as ex officio members of the church council, meaning they are on call when needed.

The members of all committees (standing and special) should be recommended by the Nominating Committee and elected by the church. Since the church brings each committee into existence, each committee reports back to the church. There should be a regular time allocated at each church business meeting for church committees to report on work accomplished.

Most of the new committees established by a church will be special committees—although it is not unusual for a new standing committee to be created. When it seems desirable to form a new committee:

1. Determine the need for a new committee.
2. Formulate its purpose and duties.
3. Prepare to allocate necessary resources.
4. Present to the church for discussion and vote.
5. Submit personnel needs to the Nominating Committee.
6. Present committee members, with chairperson designated, for church approval.
7. Educate new committee members.

Figure 2.20

DUTIES OF A COMMITTEE MEMBER

1. Know the purpose, duties, and members of the committee.
2. Be present and on time for meetings.
3. Participate in discussions.
4. Contribute to the planning and achievement of activities/projects.
5. Complete assignments as agreed upon.
6. Keep the committee chairperson informed about progress on assignments
7. Report on assignments at committee meetings.

Figure 2.21

DUTIES OF A COMMITTEE CHAIRPERSON

1. Know the purpose, duties, and members of the committee.
2. Request and administer committee budgeting.
3. Serve as an ex officio member of the church council.
4. Plan the agenda for each meeting of the committee.
5. Conduct meetings.
    *   Each meeting should have a purpose.
    *   Each meeting should have an agenda.
    *   Each meeting needs resources.
    *   Each meeting should plan for follow-up.
    *   Each meeting should be reported.
6. Supervise the work of the committee secretary.
7. Assign responsibility to committee members for follow-through actions.
8. Lead the committee to:
    *   identify and schedule some activities/projects.
    *   develop a sequence of actions.
    *   prepare a timetable.
    *   determine the resources needed.
    *   complete activities/projects.
9. Report committee action(s), as appropriate, to the church council and/or the church business meeting.
10. Collaborate as necessary with church staff members, church officers, church council, program directors, and other committees.

Figure 2.22

GUIDELINES FOR EFFECTIVE COMMITTEE WORK

1. Maintain a rotating membership for all *standing* committees, with one third of the members rotating off each year.
2. Maintain nonrotational membership on all *special* committees, that is, all members serve until the work of the committee is completed or the committee is disbanded by church action.
3. Limit committee membership to only one *standing* committee and, if desirable by the church, to one *special* committee. (Make exceptions only in unusual circumstances.)
4. Have the Nominating Committee recommend members for committees, standing *and* special, to the church. The Nominating Committee should staff newly created committees with at least three members, with one third of the membership rotating off each year. Add additional members (in any quantity) as necessary, but maintain rotational membership for all committees.
5. Usually a committee member should not be reelected to same standing committee for a period of one year following a three-year term. However, a year of ineligibility should not be mandatory. Need and willingness to serve should be the primary considerations.
6. Have the Nominating Committee designate the chairperson of each committee. (This should be done when the committee members are presented to the church for election. Chairpersons of standing committees should be designated to serve one year. Chairpersons of special committees should be designated to serve until the committee completes its work or is disbanded by church action.)
7. Assign a church staff member to each committee to act as advisor and consultant. (In a single staff church, there should be no more committees than the pastor can counsel and advise adequately. If necessary, consider asking other key leaders for assistance.)
8. Be certain each chairperson understands that he or she—not pastor or any staff member—is to lead the committee and that committee members—not the pastor or any other staff member—are to do the work.
10. Prepare a job description for every committee and provide a copy to every committee member. In preparing job descriptions:
    *   Use available material and information as a guideline (church practice, church bylaws, pamphlets, books, and resources from other churches).
    *   Write with *your* church's needs in mind.
    *   Secure committee approval on all parts of each description.
    *   Copy the job descriptions and present them to the church business meeting for approval.
    *   Make them a part of the bylaws or put them in a handbook to give to each church family.
    *   Update the descriptions periodically as the church situation changes.
11. Provide orientation for new chairpersons and new committee members.
12. Meet with the chairperson of each committee periodically to discuss the work of the committee and to coordinate activities.
13. Set aside one night a month (or quarter) as the committee meeting night. (For example, the second Wednesday of each month before prayer service. Do not expect committees to have unnecessary meetings. Whether the various committees meet should be left to the discretion of each chairperson. Make the

chairperson responsible for seeing that members know whether the committee is to meet.)

14. Instruct committees to report directly to the congregation during a regular business meeting when necessary or upon request. (Every committee should report at least quarterly.) Reports that involve major recommendations or require major decisions by the church should be shared with the church staff/church council and deacons for review and/or response prior to the business meeting. Committee reports to the church are beneficial because they:
   - inform the church about the work of a committee;
   - develop a spirit of achievement; and
   - provide promotion for the work of a committee.

Figure 2.23

NOMINATING COMMITTEE

PRINCIPLE FUNCTION: to lead the church in securing staff for all church-elected leadership positions filled by volunteers; to approve all volunteer workers before they are nominated to serve in church-elected positions.

RELATIONSHIPS AND RESPONSIBILITIES

1. Committee chairperson serves as ex officio member of the church council, contributing and receiving information related to the work of the Nominating Committee.

WITH COMMITTEES

1. Study the work responsibilities of all committees to understand the nature and scope of their work.
2. Counsel with the chairperson of each committee to determine present and/or future leadership needs.
3. Contact and enlist all nominees *prior to* presentation for election.

WITH CHURCH OFFICERS

1. Study the work responsibilities of all church officers to understand the scope of their work.
2. Contact and enlist all church officer nominees *prior to* presentation for election.
3. Chairperson of committee informs moderator of reports to be made in the church business meeting.
4. Chairperson of committee gives a copy of any reports made during the church business meeting to the church clerk for permanent record in the minutes of the church.

WITH PROGRAM DIRECTORS

1. Study the work responsibilities of all directors to understand the nature and scope of their work.
2. Contact and enlist all director nominees *prior to* presentation for election.
3. Counsel with each director to determine present and/or future leadership needs.
4. Assist directors in contacting and enlisting nominees *prior to presentation* for election.

Note: Program directors should serve on the Nominating Committee.

WITH CHURCH STAFF

1. Counsel with staff members to determine present and future leadership needs in the church and in developing plans to satisfy those needs.
2. Work closely with staff members in discovering potential leaders.

WITH CHURCH BUSINESS MEETING

1. Make periodic reports on the work of the Nominating Committee.
2. Answer questions about the work of the Nominating Committee.
3. Recommend all members of every standing committee.
4. Recommend all members of every special committee.
5. Recommend all members of deacons or related groups.
6. Designate chairperson of each standing committee annually.
7. Designate chairperson of each special committee when committee is elected.
8. Recommend all church-elected leadership for programs such as Sunday school, discipleship training, missions, and music ministry.
9. Recommend all church officers.

Figure 2.24

PERSONNEL COMMITTEE

PRINCIPLE FUNCTION: to assist the church in administrative matters related to all employed personnel.

RELATIONSHIPS AND RESPONSIBILITIES

WITH COUNCILS

1. Committee chairperson serves as ex officio member of the church council.

WITH COMMITTEES

1. Consult with the Finance Committee in developing and budgeting salary schedule and benefit provisions for all church staff members *annually.*
2. Consult with the Finance Committee in budgeting for any additional church staff members.

WITH CHURCH OFFICERS

1. Committee chairperson informs moderator of reports to be made in the church business meeting.
2. Committee chairperson gives a copy of any reports made during the church business meeting to the church clerk for permanent record in the minutes of the church.
3. Committee chairperson keeps the church treasurer informed regarding budgeted salary and benefit provisions for all staff members.

WITH CHURCH STAFF

1. Work with all staff members to:
   - prepare and update job descriptions *annually.*
   - negotiate a salaries schedule and benefit provisions *annually.*
   - develop church policies and procedures relating to church staff personnel.
   - discuss needs for additional church staff positions.

2. Consult with appropriate staff member(s) in locating, interviewing, and recommending additional church staff personnel.
3. Assess job performance of each staff member at least *annually* (and be sensitive to job insecurities that may plague them).

WITH CHURCH BUSINESS MEETING

1. Make periodic reports on work of the Personnel Committee.
2. Answer questions about the work of the Personnel Committee.
3. Recommend all employed personnel for every church staff position.
4. Recommend administrative policies and procedures for all employed personnel.

Figure 2.25

FINANCE COMMITTEE

PRINCIPLE FUNCTION: to plan and promote stewardship education in all areas of church life and to lead the church in budget planning, promotion, subscription, and administration.

RELATIONSHIPS AND RESPONSIBILITIES

WITH COUNCILS

1. Committee chairperson serves as ex officio member of the church council.
2. Develop and recommend to the church council an overall stewardship education and promotion plan.

WITH COMMITTEES

1. Review with chairpersons periodically the expenditures of committees to ensure correspondence with budget allocations and budget adjustments.
2. Consult with the chairperson of each committee annually to determine financial resources needed by each committee for its work during the following year.

WITH CHURCH OFFICERS

1. Committee chairperson informs moderator of reports to be made in the church business meeting.
2. Committee chairperson gives to church clerk a copy of any reports made during the church business meeting for permanent records in the minutes of the church.
3. The church treasurer serves as an ex officio member of the Finance Committee.

WITH PROGRAM DIRECTORS

1. Review with each director periodically the expenditures of the organization in terms of budget allocations and budget adjustments.
2. Consult with each director annually to determine financial resources needed by each organization for its work during the following year.

WITH CHURCH STAFF

1. Consult with appropriate church staff member(s) in the planning, promotion, subscription, and administration of the church budget.

2. At least one church staff minister serves as staff advisor and consultant on the Finance Committee.

WITH CHURCH BUSINESS MEETING

1. Make periodic reports on the work of the Finance Committee.
2. Answer questions about the work of the Finance Committee.
3. Recommend financial policies and procedures to be practiced by the church.
4. Make recommendations concerning proposed expenditures not included in the current budget.
5. Recommend an annual church budget.

Figure 2.26

PROPERTY AND SPACE COMMITTEE

PRINCIPLE FUNCTION: to assist the church in the care of all properties and buildings; to study and recommend the use of space and furnishings as they relate to all programs and activities; to study the need and recommend acquiring property and creating space; and to administer work assigned to it.

RELATIONSHIPS AND RESPONSIBILITIES

WITH COUNCILS

1. Committee chairperson serves as ex officio member of the church council.

WITH COMMITTEES

1. Present an annual budget proposal to the Finance Committee for financial resources needed by the Property and Space Committee to accomplish its assigned work.
2. Recommend to the Personnel Committee the employment, training, and supervision needs of maintenance personnel.
3. Work with the Missions Committee to recommend acquisition and to maintain property and space for mission purposes.
4. Work with the Long Range Planning Committee in determining future property and space needs of the church.
5. Assist other church committees in responsibilities that may relate to the assigned work of the Property and Space Committee.
6. Prepare recommendations to the Finance Committee for additional and property.

WITH CHURCH OFFICERS

1. Committee chairperson informs moderator of reports to be made at the church business meeting.
2. Committee chairperson gives the church clerk a copy of any report made during the church business meeting for permanent record in the minutes of the church.
3. Committee chairperson submits purchase order to church treasurer to request finances for budgeted items.

WITH PROGRAM DIRECTORS

1. Conduct with each director an annual evaluation of space allocations to determine areas needing adjustment and enlargement.
2. Recommend to directors space rearrangement to secure maximum use for education, special activities, and worship.
3. Recommend to directors policies regarding the use of space, equipment, and properties.
4. Assist directors in recommending and maintaining proper and adequate furnishings for programs and activities.

WITH CHURCH STAFF

1. Consult with appropriate staff member(s) in conducting an annual evaluation of space allocations to determine areas needing adjustment and enlargement.
2. Consult with appropriate staff member(s) in determining space rearrangement to ensure maximum use of facilities for worship, education, and special activities.
3. Assist the church staff in arranging, equipping, and administering adequate worship space.
4. Work with the staff member responsible for supervision of the maintenance personnel in developing and recommending maintenance policies and procedures.
5. Consult with appropriate staff member(s) regarding the need and process in acquiring new space for continued growth.
6. At least one church staff minister serves as staff advisor/consultant on the Property and Space Committee.

WITH CHURCH BUSINESS MEETING

1. Make periodic reports on work of the Property and Space Committee.
2. Answer questions about the work of the Property and Space Committee.
3. Recommend policies and procedures regarding the use of space, equipment, and properties.
4. Recommend the appointment of a Church Building Survey and Planning Committee when needed and appropriate.

CHAPTER 3

Working with People
Robert D. Dale

Some ministers appear to love humanity but hate people. These folks find themselves uncomfortable in local congregations because those fellowships are just people—all kinds of people.

Interpersonal relationships provide the bridges over which ministry moves. The effective church administrator learns to build one-to-one friendships. Moreover, managers must also expand their skills in relating to work groups, ministry committees, and program councils by learning to function well in one-to-several and one-to-many settings.

Working with church people well involves a variety of administrative challenges:

- understanding congregations as service organizations,
- ministering through committees,
- paying volunteers,
- building a unified team for ministry,
- solving problems,
- managing ministry meetings,
- chairing decision-making meetings,
- relating to church staffers,
- delegating ministry opportunities,
- supervising fellow church members,
- dealing with difficult people, and
- shaping the organizational climate.

Working with volunteers in congregations requires keen relational and management skills.

UNDERSTANDING CONGREGATIONS AS SERVICE ORGANIZATIONS

Students of management study three kinds of organizations: the *for-profits*, the *governmental*, and the *not-for-profits*. Churches and other Christian institutions fit into the not-for-profit category. Management experts agree that not-for-profits are by far the most challenging organizations to administer. Since the church is both spiritual organism and human organization, congregations are doubly difficult to manage.

What are the factors that make not-for-profits and volunteer organizations so tough to manage?

- Not-for-profits exist to render a service; for-profits exist to show a profit.

- Volunteers relate to their organizations in a somewhat avocational manner.

- Not-for-profits sometimes serve the second-level goals of their members. (Churches, however, should serve ultimate goals.)

- Volunteer organizations often relate to diverse and ill-defined constituencies. Most churches are clear about their formal membership but may be unclear about the various groups of persons in the community to whom they will try to minister.

- The purpose or dream of the not-for-profit is the most serious challenge for volunteer groups. Objectives are frequently too diffuse to provide a sharp focus for management.

- Not-for-profits are judged by their members' perceptions of effectiveness. Such varied expectations and such imprecise measurements of success create virtually unmanageable work climates.

- Not-for-profits usually produce intangibles.

- The benefits to the members of volunteer organizations are often indirect and sometimes vague.

- Not-for-profits generally function within a high (but occasionally hidden) level of competition. In most communities a large number of volunteer organizations compete for the allegiance, time, and money of local residents.

- The mission of many not-for-profits is often unattainable in the short run.

- Not-for-profits customarily pay their leaders poorly and sometimes recruit their volunteers on an "anybody-we-can-get-to-take-the-job" basis.

- Not-for-profit managers must be skilled in consensus building and other political abilities.

- Not-for-profit managers stay caught between an ongoing mission and volunteers who serve part-time or once in a while.

- Volunteer organizations and their committees often find they aren't well-served by counting on their informal traditions for ways to conduct formal management responsibilities.

MINISTERING THROUGH COMMITTEES

Committees have taken a bum rap in many churches. You've heard the jokes. "A committee is a group of the unfit trying to lead the unwilling to do the unnecessary." "Keep quiet and be considered dumb; speak up, get put on a committee, and prove what everyone suspected." "The ideal committee consists of four people who don't care and a chairman who wanted to have his own way anyway." "Committees are groups that meet to decide that nothing can be done." "A camel is a horse put together by a committee."

Churches that take the "priesthood of every believer" principle seriously take committee work seriously, too. Behind most congregational ministries and services lie the efforts of a committee or committees. This imperfect method of coordinating ministry has a way of working well enough in the end to advance the mission of the congregation.

Keep these things in mind as you work with church committees:[1]

- Committees exist for the church, not vice versa. Committees have no life independent of the congregation. Committees are to help the larger body of believers implement its ministry.

- The congregation sets church policy; committees carry out established policies. Because of a committee's special knowledge of certain congregational needs, however, that committee may propose new policies or changes in existing policies to the church.

- The function of church committees is to help the congregation accomplish tasks that can't be done as well by the congregation acting as a committee-of-the-whole.

- The congregation owes its committees a job description, orientation of its chairperson and members, and a forum for reporting their work to the church.

- Orientation sessions for committees are intended to (1) discuss how committees function in this church, (2) inform committee members of their specific duties, (3) elect any officers whom the church hasn't already specified, and (4) train the committee to complete its planning, implementing, and reporting.

- Regular meetings and special meetings called by committee chairpersons should be held to ensure the consistent service of the committee for the church.

- Any committee recommendation for congregational consideration should be accompanied by full information (the problem being confronted, the options considered and rejected, and the formal recommendation), sufficient time to discuss the issue, and the resources necessary to implement the solution.

- Periodically, congregations should evaluate their committee structure in order to cover emerging needs and eliminate any gaps or overlaps in committee duties. Wasted motion is demotivating to all workers, especially volunteers who have less time to invest.

PERSONAL REWARDS FOR VOLUNTEERS

Rewards for volunteers? Doesn't that idea fly in the face of the definition of a volunteer as a person who serves freely by personal choice? Not really. It's true that volunteers do not receive wages, fringe benefits, or bonuses. But volunteers do receive emotional and spiritual rewards.[2]

Consider these personal rewards for volunteers:

(1) *Contributing to a vital cause.* Some persons find great satisfaction in being part of a goal-oriented organization. They join with other folks on the same mission and feel the exhilaration of being "on the team." These volunteers are concerned with excellence, production, problem solving, and the achievement of goals.

(2) *Enjoying the fellowship of like-minded persons.* These volunteers relish being with other persons in whose company they feel comfortable. They value warm and friendly relationships and enjoy listening, sharing information and feelings, and giving encouragement to others.

(3) *Influencing individuals and groups.* These volunteers want to be heard, like to have their advice heeded, and enjoy position and prominence. They generally hold strong opinions, are outspoken and fluent, sometimes like to debate issues and win arguments, and intend to change others. Hopefully their major concern at this point is to invest their influence in inspiring and empowering others to reach group goals.

These three categories of volunteers have been called achievers, affiliators, and power people. *Achievers* serve their volunteer organizations best by organizing new projects and programs, by solving challenging problems, and by brainstorming possibilities and options. *Affiliators* nurture and lend support by counseling, greeting, listening, and acting as hosts and hostesses. *Power people* are the movers and shakers who raise money, persuade others to join in, and generally keep the organizational structures moving forward in positive directions or backward in reactionary modes.

In other words, each of these types of volunteers is needed in churches and other volunteer agencies. Additionally, each of these volunteers receives personal rewards. Yes, volunteers are paid—in service, recognition, growth, challenge, results, love, and teamwork.

BUILDING A UNIFIED TEAM FOR MINISTRY

Teamwork is needed in the congregation anytime two or more people must work together and depend on each other. Think of managing the team-building process as a four-step sequence:

1. Sharing personal history with one another,

2. Affirming each person's gifts for and contributions to ministry,

3. Setting goals for ministry projects and programs, and

4. Celebrating the developing sense of unity (figure 3.1).

Figure 3.1

TEAM-BUILDING MODEL

It's important to treat team building as a continuing process and to use the model to design meetings when you want to enhance and maintain unity.

One key attitude in team building is making ministry results the "captain of the team." That is, group or congregational goals become the focus of team building with individual goals and other concerns becoming secondary. Several ingredients are basic to developing an effective ministry team:

• a clearly defined congregational dream;

• settings where people feel free to risk their ideas and opinions;

- cooperating rather than competing; and,
- a commitment to congregational goals.

The team-building model helps workers get acquainted, divide responsibilities, build group cohesion, heighten morale, increase creativity, and deepen loyalty. Independence then becomes *interdependence*. That's team building!

SOLVING PROBLEMS

Every organization faces problems. Volunteer organizations grapple with tough issues gingerly because these groups are glued together by a fragile bond called trust. Problem solving, then, involves the entire congregation and demands skilled management.

Problem solving can become a creative instead of a frustrating experience if a good method is used:

1. *Begin with a concise and precise statement of the problem.* Include a broad description of an ideal solution, too. Both need and hope are identified by this step.
2. *Brainstorm possible solutions by "goal wishing."* Completing the sentence "I wish that . . ." generates lots of options and lessens the need to defend our ideas. After all, anything can be wished for.
3. *Take an excursion in your mind.* Historically, great inventors and creative thinkers have used ideas and images from unrelated sources to solve their problems. For example, Edwin Land's daughter fretted about the time delay for processing photographs. This complaint stimulated him to invent the Polaroid camera. Thinking deliberately about material or events unrelated to the problem under consideration can provide the key link for solving a problem.
4. *Try a force fit.* Choose an idea from your excursion, focus on it, return to your problem, and see if something from the excursion idea helps break through to a new solution by examining its positive possibilities first and then its negative potential. If the possibilities outweigh the pitfalls, a solution is available. Personal commitment, group endorsement, and planning the details of implementation complete the problem-solving process.

MANAGING MINISTRY MEETINGS

Business managers complain that they spend as many as one thousand hours yearly in meetings. While ministers may not spend that much time in meetings, they work with volunteers and must guide meetings well or risk losing the volunteers.

Avoid extra meetings. Meetings are necessary when:

- congregation-wide concerns need to be discussed,
- consensus building is demanded,
- verbal reports must be shared,
- morale needs to be cultivated, and
- many members need to be trained at the same time.

Don't call meetings when the same information can be shared as well in writing or over the phone, essential participants will be absent, leaders can't get prepared, and the results will not justify participants' time and energy.

Not all meetings are the same. Basically, the structure of a meeting should match its purpose:

Information meetings convey basic facts and require good communication skills and a variety of methods for sharing data.

Problem-solving meetings focus on difficult questions and demand participative and consensus-building skills.

Procedural meetings announce policies and call for abilities to enhance psychological ownership.[3] An agenda and handouts should be prepared beforehand and, in some cases, circulated in advance.

Effective meeting managers have a plan or model they use in guiding the progress of the meeting itself. One helpful meeting management model moves from (1) *evaluating* the group's progress toward its mission, (2) *creating* a range of options and resources for dealing with challenges, (3) *deciding* which alternative to recommend for the congregation's consideration, and (4) *implementing* the congregation's ministry decisions and programs (see figure 3.2). This approach provides steps for leaders of conferences and meetings to follow during work sessions.

Figure 3.2

MEETING-MANAGEMENT MODEL

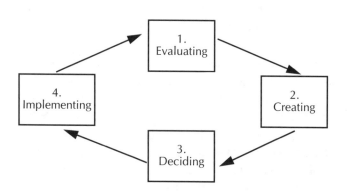

CHAIRING DECISION-MAKING MEETINGS

Formal decision-making meetings can be intimidating for the inexperienced or uncertain chairperson. Some straightforward principles can be helpful:

- Limit discussion to one subject at a time.
- Provide every member an equal right to speak, offer motions, hold office, and vote.
- Allow for full and free debate.
- Protect the rights of both the majority and the minority.
- Set a climate of teamwork, cooperation, and consideration.

The duties of the chairperson usually include (1) keeping the meeting moving according to the agenda, (2) knowing your congregation's formal documents (such as its constitution and bylaws) and its adopted parliamentary guide (such as *Robert's Rules of Order*) well enough to maintain orderliness, and (3) acting fairly and striving to preserve harmony.

RELATING TO CHURCH STAFFERS

Every church has a staff, and most church staffers nationwide are volunteers. How church leaders treat each other and work together is an important climate setter for congregations. Several principles contribute to good staff relationships:

1. Church staffers are people, not roles. Respect the God-created uniqueness of your colleagues. Help them grow, meet their needs, and reach personal and congregational goals.
2. Recognize that there are different kinds of relationships on church staffs. Some staffers' relationships revolve around what sociologists describe as "identity bonds." That is, my personality and gifts for ministry complement your gifts for ministry so that together we form a well-balanced team. Other staffers relate around "task bonds" and, therefore, focus on goals and work to be done.
3. Effective staffs blend specialist and generalist roles. The crucial issue here is that someone—usually the pastor—must maintain a corporate perspective and view the congregation's ministry in its broadest scope. Some church administrators must fill a generalist role for the congregation while others may specialize in particular ministries.
4. The larger the staff, the higher likelihood there is of relational tension. That's not to say that large staffs will inevitably disagree. But relational bonds, or primary interpersonal ties, multiply geometrically and become increasingly complicated as additional staffers are added.[4] Most of us have been led to believe "the more, the merrier"

in staff resources. The fact is that where more staffers are involved, there's more potential for complications in staff relationships.

5. Job descriptions provide a formal statement of congregational expectations for employed and volunteer staffers.

6. Adopt a healthy management style with staffers. Provide both freedom and security for workers. A dictatorial management style majors on structure and security while stifling freedom. Managers who use a "path of least resistance" approach supply freedom but no security. Balanced styles are more apt to undergird both freedom and security.

7. Take a developmental stance. Every staffer has some limitations, but most of us can grow with assistance and encouragement.

8. Provide forums for communication and mutual nurture. Structured meetings with friendly atmospheres allow for information sharing, joint learning, teamwork, and supervision.

DELEGATING MINISTRY OPPORTUNITIES

Delegation offers two positive opportunities to church managers. First, delegation allows ministers to multiply their ministries by involving others. Second, delegation lets others learn by doing. When is delegation called for?

- When someone else does the job better than you.
- When it saves the church time and/or money.
- When someone can be trained by means of the experience.

Good delegation demands a clear description of the opportunity and its limits, a large-enough and complete-enough task to challenge the person, a realistic time span for finishing the task, and agreed-upon checkpoints for reporting on progress. When delegating, let the task go; don't breathe down someone's neck while she or he is trying to share your work burden.

SUPERVISING CHURCH MEMBERS

Directly observing good supervision isn't a common experience. But several years ago I saw a first-rate example of supervision, and I was the guinea pig for the entire process. I had gone to the teaching hospital in Nashville's Vanderbilt Hospital for an eye examination. There I was treated by an ophthalmologist and a young intern on his first day of rotation in the eye clinic. The doctor would carefully explain what he was going to do and what he'd be looking for. After checking me himself, he would turn to the trainee and ask, "What do you see?" Sometimes the doctor would say, "See that? If his eyes were abnormal, they would . . ." and he'd proceed to describe what a diseased eye would look like. The step-by-step process and the careful instructions kept my usual "doctor's office anxieties" at a minimum.

Suddenly, I became very worried. The doctor announced that he was ready to dilate my eyes and asked the intern, "Will his pupils get larger or smaller?" I was horrified when the intern answered incorrectly. I knew more about this process than the young doctor-to-be!

Then my lesson in good supervision emerged. The ophthalmologist patiently and gently explained the physiological reaction that would take place in the patient. His attitude calmed me as well as teaching the young intern without embarrassing him. Good supervision combines gentleness with firmness.

This experience demonstrated supervision for me. Supervision, especially in a volunteer organization, is a supportive relationship. In other words, supervision calls for a comfortable but structured relationship. Typically, we have thought of supervision as a boss-employee tie with authority as the lever for change. Supervision is actually more of a mentor-novice relationship. The mentor serves as sponsor, guide, guru, model, and cheerleader. The novice, on the other hand, receives encouragement, nourishment, guidance, and proven ways of working. Supervision is a reciprocal relationship—like a two-person rail cart that requires both persons' efforts to move it down the track. The end result of supervision is growth for both the novice and the mentor.

Supervision blends learning by example, practice, and feedback: (1) Pastors and other church staff ministers who supervise volunteer leaders and workers must be willing to put their ministry on display and allow others to look over their shoulders. The opportunity for novices to observe and question is an invaluable learning experience. (2) The practice of ministry is learning by doing. Much of it is on-the-job training. What's second nature to the veteran in ministry can be broken down into bite-sized hunks for the less experienced. (3) Feedback extends self-evaluation into objective, behavior-based change. Feedback allows failure to become a base for learning. Effective supervisors affirm first and then confront with caring directness.

Several mistakes are common to supervision in the church:

- trying to become a supervisor without having been supervised
- making hasty selections of workers
- allowing jobs to expand without planning
- failing to keep work assignments clear
- bossing rather than coaching
- avoiding necessary discipline
- neglecting to train workers

These mistakes can be deadly for congregational health whether the supervisees are church staff ministers or volunteer teachers, officers, and committee workers.

DEALING WITH DIFFICULT PEOPLE

Every church has members who are abrasive to the larger congregation. They aren't emotionally unbalanced; they're just relationally out of step with the mainstream of the church. These folks may become a threat to congregational health if they try to take control of the congregation's atmosphere and mission. In fact, controlling behavior is a primary mark of the difficult person.[5]

Difficult people fall into two broad categories: *aggressives* and *passives*. Aggressive controllers include *hostile persons, cliques,* and non-communicating *"crazymakers."* Passive controllers include *apathetic persons, lonely people,* and *traditionalists.* Aggressives try to dominate the agenda of their congregations; passives place a drag on the mission and momentum of their congregations.

Which of these six difficult types is hardest to work with in ministry? All are tough to deal with, but the most difficult depends on you. Generally, the most offensive persons to us reflect the darker, more shadowy sides of our own personalities. We often have difficulty with the same aspect of the behavior of others that we fear in ourselves.

A general strategy for coping effectively with difficult persons must be broad-based and constructive. Consider these actions:

- Pinpoint the problem. What exactly is the issue that's calling out the controller(s) and creating the tension in the congregation?

- Rate the relationship. How strong are the ties between the controller(s) and the leaders of the congregation?

- Count the costs of negative behavior within the congregation. Can the controlling actions be ignored, or must they be confronted?

- Search for a solution. What options are available for dealing with controlling behaviors?

- Covenant for continuity. Can an agreement be reached that will allow the congregation to advance toward its ultimate mission?

Each of the difficult persons mentioned above displays controlling actions differently. *Hostiles,* for example, control their groups by daring to "be bad" in an institution that has a "nice" self-image. Their belligerence and demanding confrontiveness set the emotional tone for relating. If we avoid conflict or naively assume that hostiles will eventually ease the tension, we give the hostile member an important measure of control.

Cliques control a congregation's atmosphere for good or ill. Negatively, cliques gather for protection, revenge, or warfare. Positively, cliques lend status or share information with their members.

Crazymakers control communication processes by changing the subject, overloading the conversation with multiple issues, and contradicting. When we try to communicate with crazymakers, we are thrown off balance

SECTION TWO:

How a Minister Performs Administrative Responsibilities

CHAPTER 4

Administering Personnel
William G. Caldwell

Churches should employ personnel only after careful study of how to choose and administrate them. Proper treatment of personnel has become increasingly important as legal and ethical issues have developed. Churches can no longer ignore concerns that are being faced in other places of employment.[1]

Most congregations spend at least half of their income for paid staff. These costs are found in several places in the budget rather than in one general account. The total amount of staff compensation generally includes items like salaries, wages, total benefits, worker's compensation, Christmas bonuses, and Social Security. When calculating staff costs, include the ministers, support personnel, secretaries, custodians, food service workers, musicians, child care staff, and employees of any subsidiary programs directly managed by the church, such as a kindergarten.

It is not possible, however, to say 50% is the minimum or maximum amount that should be budgeted for personnel. Each congregation must determine its staff needs (paid and volunteer) and balance the costs among other financial priorities, like missions, facilities, and church programs.

Since such a sizable percentage of expenditures relates to the church staff, it becomes imperative that the church understand the dynamics of personnel management. It is a spiritual responsibility not only to use God's money wisely but to be a partner in the life and work of each staff member regardless of the tasks assigned.

ESTABLISHING A PERSONNEL COMMITTEE

A Personnel Committee, or another similar group, studies the staff needs of the church, develops personnel policies, and administers the policies on behalf of the church. The committee should be made up of six to nine church members with the pastor serving ex officio. These members should be spiritually mature, sensitive to the needs of persons, and willing to become knowledgeable in human resources development.

The Personnel Committee is responsible to the church for developing and recommending policies relating to the paid staff members and their work. Their duties include the following:

1. Study the needs for future personnel.
2. Develop and keep current all position descriptions.
3. Develop and maintain an organization chart and personnel policy.
4. Develop a process for employment of personnel.
5. Recommend to the church a salary and benefit plan, consulting with the finance committee.

DEVELOPING PERSONNEL POLICIES

Every church, regardless of size, should have personnel policies. In the small church with a bi-vocational pastor, policies will be very simple. Larger churches will want to develop a personnel policy manual to assure productivity and to avoid organizational and legal problems.

Policies should cover as many aspects of personnel administration as possible. Differences in policies for ministerial and support staff should be clearly identified. Any unwritten policies, which have become tradition, must be dealt with. Consider this list of areas to be included:

- Insurance provisions—health, life, worker's compensation, and disability
- Retirement provisions
- Social Security provisions
- Vacations
- Holidays
- Leave provisions—sickness, death, study time, military, jury duty, etc.
- Time away for professional development and leadership for other groups
- Salary and benefits plan
- Performance analysis procedures

A church may have a need for additional areas to be considered. See the *Sample Personnel Policy Handbook* at the end of this chapter.

After the policy manual has been developed, it is wise to present it to the church and implement it at a specific date. This should allow time for the staff members to be informed concerning the document and to understand its use. Any new staff members will be instructed concerning its contents. An annual review should be conducted by the personnel committee to keep the policies up-to-date and applicable when circumstances warrant changes.

DESIGNING A STAFFING PLAN

Every church needs a written process for developing a staff based on its vision and approach to ministry. There is no magic formula for doing this. No predetermined membership size or budget amount can be used to add a staff member. The changing nature of a church or the community must be taken into account along with the financial and human resources available.

The Personnel Committee should consider questions like these:

1. What task is to be accomplished with this new staff member? Does the task match our objective? Do we have adequate resources?

2. Why is it important to the church? Is this position really needed? Would a part-time position work?

3. Where will the new staff member work? Is office space currently available?

4. When will the staff member begin work?

5. What skills will this person need?

6. What will happen if we don't get this person?

WRITING JOB DESCRIPTIONS

An important part of any personnel process is the writing of job or ministry descriptions. Equally as important is using these descriptions regularly and keeping them updated and accurate. Good job descriptions assure that persons know what is involved in a job; clarify expectations of the job; provide lines of authority for supervision; and improve morale as persons feel good about what they are expected to do.

The supervisor should be involved in writing job descriptions. In some cases, this would be in conjunction with a committee assignment. A job description should include four pieces of information: the job title; a principal function statement; the identification of the person's supervisor; and a listing of the responsibilities and duties in a summary fashion. Although the job description is written before the search process begins, it is often helpful to allow the new employee to have input into the document when beginning work. The basic assignment would not change, but some of the new person's abilities might be better utilized. When a vacancy occurs, the job description should always be evaluated and revised.

Samples of job descriptions are included at the end of this chapter.

DEVELOPING A SALARY PLAN

Establishing a salary plan is often overlooked in dealing with staff personnel. Many churches pay "whatever it takes" when dealing with a new staff member. In larger churches with several staff members, this can be a serious problem because there is no attempt to base salary provisions on the responsibilities of the job. Any church can benefit from a formal, well-thought-out process for determining salary amounts.

Here are six things to consider in developing a salary plan.

1. Use current, accurate job descriptions for each position. Knowing the responsibilities and duties of each person is the only way to begin to know a salary amount.

2. Rank each full-time position according to the level of responsibility. For example, supervision of others, independent decision making, and highly technical skills indicate high levels of responsibility. Positions with similar responsibilities should have a similar rank.

3. Survey comparable community and church positions to discover salary amounts. In conducting the survey it is important to ask about positions according to the work being done, not the title being used. The base or beginning salary for each position is what is needed.

4. Decide on a beginning salary amount for each position starting at the bottom of the ranking. Make certain that the position identified as the one with the least responsibility is still provided a living wage in your community. Part-time positions will have to be adjusted accordingly. The beginning salary will take into account any minimum requirements for experience and training.

5. Consider a maximum salary for each position, if desired. Some plans use a 25–35 percent range between the minimum and the maximum amount. This would allow for a dollar-amount step increase for each year a person is employed. A percentage-based amount can also be used for salary adjustment. The increase should be determined based on continued service, additional training received, performance goals achieved, or a combination of these.

6. Adjust the salary amounts annually to reflect the community cost-of-living changes. If it is determined that a three percent increase is necessary to keep up with inflation, then all beginning salaries in the plan would be increased by that amount and present salaries would be adjusted accordingly.

FILLING STAFF VACANCIES

Staff vacancies are filled primarily in two ways: through an *application and hiring* process and through a *search and call* process. The former is used to fill non-ministerial positions, while the latter is the way vacancies for pastors, associate pastors, ministers of education, ministers of music, and other ministers are filled. Usually, the supervisor is responsible for securing support staff members and reporting their employment to the proper committee or to the church.

These two processes require different procedures. First, the steps for application and hiring:

1. Prepare/update job description, qualifications, and salary plan.

2. State requirements for religious faith, moral conduct, or church affiliation as applicable.

3. Prepare an application form and solicit applicants (see figure 4.1. p. 81).

4. Conduct interviews with applicants meeting qualifications.

5. Test for job skills if appropriate.

6. Prepare reference follow-up form; secure references on selected applicants. (see figure 4.2. p. 83).

7. Choose best person for the job and conduct an in-depth interview. Follow up on references, discuss details of the job, review salary and benefits, and determine whether to offer the job. Other tests may be appropriate after the job is offered, such as drug testing or physical examinations. In small to medium-size churches, the person to whom the worker will report usually conducts the interviews and approves hiring. In larger situations, the screening process to this point may be done by someone else. Either way, the supervisor of the new worker must be *involved* in the final screening, interview(s), and choice of the worker.

8. Review all information and make a choice. (See the information in figure 4.3 p. 83, "Evaluating Potential Employees.")

The search and call of staff ministers is a more complicated process. Procedures vary from denomination to denomination and even from church to church. Some churches don't conduct a search because a new minister is assigned to them. The following information describes typical procedures.[2]

The Personnel Committee or one similar will begin the search for the approved staff member. There also is the possibility that the committee or congregation will ask that a special ad hoc search committee be appointed/ elected to assist in seeking the new staff member.[3]

Where are prospective staff ministers found? Many religious organizations and denominational offices have minister relations departments that assist churches with prospective workers. Seminaries and divinity schools always provide this service. Résumés are kept current and on file to provide personnel committees with helpful information.

Calls can be made to friends and denominational workers in other areas to secure names of prospects. Encourage church members to share names of people who have impressed them.

Churches often employ staff members who are already employed by other churches. They should not, however, overlook faculty and staff members from seminaries and colleges, and employees of denominational agencies. Sometimes these well-qualified people will feel God's call to return to the local church.

Churches should not hesitate to interview and call recent graduates who have prepared for ministry. Many of these well-trained and highly motivated people are ready to make a lasting contribution to God's work in the local church. If the prospect has had church staff responsibilities before or during school days, the possibility for significant contribution is greatly enhanced in the first full-time church.

Once recommendations have been obtained and evaluated, it is essential that full information be secured for the most promising prospect(s). Some feel that the prospective staff member should be thoroughly investigated before any formal contact. Others prefer a conference call or an informal, get-acquainted visit in the home or office of the prospect. It seems best to have consent from the person before beginning any formal investigation.

In the contacts/conferences that follow, great care should be given in describing the church, the position, other staff members, the people, prospects for growth, and how the prospective staff member can aid the church. Discuss negative as well as positive factors related to the position and the church. If God leads the church and the prospect to each other, this honesty and openness will have long-term dividends.

Above all, don't make unrealistic promises or develop unrealistic expectations. Good decisions are based on accurate information and clear understandings of the ministry potential for the person and the church.

A poor decision can be detrimental to the fellowship, future growth, ministry, and financial program of the church. Churches need God-called men and women to provide leadership. Consequently, the search committee and the congregation will be called to prayer in seeking the leadership of the Holy Spirit in this strategic matter. Don't rush the process until there is a strong consensus that God is leading.

Here are specific questions that the prospective minister and the search committee should ask themselves in the evaluation process:

1. Does the prospect display leadership skills? Today's churches demand people who can lead. Is the prospect too slow to keep up with the people or so visionary so as to be too far in front? Does the staff member have basic traits of leadership such as truthfulness, honesty, willingness to work, interest in people?

2. Is there an overwhelming sense of God's call evident in the prospect? The dynamic church in today's society demands a high calling from God.

3. Is there a strong commitment to teaching and preaching God's Word? This is absolutely imperative in the life of a prospective leader.

4. Is the person flexible while remaining true to the Bible? "Rolling with the punches" seems to be a necessary trait of church leaders. Changing programs to meet needs is most helpful in today's churches.

5. Is the prospective staff member a generalist? This trait is helpful in local churches. A staff member who is interested in and helpful toward all church programs is important.

6. Are there indicators of continued growth in the individual? Staff members need an ongoing program of education and updating of knowledge. This is a key point of leadership in progressive churches.

7. Is there an evident love for people and their needs? The staff member who stays secluded day after day will have a difficult time in relating to the real-life needs of people.

8. Is the person capable of being an example of morality to the congregation? Issues of personal morality must be addressed.

After the committee members come to the conclusion that the prospect may be the person God would have in their church, they are ready to take the final step in the search process. This step is twofold.

First, the prospect must come to the same conclusion. There must be enough interest to make a visit, meet the people and—along with the church—consider the possibility of an invitation to join the staff. After this has been done, the prospective staff member will need to seek God's will in the matter.

Second, the church members should have an opportunity to meet the prospective staff member. The leaders with whom the staff member would have the most exposure should assuredly have dialogue with the prospect. The future effectiveness of the staff person can be harmed or enhanced by the way this get-acquainted visit is conducted.

At the conclusion of the visit, the church also will need to seek God's will and decide whether to invite the prospective minister to join the staff. If an invitation is extended, compensation according to the salary plan should be stated clearly to both church and future employee. There should be a general agreement as to the position expectations and performance standards. If the church approves and the staff member accepts, both parties then begin to establish the new partnership.

ORIENTING A NEW EMPLOYEE

The new staff member needs a knowledgeable person to assist in getting acquainted. The logical person to do this is the immediate supervisor. Some explanation of what has happened since the last person in the job left may be helpful. In the case of a new pastor, the search committee chair or other assigned person(s) should assist with the orientation.

Here are the things you should include when orienting a new staff member.[4] Make adjustments depending on the level of experience and background of the individual, and spread activities over several days.

1. Introduce staff members and tour the church facilities.

2. Tell how the staff is organized to carry out the church's programs and ministries.

3. Describe the church's programs, ministries, calendar of events, and schedule of services, and interpret the personality of the congregation; review the church's history.

4. Review how the church operates through its various organizations, councils, or committees.

5. Explain specific policies on drug use, sexual harassment, and ethical conduct.

6. Explain employee benefits, personnel policies, salary plan, pay dates, work hours, holidays, and other pertinent items. Special tax considerations for ministers should be discussed.

7. Review and explain job duties.

8. Tour the community; introduce the new person to important business contacts relating to the job, such as the postmaster, printer, bank officials, and social service representatives.

THE STAFF AS A TEAM

One of the distinguishing features of an outstanding church staff is unity of purpose. This unity should include all members of the staff, support staff members as well as ministerial staff members.

If a church staff is to be effective, it should have the same characteristics that a competitive sports team has.[5] The members will form a cohesive whole that is greater than the sum of its parts. Staff members will be interdependent with each person supporting others on the staff. This interaction is stimulating and enjoyable to all those who are involved.

In most team sports each member of the team relates to every other member of the team. Instead of hierarchy, as one would have in a military structure, there should be a broad-based equality on a church staff. Even though at a given time one member of the team may be more important to the outcome of the contest, there is general recognition of equality. Good relationships, then, will be foundational to effective ministry. (See the chapter on staff relations for additional information.)

Today's most productive church staff teams have four key characteristics that mark their effectiveness:

1. *Appreciation.* Church-wide love and appreciation for the individual staff member lead to staff security in work and in relationships; these lead to an enhanced team effort.

2. *Responsible freedom.* This is freedom to be creative; freedom to inno-
   vate; freedom to pioneer; and freedom to fail. A loving congregation
   will understand that the staff leader may sometimes miss projections,
   fail in developing an organization, or misread the needs of the people.

3. *Understanding.* Staff members grow through an understanding of
   themselves, others on the staff, and the people they lead. They grow
   as they understand the objective of the church and its goals. They
   grow by playing on the team to achieve those goals.

4. *Cooperation.* All staff members pull together in support of each
   other's work as well as of the total life of the church. This type of
   cooperative spirit nurtures staff members in their own sense of purpose and fulfillment as servant leaders.[6]

INDEX

PERSONNEL FORMS, JOB DESCRIPTIONS, AND PERSONNEL POLICY HANDBOOK

Figure 4.1

APPLICATION FORM

_____CHURCH

| Date | Position you are applying for: |

Are you available for:
full-time_____
part-time _____
temporary work _____
Were you referred by a current or former employee? yes ___no___
If so, who? _____

I. PERSONAL DATA

Name (last)_____(first)_____(middle)_____
Address (street) _____
(city) _____
(state) _____
(zip) _____
How long at this address? _____
Phone Number _____ Social Security Number _____
Prior Address _____ How long? _____

II. EDUCATION

(Complete only if job has educational qualifications.)
High School Diploma: yes_____ no_____ ; if yes, when?_____
Business College: yes_____ no_____ ; where located? _____
University or College: yes_____ no_____ ; if yes, did you graduate?
What was your major? Minor? _____
Name and location of college _____
School or college activities in which you engaged? _____

III. EMPLOYMENT HISTORY

(Start with present or most recent job)
Are you presently employed? yes _____ no _____
May we contact your present employer? _____ now _____ later _____no
1. Name of Employer _____Address _____ Worked from _____ to _____
   Supervisor _____ Monthly salary or hourly rate: start _____ end _____
   Type of work performed _____ Reason for leaving_____
2. Name of Employer _____Address _____ Worked from _____ to _____
   Supervisor _____ Monthly salary or hourly rate: start _____ end _____
   Type of work performed _____ Reason for leaving_____
3. Name of Employer _____Address _____ Worked from _____ to _____
   Supervisor _____ Monthly salary or hourly rate: start _____ end _____
   Type of work performed _____ Reason for leaving_____

IV. JOB DATA

Name of Employer _____ Address _____
(Check areas in which you have had experience or training)

_____ Typing (Speed _____WPM)	_____ Receptionist
_____ Word Processor	_____ Writing and Editing
_____ Transcribing Machine	_____ Supervisor
_____ Bookkeeping	_____ Custodian
_____ Duplicating Machine	_____ Other:

Figure 4.1

APPLICATION FORM (continued)

V. CHURCH LIFE

Denomination_____

Name of Church (Where you hold membership) _____

Location _____

What church activities did (do) you participate in? _____

What positions in a church have you volunteered for or been employed for: _____

VI. WORK HISTORY

Have you ever had a license suspended or revoked by a professional body or state agency?
____yes ____no. If so, explain circumstances _____

_____

How many days were you late to work last year? _____

How many days were you absent from work last year? _____

VII. CRIMINAL RECORD

Other than a minor traffic offense, have you ever been convicted of a crime? yes ___ no ___
If so, please explain: _____
Are you currently involved in any legal proceedings? yes ___ no ___
If so, please explain: _____

VIII. REFERENCES

(Do not list relatives or former employers)

1. Name _____ Address_____
   Occupation _____ Years Known _____
2. Name _____ Address_____
   Occupation _____ Years Known _____
3. Name _____ Address_____
   Occupation _____ Years Known _____

IX. ADDITIONAL INFORMATION

Please give us any additional information you desire about your education and experience (include any special talents). Please list any personal characteristics that you feel would prepare you for this position.

Employment terms: I understand that this church is an "at-will" employer and that employment may be terminated at any time with or without cause. This status is not to be altered unless we enter a contract that specifically addresses and replaces the "at-will" employment status.

Applicant's Signature _____ Date_____

REFERENCE RELEASE:

The information I have provided is accurate and true and I understand that any false information is grounds for termination. I authorize the verification of this information with all former employers, references, and other appropriate persons. I will not take action against anyone releasing the requested information.

Applicant's Signature_____ Date_____

Figure 4.2

EMPLOYMENT REFERENCE CHECK

Name of Applicant _____

Position under consideration _____

Person contacted for reference _____

Firm/Church_____ Phone_____

Employment period covered: From_____ to _____

The above person has given your name as a reference and signed a release giving us permission to contact you. Please complete the confidential questions below and return in the enclosed, postage-paid envelope. Thank you!

Person conducting reference check _____ Church _____

1. In what capacity did you know the applicant and for how long?_____
    Were you the immediate supervisor? _____yes _____no
2. What was the job title? _____
    What specifically was done as a part of the job? _____
3. How would you rate (a) performance? _____
    (b) supervisory abilities?_____
    (c) independent work? _____
    (d) creativity?_____
4. How did this person get along with others? _____
5. Any unusual work habits? _____
6. What were the circumstances under which the person left?_____
    _____Is this person eligible for rehire? Yes_____Any qualifications?
    No_____Why? _____
7. Describe the strong points? General _____
    Technical_____
8. Are there any negative aspects or weaknesses? _____
9. Did this person have the skills required for the job? _____yes _____no
    If not, explain._____
10. Please list any other names we might contact for a reference.
    Name _____ Address _____ Phone _____
    Name _____ Address _____ Phone _____
    Name _____ Address _____ Phone _____
11. Any additional comments:
    Signed _____Title _____Date _____

Figure 4.3

EVALUATING POTENTIAL EMPLOYEES

1. Is the applicant a Christian? Participating in a local church? Living and acting responsibly? Does applicant have a good character and reputation?
2. Is the applicant neat? Alert? Have good posture? Good facial expression?
3. Is the applicant tactful? Courteous? Confident? Warm? Enthusiastic? Cheerful? Optimistic? Animated? Humorous?
4. Does the applicant have good pronunciation? Enunciation? Vocabulary? Grammar? Have good expression? With clarity? Act in an organized manner?

5. Does the applicant have good educational and professional backgrounds? Can do the job at an acceptable level now or with training?
6. Has the applicant exhibited mental effectiveness? Good personality? Skill in getting along with people? Good insight?
7. In short, beginning with your initial contact, did you immediately sense that this person would fit in well and is qualified for the job?

Figure 4.4

PASTOR

PRINCIPAL FUNCTION: The pastor is responsible to the church to proclaim the gospel of Jesus Christ, to preach the biblical revelation, to engage in pastoral care ministries, to provide administrative leadership in all areas of church life, and to act as the chief administrator of the paid staff.

RESPONSIBILITIES

1. Plan and conduct the worship services; prepare and deliver sermons; lead in observance of ordinances.
2. Lead the church in an effective program of witnessing and in a caring ministry for persons in the church and community.
3. Visit members and prospects.
4. Conduct counseling sessions; perform wedding ceremonies; conduct funerals.
5. Lead the church in planning, organizing, directing, coordinating, and evaluating the total program of the church.
6. Work with deacons, church officers, and committees as they perform their assigned responsibilities.
7. Act as moderator of church business meetings (unless a layperson is elected as moderator).
8. Cooperate with denominational leaders in matters of mutual interest and concern; keep the church informed of denominational development; represent the church in civic matters.
9. Serve as chief administrator of the paid church staff; supervise the work of assigned paid staff workers.

Figure 4.5

MINISTER OF EDUCATION

PRINCIPAL FUNCTION: The minister of education is responsible to the church, supervised by the pastor, for providing staff leadership to the entire church educational program. This involves assisting church program leaders in planning, conducting, and evaluating a comprehensive ministry of Christian education in support of the mission and objectives of the church.

RESPONSIBILITIES

1. Lead the church in planning, conducting, and evaluating a comprehensive program of Christian education.
2. Serve as educational resource person and advisor to the leaders of church program and service organizations.

3.   Serve as educational resource person and advisor to the committees of the church as requested.
4.   Work within the church process to select, enlist, and train qualified leaders.
5.   Coordinate the production of informational and public relations materials, such as church publications and news releases.
6.   Develop special educational and training projects such as camps, retreats, and study seminars for various age groups within the congregation.
7.   Lead the church to be aware of the educational and curriculum materials available and lead the church to choose the most suitable.
8.   Prepare an estimated annual education budget and administer the approved budget.
9.   Assist the pastor in planning, conducting, and evaluating congregational services as requested.
10.   Serve on the church council or coordinating group.
11.   Supervise appropriate church staff members as assigned, such as age-group directors, recreation leaders, educational secretary, and custodian.
12.   Cooperate with denominational leaders in promoting activities of mutual interest.
13.   Keep informed on methods, materials, principles, procedures, promotion, and administration as related to the education program.
14.   Perform other duties as assigned by the pastor.

Figure 4.6

MINISTER OF MUSIC

PRINCIPAL FUNCTION: The minister of music is responsible to the church, supervised by the pastor, for the development and promotion of the music program of the church.

RESPONSIBILITIES

1.   Direct the planning, organizing, conducting, and evaluating of a comprehensive music program including choirs, vocal and/or instrumental ensembles.
2.   Supervise the work of assigned paid staff workers.
3.   Cooperate with the church process to enlist and train leaders for the church music ministry, including graded choir workers, song leaders, and accompanists for the church education organizations.
4.   Lead in planning and promoting a graded choir program; direct and coordinate the work of lay choir directors; direct adult, youth, and other choirs as needed.
5.   Serve as a member of the church council or coordinating group; coordinate the music program with the organizational calendar and emphases of the church.
6.   Assist the pastor in planning all services of worship.
7.   Arrange and provide music for weddings, funerals, special projects, ministries, and other church-related activities upon request.
8.   Plan, organize, and promote choir tours, mission trips, camps, festivals, workshops, clinics, and programs for the various choirs.
9.   Supervise the maintenance of the music library, materials, supplies, musical instruments, and other equipment.
10.   Keep informed on music methods, materials, promotion, and administration.
11.   Prepare an estimated annual music budget and administer the approved budget.

12. Cooperate with denominational leaders in promoting activities of mutual interest.

13. Perform other duties as assigned by the pastor.

Figure 4.7

BUSINESS ADMINISTRATOR

PRINCIPAL FUNCTION: The business administrator is responsible to the church, supervised by the pastor, for administering the business affairs of the church.

RESPONSIBILITIES

1. Establish and operate an efficient plan of financial record keeping and reporting; develop bookkeeping procedures.

2. Prepare financial information for the Finance and Budget Committees and treasurer of the church.

3. Serve as resource person regarding legal and business matters of the church; study annually the insurance program and make recommendations, if any.

4. Serve as church purchasing agent; approving and processing requisitions and purchase orders.

5. Maintain records on church staff personnel; establish and maintain records of equipment and facilities.

6. Administer church-adopted policies and procedures concerning the use of all church properties and facilities.

7. Assist Building Committee in its relationships with architect, contractors, and others in building, remodeling, and equipping church buildings.

8. Work with the Property and Space Committee in preparing an annual budget of maintenance and equipment needs.

9. Supervise workers in the maintenance and repair of all physical properties; establish and implement cleaning, painting, renovating schedules; operate within approved budget.

10. Supervise the operation of food services.

11. Supervise assigned office personnel.

12. Perform other duties as assigned by the pastor. Several of the duties are usually included in the minister of education's position description when the church does not have a business administrator. Many of the jobs indicate supervision by the business administrator. This would change to office manager, minister of education, building superintendent, or other staff person if there is no business administrator.

Figure 4.8

MINISTER OF YOUTH

PRINCIPAL FUNCTION: The minister of youth is responsible to the church, supervised by the minister of education, for assisting church program organizations to develop a comprehensive program of youth education.

RESPONSIBILITIES

1. Counsel with church program organization leaders in planning, conducting, and evaluating a youth education ministry and in enlisting appropriate youth workers.

2. Conduct special training projects for youth workers in proper relationship to discipleship programs.

3. Advise in the use of program materials, equipment, supplies, and space by youth groups in all church program organizations.

4. Work with the director of the recreation service to provide needed services.

5. Plan and conduct special projects (such as camps and retreats) for youth program organization groups.

6. Work with organization leaders to coordinate visitation for the youth division and lead workers to visit prospects and absentees.

7. Develop a proposed budget for youth ministry and administer it when approved.

8. Work with program leaders and teachers and appropriate staff members to resolve philosophical, procedural, and scheduling problems in the youth division.

9. Perform other duties as assigned by the minister of education.

Note: This description could be used for any age-group specialist; simply substitute the appropriate age group for "youth."

Figure 4.9

SECRETARY

PRINCIPAL FUNCTION: Perform general office work, under the supervision of the business administrator, in relieving supervisor of minor executive and clerical duties.

RESPONSIBILITIES

1. Transcribe dictation; type sermons; use word processing equipment as required.

2. Perform general office work; maintain supplies and various files; keep records and compile these into periodic or occasional reports.

3. Review, open, and distribute mail; prepare routine answers without direction for approval and signature; answer routine letters in absence of the supervisor.

4. Act as required during supervisor's absence in making decisions or taking any necessary action not requiring supervisory approval.

5. Exercise tact, courtesy, and diplomacy in receiving callers, personal or telephone; keep calendar of appointments.

6. Notify committee members of meeting dates.

7. Edit and prepare bulletin copy.

8. Order literature and office supplies.

9. Assist in training new office workers.

10. Perform other duties as assigned by the business administrator.

Figure 4.10

ORGANIST AND MUSIC ASSISTANT

PRINCIPAL FUNCTION: The organist and music assistant, supervised by the minister of music, serves as organist of the church and assists in the music ministry.

RESPONSIBILITIES

1. Play for all services of the church, both regular and special.
2. Serve as accompanist for choirs, ensembles, and soloists in regular and special rehearsals and performances, as assigned.
3. Play for weddings and funerals, as requested, and with the approval of the minister of music.
4. Assist in planning worship services, choir rehearsals, and special music events.
5. Plan and give direction to a training program designed for developing organists and pianists in the church.
6. Maintain a regular schedule of organ practice and study.
7. Prepare workbooks and study materials for the graded choirs as assigned.
8. Perform other duties as assigned by the minister of music.

Figure 4.11

MINISTER OF EDUCATION AND MUSIC

PRINCIPAL FUNCTION: The minister of education and music is responsible to the church, supervised by the pastor, for the development and promotion of the educational and music programs of the church.

RESPONSIBILITIES

1. Direct the planning, coordinating, conducting, and evaluating of comprehensive educational and music programs based on program tasks.
2. Supervise the work of assigned paid staff members.
3. Lead in enlisting and training volunteer workers.
4. Organize and direct a church-wide visitation program.
5. Assist the pastor in planning all services of worship; arrange and provide music for weddings, funerals, special projects, ministries, and other church-related activities upon request.
6. Maintain personnel records of all paid staff workers; maintain music library, materials, supplies, musical instruments, and other equipment.
7. Serve as the purchasing agent for the church as assigned.
8. Develop projects such as mission trips, festivals, youth camps, retreats; plan activities for senior adults.
9. Edit church publications as assigned.
10. Assist the chairpersons of the various church committees; serve as ex officio member of church committees as assigned.
11. Prepare an annual program ministry budget for approval; administer the approved budget.
12. Keep informed on educational and music methods, materials, promotions, and administration.
13. Cooperate with denominational leaders in promoting activities of mutual interest.
14. Perform other duties as assigned by the pastor.

Figure 4.12

MINISTER OF ACTIVITIES/DIRECTOR OF RECREATION

PRINCIPAL FUNCTION: The minister of activities/director of recreation is responsible to the church, supervised by the minister of education, for leading the church in planning, conducting, and evaluating a program of recreation for church members and other persons in the community.

RESPONSIBILITIES

1. Direct the planning, coordination, conducting, and evaluation of recreation activities in the church.
2. Coordinate and administer activities in the church's recreation center, as assigned by the church.
3. Work with the church process to recruit and enlist workers for the church's recreation program.
4. Plan and coordinate training for all volunteer recreation workers.
5. Coordinate the recreation activities with the calendar and emphases of the church.
6. Serve as recreation resource person and advisor to organizations of the church as requested.
7. Lead the church to provide equipment and supplies needed in the recreation activities.
8. Supervise the inventory, care, repair, and storage of recreation equipment and supplies.
9. Provide representation for the church in planning, conducting, and evaluating recreation activities that involve other churches and groups.
10. Prepare a proposed recreation budget and administer it after approval.
11. Perform other duties as assigned by the minister of education.

Figure 4.13

FINANCIAL SECRETARY

PRINCIPAL FUNCTION: Maintain the church financial records and prepare financial reports, under the supervision of the business administrator.

RESPONSIBILITIES

1. Receive, count, and deposit all church offerings, with appropriate committee help.
2. Post receipts and disbursements of all accounts according to financial system.
3. Post offerings weekly to individual accounts; file envelopes.
4. Prepare bank reconciliation statements monthly.
5. Prepare monthly and annual financial reports for Finance Committee and church business meetings.
6. Prepare quarterly and annual tax reports.
7. Check and total all invoices when approved; inform responsible persons of their budget expenditures.
8. Receive and answer queries concerning financial matters; maintain file of invoices, correspondence, and reports.

9. Prepare and issue checks to staff members, designations, and organizations in accordance with church policy.
10. Mail pledge cards, stewardship letters, and envelopes to new members.
11. Requisition and prepare all forms and records for the annual stewardship emphasis.
12. Perform other duties as assigned by the business administrator.

Figure 4.14

STENOGRAPHER

PRINCIPAL FUNCTION: Transcribe dictation, use word processing equipment and perform general office work, under the supervision of the business administrator.

RESPONSIBILITIES

1. Transcribe dictation; use word processing equipment.
2. Perform general office work; maintain files and supplies; keep records and compile these into periodic reports.
3. Type copy for reproduction.
4. Receive visitors; arrange appointments and keep calendar of appointments.
5. Receive and distribute incoming mail.
6. Answer the telephone.
7. Assist in mailing out the bulletin.
8. Perform other duties as assigned by the business administrator.

Figure 4.15

CLERK-TYPIST

PRINCIPAL FUNCTION: Maintain office files, records, and schedules; make requisitions, prepare reports, and type copy, under the supervision of the business administrator.

RESPONSIBILITIES

1. Maintain office files, program records, and schedules.
2. Fill out requisition forms.
3. Prepare reports periodically or as directed.
4. Do routine typing and compose routine letters.
5. Correct mailing lists; prepare mailing labels as needed.
6. Operate duplicating machine.
7. Take and transcribe dictation, as assigned.
8. Answer telephone and serve as receptionist, as assigned.
9. Perform other duties as assigned by the business administrator.

Figure 4.16

TYPIST

PRINCIPAL FUNCTION: Type routine copy; address envelopes; use word processing equipment as required, under the supervision of the business administrator.

RESPONSIBILITIES

1. Type routine form letters, copy, records, record cards, and reproduction masters.
2. Address and stuff envelopes.
3. Perform routine clerical work as assigned.
4. Answer the telephone, as assigned.
5. Sort and deliver incoming mail, as assigned.
6. Perform other duties as assigned by the business administrator.

Figure 4.17

CHURCH HOSTESS

PRINCIPAL FUNCTION: Oversee the operation of the kitchen and dining areas for all food services, under the supervision of the business administrator.

RESPONSIBILITIES

1. Plan meals; purchase, prepare, and serve food for all scheduled meals and snacks and for social functions as requested.
2. Supervise assigned personnel; enlist and direct volunteer workers; train workers in proper food preparation and service.
3. Maintain high standards of sanitation in cleanliness of cooking utensils, dishes, glasses, silverware, and in food handling, preparation, service, storage, and so forth, to assure compliance with local health and sanitation laws; maintain clean work areas, storage bins, and so forth.
4. Prepare proposed food service budget; administer it when approved, maintaining accurate records in costs and operation.
5. Maintain up-to-date inventory of food supplies.
6. Arrange for the servicing, repairing, and replacing of equipment in the kitchen as needed.
7. Work with the building superintendent on table and room arrangements for all meals and social functions.
8. Perform other duties as assigned by the business administrator.

Figure 4.18

CUSTODIAN

PRINCIPAL FUNCTION: Maintain clean buildings and grounds; make minor repairs, under the supervision of the business administrator.

RESPONSIBILITIES

1. Sweep, mop, buff, clean, and wax floors according to schedule; dust furniture and equipment; wash walls and windows and vacuum carpets as scheduled.
2. Maintain clean rest rooms; replenish tissue and towels; empty waste cans.
3. Request cleaning and maintenance supplies and equipment as needed.
4. Operate heating and cooling equipment according to schedule and instruction.
5. Open and close building daily as scheduled.
6. Mow grass; trim shrubbery, maintain clean church entrance, sidewalk, and parking areas.

7.   Check with church office or supervisor daily for special assignments.
8.   Move furniture, set up tables and chairs for suppers, banquets, and other similar occasions; set up meeting areas for regular and special activities.
9.   Make minor electrical, plumbing, and equipment repairs as requested.
10. Paint walls, furniture, and equipment.
11. Perform messenger service.
12. Perform other duties as assigned by the business administrator.

Figure 4.19

PERSONNEL POLICY HANDBOOK

CONTENTS

CHURCH EMPLOYEE CATEGORIES

Employee categories are defined below. These terms will be used throughout this handbook in relation to certain practices and benefits.

1. *Called Staff*

    Full-time: Positions relating to the primary ministries of the church that include, but are not limited to:
    - Pastor
    - Minister of Education and Administration
    - Minister of Music and Outreach

    Part-time: Persons employed to direct a ministry of the church for a specified number of hours each week that include, but are not limited to:
    - Organist
    - Pianist
    - Children's Minister
    - Youth Minister

2. *Support Staff*

    This category includes:
    - Secretaries, Custodian/Maintenance, Kitchen Employees

    Probationary: A period of 60 days will apply to all categories of Support Staff.

    Regular: Employees who have been with the church more than 60 days and who work at least 37½ a week.

    Part-Time: Employees who have been with the church more than 60 days and who regularly work at least 20 hours per week but less than the normal full-time schedule.

    Temporary Part-Time: Employees who do not normally work on a regular schedule or who may be employed for a relatively short period of time.

EMPLOYMENT PROCEDURES

1. *Called Staff*
    a. Personnel Committee selects a subcommittee to help recruit for each vacant position with the exception of the pastor.
    b. Review and/or possibly amend the position description. Recommend any change in the position to the church.
    c. Develop a selection criteria based upon the perceived job, experience, and educational requirements of the position. A pay-benefit study may be conducted.
    d. Dissemination of pertinent position information to possible resources (e.g., seminaries, denominational offices, past staff members).
    e. Review all applicants against the selection criteria. Additional information may be requested as the review process proceeds.
    f. Recommend to the full Personnel Committee a priority listing of applicants based on qualifications. The full committee may amend the listing.
    g. Interview and/or review "in view of a call" the applicants in priority order.
    h. Recommend most qualified applicant to the church.

2. *Support Staff*
    a. When a vacancy occurs, the supervisor will review and/or possibly amend the position description.
    b. The supervisor will review all applicants in view of the qualifications needed for the position, and select the one who will best suit the job.

TERMINATION PROCEDURES

1. Voluntary Termination
    a. Two (2) weeks written notification must be given prior to the effective date of resignation. Failure to make proper notification could result in the loss of any accumulated benefits.
    b. In the case of called staff, the resignation must be announced at a church meeting.
2. Involuntary Termination
    a. Any church employee may be terminated involuntarily for unsatisfactory performance, failure to support church programs, failure to adhere to established personnel procedures or behavior unbecoming a Christian (as determined by vote of the church).
    b. Support staff may be terminated by his/her supervisor with the approval of the Personnel Committee.
    c. Called staff members may be terminated by the church. Such action may be initiated by the pastor and the Personnel Committee.
    d. Called staff terminated involuntarily may be given up to three (3) months severance pay and benefits as determined by the Personnel Committee.

OTHER EMPLOYMENT AND INTERIM POSITIONS

1. A called or full-time employee may not be employed in another job (inside or outside the church) without the written consent of the pastor and Personnel Committee.
2. The Personnel Committee and the pastor may employ an "interim" or "supply" staff worker in the event that a staff position is vacated.

WORKING RELATIONSHIPS

1. The pastor will supervise all called staff members.
2. The minister of education and administration will supervise all support staff members and the day care director.
3. The minister of music and outreach will supervise the organist and pianist.

LEAVE OF ABSENCE

1. Support staff: A leave of absence must be approved by the supervisor and the Personnel Committee.
2. Called staff: A leave of absence must be approved by the pastor, the Personnel Committee, and the church.

SCHOOL ATTENDANCE

School attendance during normal working hours must be approved by the pastor and Personnel Committee.

WORKING CONDITIONS

1. Normal office hours are 8:00 A.M.–5:00 P.M. All full-time employees are expected to work a minimum of 37½ hours per week. Part-time employees will post a schedule of working hours not adhering to the normal working hours.
2. Breaks:
    a. A lunch break will normally be one (1) hour. Longer periods of time must be approved by the supervisor and normal hours adjusted.

b. A fifteen (15) minute break may be taken in the morning and one in the afternoon. Working hours may not be adjusted for shorter breaks.

c. Overtime is considered an exceptional working condition and must be approved by the supervisor and/or the Personnel Committee if compensatory time or pay is to be granted.

d. All work will normally be performed in the location appropriate for the activity (e.g., all office work is to be done in the office). Any deviation from this pattern must be approved by the supervisor and/or Personnel Committee.

e. Full-time called staff members will be allowed two (2) days off per week (not to include Sunday). Only one day will be taken between Monday and Friday and must be scheduled on a permanent basis with exceptions being scheduled at least one week in advance. Days off not taken may not be accumulated.

PAY POLICIES

1. Called staff and support staff will be paid biweekly. Pay periods will end on Saturday for support staff and on Sunday for called staff.
2. Checks will be issued on Wednesday following each ending pay period.
3. Initial employment pay-benefits will be recommended by the Personnel Committee to the Finance and Stewardship Committee. The Finance and Stewardship Committee will approve and/or amend the pay benefits, based upon the financial resources of the church, and include these with the position description for final approval by the church.
4. Raises/benefits will be recommended to the Finance and Stewardship Committee by the pastor and Personnel Committee.
5. Raises/benefits for the pastor will be recommended to the Finance and Stewardship Committee by the deacons.
6. Raises/benefits for all staff will be reviewed annually in time to be included in the January 1 budget.
7. The church participates in the Social Security program for all employees. Qualified ministers relate to Social Security on an individual basis as self-employed persons.
8. Worker's compensation insurance coverage shall be provided for all employees and ministers.

BENEFITS FOR FULL-TIME CALLED STAFF

1. Vacations:
   After six (6) months of service—five (5) working days and one (1) Sunday.
   One (1) to four (4) years of service—ten (10) working days and two (2) Sundays.
   Five (5) to ten (10) years of service—fifteen (15) working days and three (3) Sundays.
   Ten (10) years plus of service—twenty (20) working days and four (4) Sundays.
   Vacations may not be declined during successive years.
   Vacations not taken within the year of eligibility will be lost except as approved by the Personnel Committee in writing.
2. Sick Days:
   Provisions for sick days are determined by the Personnel Committee.

3. Revivals and Speaking Engagements:

    Four (4) weeks including Sundays (not consecutive) may be taken to serve
    as guest minister or a leader or participant in training conferences, classes,
    conventions, etc. Consecutive Sundays must be approved by the Personnel
    Committee.

4. Holidays:

    Nine (9) holidays* per year as follows:

    New Year's Day

    Memorial Day

    Good Friday

    July 4

    Labor Day

    Thanksgiving Day and the following Friday

    Christmas Eve and Christmas Day

    *When the holiday falls on Saturday and/or Sunday, adjustments will be
    made.

5. Leave of Absence:

    A leave of absence without pay may be granted upon the approval of the
    Personnel Committee and the church. A leave of absence may not be
    granted for more than 45 days.

6. Military Leave

    Military leave, not to exceed two (2) weeks, will be granted to any person
    who is active in the National Guard or Reserves.

7. Bereavement Leave

    Three (3) days bereavement leave may be granted in the death of an imme-
    diate family member: spouse, children, and parents. Additional time may be
    granted by the Personnel Committee.

8. Maternity Leave

    A leave of absence not to exceed twelve (12) weeks may be taken. The
    church shall continue only insurance benefits during such leave. No salary
    will be paid during the leave of absence except for remaining sick leave and
    vacation time. Additional time with or without pay may be granted by the
    Personnel Committee.

9. Study Leave

    Upon completion of each ten (10) years of service, the pastor and other
    full-time called staff become eligible for a study leave.

    The pastor may be granted up to twelve (12) weeks leave in addition to other
    time off with full pay to engage in study. Other full-time called staff mem-
    bers may be granted up to nine (9) weeks in addition to other time off.

    The Personnel Committee may secure an interim supply for the staff
    member on leave.

    A study leave agenda must be approved by the Personnel Committee.

10. Jury Duty

    Employees are encouraged to cooperate in civic responsibilities. The
    worker on jury duty will receive full pay in addition to jury fees.

11. Anniversary Recognition

    Anniversary recognition shall be observed on the 1st, 5th, 10th, 15th, etc.,
    anniversaries. A church-wide reception will be held to recognize each min-
    ister on these occasions.

BENEFITS FOR FULL-TIME AND PART-TIME
SUPPORT STAFF

1. Vacations:

    Five (5) working days may be taken after six (6) months of service.

    Ten (10) working days may be taken after one (1) year of service.

    Fifteen (15) working days may be taken after ten (10) years of service.

    Organist and Pianist Vacations:

    > One (1) week may be taken after six (6) months of service.

    > Two (2) weeks may be taken after one (1) year of service.

    > Three (3) weeks may be taken after ten (10) years of service.

    Vacations may not be declined during successive years.

    Vacations not taken within the year of eligibility will be lost except as approved by the supervisor and Personnel Committee.

2. Sick Leave:

    Five (5) working days per year are allowed for the illness of the employee or immediate family. Upon completion of three (3) years service, two (2) weeks are allowed. Additional time off may be granted by the Personnel Committee.

    Organist and Pianist Sick Leave:

    > One (1) week per year is allowed for the illness of the employee or immediate family. Upon completion of three (3) years service, two (2) weeks are allowed. Additional time off may be granted by the Personnel Committee.

3. Holidays:

    Nine (9) holidays* per year as follows:

    New Year's Day

    Memorial Day

    Good Friday

    July 4

    Labor Day

    Thanksgiving Day and the following Friday

    Christmas Eve and Christmas Day

    *When the holiday falls on Saturday and/or Sunday, adjustments will be made.

4. Bereavement:

    Three (3) days bereavement leave may be granted to an employee in the case of a death in the immediate family: spouse, children, and parents. Additional time may be granted by the Personnel Committee.

5. Absences:

    The supervisor must be informed prior to the employee's absence. Absences for personal reasons are discouraged but in emergencies must be approved by the supervisor.

6. Maternity Leave:

    A leave of absence not to exceed twelve (12) weeks may be taken. The church shall continue only insurance benefits during such leave. No salary will be paid during the leave of absence except for remaining sick leave and vacation time. Additional time with or without pay may be granted by the Personnel Committee.

7. Jury Duty:

    Employees are encouraged to cooperate in civic responsibilities. The worker on jury duty will receive full pay in addition to the jury fees.

CHAPTER 5

Office Administration

Bruce P. Powers

A church office is the nerve center of a congregation's life. It is a support system for church staff members and volunteer leaders, a communication center for church life, and a business location for transacting church affairs. It is at the center of support services for church administration.

PURPOSE OF THE CHURCH OFFICE

The purpose of the church office is to provide support services that assist the congregation in achieving church-approved goals. Under the guidance of designated leaders, tasks will be organized and performed in such a manner as to enable a church and its leadership to function effectively and efficiently.

The church office is the administrative center for the congregation as well as the major contact point for members throughout the week.

CHECKPOINTS FOR OFFICE ADMINISTRATION

There are five major areas to consider: location, environment, facilities, equipment, and work systems. General guidelines for each of these will be given. Keep in mind, however, that you will have to determine specific ways to apply these in your situation. The number of church staff members, the availability of facilities, and financial considerations influence the extent to which a church can provide centralized support services.

LOCATION

Where is your church office? It should easily be accessible by church members *and* by persons not familiar with your facilities. Parking should be nearby, access by young and elderly should be easy, directional signs

should point the way, and the area should be convenient to other offices and work rooms.

Pretend you are a newcomer to town and that you are going to the church office to get information about worship services. Drive up to your church and approach it as a newcomer would. What would you see? Where would you park? What entrance would you use? What signs would tell you where to go? What would you think of the church before even reaching the office?

ENVIRONMENT

As you walk into your church office, what impresses you? Does it appear orderly? And would you know where to stand or sit, or where to get information if you were a stranger. How would you be greeted, and by whom?

The personality of an office is just as important in relating to people as your personality is to you. The environment of your church office elicits a positive or negative feeling, it gives confidence or doubt, it can inspire trust or encourage suspicion about the quality of administrative leadership in a church.

Most often mentioned in office manuals are the needs for:

- clean and uncluttered work areas;
- clean and attractive reception/waiting area;
- clean and well-maintained furnishings;
- clean and well-maintained floors, walls, and ceilings;
- adherence to published office hours;
- warm, personal greeting when a guest enters.

Office consultants would tell many of us: clean up, throw away, paint, and spend a little money on attractive furnishings.

FACILITIES

An office can be a corner of a room, or it can be a suite of offices, workrooms, and storage areas. One basic principle overrides all others: everything must be functional—it must help you do your job! The church office must not be a catch-all location for old literature, athletic supplies, out-of-date equipment, and a place to retire used furniture that someone donated.

A basic administrative guideline is, *a place for everything, and everything in its place*. This is pretty good advice. You need a reception area, work stations (desks or tables), walkways, work areas, and storage facilities. Each of these requires decisions about what is needed, where it should be located, and how best to manage the work flow.

Reception Area. This area should be immediately inside the entrance to the office, and it should be separated from the work area by a reception desk, counter, planter, or some other device. Items needed include: at least two comfortable chairs, a table, lamp (or good overhead lighting), a place to hang coats, and a small trashcan. Keep some current church literature and brochures about your church on the table.

The secretary or receptionist should have line-of-sight vision of the entrance in order to greet any visitor immediately. Seats in the reception area should be arranged so that persons waiting are not looking directly at the work areas; in this way jobs can continue without office workers appearing rude.

Guidelines for the Reception Area

1. Greet each visitor and determine what he or she needs.
2. If the visitor has an appointment, ask the guest to be seated while you notify the appropriate person.
3. If the person has an information or work request, determine immediately whether you can handle the request or need to refer it. Most requests will be routine, and you can handle according to established procedures. If you are not sure how to handle a request, write down the information and inform the person when and to whom you will channel the request.
4. When a visitor is kept waiting, tell the person you are sorry and give a reason if appropriate. Don't let a person sit and wonder why the delay.
5. Keep a record of visitors, requests, and work you perform on a drop-in basis. Use a daily calendar or appointment sheet. This is invaluable if you are asked to tell about something that was said or done, if you need to assess the work flow in the church office, or if you need to recall the details later when you are doing some work that someone had requested.
6. Keep the area fresh and clean. Live plants, up-to-date reading materials, a box of tissues, and attractive furnishings will make a good impression for your church.

Work Stations. Desks, tables, and chairs should be at a comfortable height: desks, 29–30 inches; typing or keyboard tables, about 26 1/2 inches; and chairs, adjustable from 17 to 21 inches. Chairs must be comfortable in size and in design. It is unwise to use cheap chairs to save a little money and lose efficiency due to poor back support.

The size and design of furniture should be appropriate for the work to be performed. Consider the size and number of machines and other devices that must regularly be within reach of the person working at a particular place. If you are outfitting a new office, consult with an office supplier to determine what might be appropriate in your situation. If you are going to evaluate a current arrangement, discuss needs with those who use the equipment. Be sensitive to expressions of back and shoulder discomfort, eye fatigue, and inability to concentrate for extended periods—signs often related to design of work areas.

Guidelines for Work Areas

1. Determine what needs to be done at each work station, the appropriate furniture, necessary equipment, and the resources that need to be nearby.

2. Design each work area so that all major items (phone, primary work machines, etc.) are within a radius of about three feet from the worker. A swivel chair with rollers is preferable for many situations; this allows quick, easy access to secondary resources (file cabinet, supply shelf, etc.) within about six feet. The distance from the floor should range between 6 and 54 inches, with the ideal being within 12 inches of the desktop.

3. Locate large and/or noisy operations away from the central office. In a small church, this may be in the next room. In a big church, locations most appropriate for the operations should be selected. Be sure to check the lighting, power, heating/cooling, and communications needs for remote office functions such as printing, addressing and mailing, literature processing, and such before making any final decisions.

4. Storage areas of often-used supplies should be in the immediate area where they are used. For example, word processing supplies should be at or near the desks and word processing machines or terminals, printing supplies in the printing/duplicating area, and financial materials in the area or office where such matters are handled. In a small church, you need a main storage cabinet; this would be located so that a secretary could secure paper or a typing ribbon without leaving the phone or reception area unattended. For all storage areas, label the location on each shelf or in each drawer for all items kept on hand. When the supply of a certain item is low, it will be easy to determine what is needed and reorder. A storage area for coats, umbrellas, lunches, and other items belonging to workers should be provided in a convenient but out-of-sight location.

5. Arrange work stations so that there is a minimum of distraction to a worker when someone walks by. In general, arrange a walkway on one side of a work area rather than through it. Whenever possible, arrange a divider at least 54 inches high between work stations to provide privacy, control the noise level, and avoid distractions. Make sure that all areas have good overhead lighting (preferably fluorescent) and adequate ventilation.

6. Evaluate your office arrangement whenever new workers come or there is a change in work assignments, equipment, or quality/quantity of work. Experiment with various arrangements by using graph paper or a computer design program to sketch out the possibilities.

OFFICE EQUIPMENT

The administrator's concern with equipment primarily is at the point of how best to speed up the work. An office could function without any electronic or mechanical assistance; but how nice it is to have labor-saving devices that improve efficiency. Each church has to determine what it is willing to invest in order to make its work easier, get it done faster, or do more of it.

One caution: The quest for improved efficiency through the use of electronic devices must not result in a loss of the *personal touch of ministry* extended to people through the church office.

Church office equipment generally helps us to do one of the following tasks:

• Word processing

• Financial reporting

• Data filing and sorting

• Duplicating

• Communicating

In each of these areas, there is a great variety of equipment ranging from simple, cheap, and slow to complex, expensive, and fast.

Work can be done well at a number of levels, for example word processing: by hand, mechanical typewriter, electric typewriter, "memory" typewriter, word processing computer, and oral/character recognition processors. Price range is from a few cents to several thousand dollars. Personnel time may range from ten minutes per letter to about three minutes; a second or slightly revised copy, thirty seconds to ten minutes. A typed bulletin that takes one hour to complete a perfect master on a typewriter takes twelve to fifteen minutes on a computer.

Consider the following options when making decisions about equipment.

Word Processing. As a general guideline, ten hours devoted to typing by an efficient worker with a typewriter can be reduced to three to five hours with a word-processing computer and printer. The real value of the computer is that corrections and changes can be made on a screen and fresh, original copies produced quickly. New copies might be typed at 50–70 words per minute; but a computer and laser printer can produce the same material error-free in a few seconds. Visit a computer dealer to compare work speed, print quality, and price ranges for various options.

Another consideration is the storage that is available with many electronic devices. After items are prepared the first time, they can be stored on a disk until you need them again, desire to revise them, or choose to delete them—all with very little time and trouble.

Take the church bulletin, for example. Prepare it one time and store it; the next week, push a button and it will appear on a screen. Type over the incorrect parts with the new date, hymns, sermon title, and announcements; press a button and a perfect master is printed. You just saved three-fourths of the time it would have taken to prepare one without the saved version.

Financial Reporting. The same examples given for word processing could be given for financial reporting. The only difference is that much more time can be saved. Rather than using a journal, finding and entering figures by hand, and performing calculations on a separate machine, a computer works this way:

1. A spreadsheet or budget form is displayed on the screen.

2. Figures are entered using the calculating keys on the computer keyboard.

3. Push a key and all of the entries are automatically calculated or readjusted in a matter of seconds.

4. Push a key and an accurate report is printed.

Data Filing and Sorting. Two types of filing cabinets are in general use in church offices. One is the traditional stacked-drawers model that files materials front to back. A newer style—called a lateral file—opens on the side, and file folders are placed side by side as if on a shelf. This design makes it easy to get to a large number of files without pulling and pushing drawers. If you wish, you can pull down a sliding cover over the materials.

Sorting devices for information are rather rare. Usually, materials will be sorted before filing, as in the case of a prospect list sorted by age groups, and then left in that form in a notebook, card file, or folder. To help with this task, most administrators have used codes like colors or symbols to faciliate what basically has been a manual operation.

The computer has revolutionized filing and sorting. With any information that must continually be updated, combined, sorted into parts, or in any way rearranged, a filing program on a computer will prove invaluable. Computer files can be used for membership rolls, financial records, sermons, ideas, prospects, visitation records, pastoral calls, sick lists, appointment schedules—in fact for anything that you might normally write on paper and stick in a file folder. All of this is encoded by typing the information on a screen, then recording it in an electronic file system. The most useful systems save the information internally and also allow you to transfer the data from machine to machine through a network or on a disk.

A membership record could be keyed to print out names sorted by ZIP code, age, vocation, and so forth. A talent file could within seconds list prospects for a vacant position. A sermon file could display a message preached in the past; it could be updated, added to, parts could be deleted, and a fresh, *new* sermon produced in a short period of time. Do you need to list new members in an alphabetical file? Simple. Type the information and tell the computer to insert it in the correct places. The insertions are made, and all material is automatically resorted to produce an accurate, up-to-date list. Want a fresh copy? Press a button.

Duplicating. A great variety of equipment is available to make multiple copies. For the usual items such as bulletins and newsletters, a photocopy machine is suitable. If paper of different sizes and textures is desired or collation is needed, more sophisticated equipment is required. Commercial printers are often used for thousands of copies or color materials. Consequently, you must determine the types of materials that need to be duplicated in your office and those that might be taken to a printing specialist.

In order to make decisions about duplicating in your office, list the items and the number of copies that need to be made during a typical month. Then discuss your needs with an office supply specialist.

Communicating. The basic equipment for communication is the telephone. However, the traditional use of one line with several extensions has been replaced by several options that are more efficient and very cost-effective.

Of course, there is still the need for that basic phone service line to the church office. This is provided through your local communication company. But once the line is installed, you may make whatever decisions you wish since all equipment can be purchased or leased from any source.

Guidelines for Communicating

1. Invest in quality equipment supported by good service. Inquire about the reputation of dealers in your area before making *any* decisions. Visit or call several churches similar to yours and discuss the good and bad features of their systems. Inquire about costs, reliability, and suggestions based on their experience.

2. In a small office, consider one desk phone and extensions as needed. If a private extension is needed, such as in a minister's study, arrange for an intercom on the phone system.

3. In larger offices that have several rooms and/or private working areas, you must have a switchboard to direct calls. Switchboards no longer are large and unsightly; they may take little more space than the phone and a large box of tissues. Discuss options for this with several vendors; secure proposals with specific bids. Consider leasing *and* purchasing.

4. Buy at least one good cordless phone, with a range of at least 700 feet and an intercom feature. This can be plugged right into a phone plug and used as an extension phone. Whenever someone has to work

away from the office, the portable handset can be carried. The church phone can be answered from this handset, or the person can be paged from the location of the phone's base. Some models offer multiple handsets that can operate from the same base.

5. Consider installing an answering and message machine. This device can be used very effectively to "tend the office" and to provide information about the church and scheduled activities when the office is closed. Callers can be greeted courteously by a recorded message, then asked if they would like to leave a message for someone. Note: Make your recorded messages short and personable, then tell callers how to leave a message. Always check the recorded message file as soon as possible after returning to the office and respond promptly to messages.

6. Consider placing answer-only phones and/or pay phones in locations where a phone is needed but use cannot be monitored, such as in a fellowship hall or in a gym.

7. A facsimile (FAX) machine is useful to send or receive copies needed quickly. If it is to be used frequently, buy one that prints on regular sheets rather than rolled or treated paper.

8. Scanning devices connected to computers can be used to transmit printed materials into electronic files for storage, editing, or transmitting to other locations via FAX.

9. Consider a multiple-use device that combines several functions such as phone, FAX, message center, and printer. Office supply stores can provide information as well as describe how properly equipped computers can perform these same functions.

Audit of Equipment Needs. Whenever there are questions about the efficiency and effectiveness of office functions, an audit can help to determine what equipment is appropriate for the job. The forms in figures 5.1and 5.2 can be used to evaluate either proposed or existing equipment needs.

Guidelines for Equipment Audit

1. Determine:
   - What needs to be done?
   - Who will do it?
   - How fast does it need to be done?
   - What level of quality is necessary?

2. According to the availability of resources, choose the most efficient equipment for the work that needs to be done. Consult with several

Figure 5.1

AUDIT OF EQUIPMENT NEEDS

WHAT NEEDS TO BE DONE? (What results do you expect?)	BY WHOM? (Name the person or position)	HOW FAST? (Rate from 1–10) Now Needed	QUALITY LEVEL NEEDED (Rate from 1–10) Now Needed	TOTAL POINT DIFFERENCE
1.				
2.				
3.				
4.				
5.				
6.				
7.				

Instructions

Complete the above information for each specific job function that requires equipment. Rate the present speed and quality on a scale between 1 and 10 with 1 the lowest. Then rate the *needed* performance level from 1 to 10. Subtract the *now* score from the *needed* score on each line; add these two numbers and enter the sum under *Total Point Difference.*

PRIORITY ITEMS (List the above needs in order from the highest score to the lowest.)

1.

2.

3.

4.

5.

6.

7.

Figure 5.2

EVALUATION OF EQUIPMENT OR SOFTWARE

EVALUATION OF EQUIPMENT OR SOFTWARE FOR:_____(job)
NAME OF EQUIPMENT OR SOFTWARE:_____
VENDOR OR SUPPLIER:_____

REQUIREMENTS FOR THIS ITEM	EVALUATION (USE A SCALE FROM 1–10)			COMMENTS FOR OR AGAINST
	References From Users	Vendor Literature	Demonstrations You Have Seen	
SPEED				
QUALITY				
EASE OF USE				
EASE OF LEARNING				
EASE OF MAINTENANCE				
POINT AVERAGE	ESTIMATE THE VALUE OF THIS ITEM BASED ON THE COST:			__SUPERIOR __GOOD __FAIR __POOR
SIGNED	POSITION			

vendors (such as office equipment, computer supply, and communication companies) to get acquainted with equipment options and to secure recommendations. Meanwhile, discuss needs with knowledgeable business persons in your church.

3. Evaluate possibilities with workers who would be affected.
4. Work through the normal decision-making channels in your church to secure and/or replace equipment.
5. Use only reputable dealers that have a reputation for service and attention after a sale. Avoid trading after-the-sale assistance for a few dollars' savings; the best price must be determined over the life of the equipment.
6. A fireproof safe or filing cabinet is absolutely necessary for securing valuable records.
7. As you add or change equipment, keep at least one typewriter in service. Typewriters are more efficient than computers for short-work items like addressing an envelope or filling out a form. Volunteers

helping out in the office can use a typewriter, and you will have a
back-up machine for typing when the other equipment is being serviced.

8. When considering computer applications, keep these points in mind:

- Even with a good computer, you still need good manual procedures. Computers operate best when office information systems
are well designed and understood.

- A new computer or program will not fit exactly your present methods; adjustments in work flow and duties will be necessary.

- Computers help *good* workers. They can only extend and enhance
the skills of those using them. Don't count on a computer to make
up for poor performance of a worker.

- While your office is adjusting to a computer, demands will be
greater for those learning how to operate the equipment and use
the system. Be patient.

- You must evaluate the specific needs of your office. Then, if you
desire to move toward new computer applications, evaluate the
programs (software) that are available. Find those that best meet
your needs, then consider the equipment (hardware) that will operate the programs.

WORK SYSTEMS

On the following pages you will see a variety of work systems that
could be used in your office. Each of them obviously must be part of a
larger operation; everyone and everything in an office must work together
for the benefit of the church.

Review these ideas, consider your existing systems, then determine
what you might want to revise. In some cases you can take the suggestions
and use them with very little adaptation. In others, you will want to consult
the suggested resources and then work out your own version. Either way,
good administrative practice requires that those who are involved in doing
the work be involved in making decisions about how to improve.

Office Protocol. Review and/or determine the items in figure 5.3 for
your situation. Write in the general expectations. Discuss them with those
involved; then prepare a final copy that can be distributed and used as a set
of guidelines for office protocol.

Figure 5.3

GUIDELINES FOR OFFICE PROTOCOL

Office hours—

Dress code—

Reception duties—

    How to greet callers:

    On the phone—

    In person—

Titles: when and what titles to use (Mr., Mrs., Dr., Rev., etc.):

    In reference to ministerial staff—

    Church members—

    Outsiders—

How to handle requests—

Message taking procedure—

How to handle emergencies—

What to do when someone is angry or demanding:

    Member—

    Visitor—

    Business or civic representative—

    Vagrant—

What to do when you:

Are sick—

Are angry—

Have a conflict with a co-worker—

Expectations about supervision—

Expectations about confidentiality—

Telephone/Communications

1. If possible, the same person should do all the answering, forwarding of calls, and message taking. In case this person is unable to answer, agree that anyone in the office will answer after three rings. Be sure *all* personnel are trained in how to answer the phone and what to say. Few things are worse for your image than a gruff "Hello!" followed in a few seconds by, "I don't know."

2. Identify the church, then yourself, and ask, "May I help you?"

3. Do not keep a person waiting. If a caller cannot be helped or connected right away, arrange to take a message or to call the person back. Avoid placing a person on "hold."

4. Use a standard form such as illustrated in figure 5.4 to record all messages.

Figure 5.4

OFFICE MESSAGE FORM

TO	DATE	TIME
FROM	TELEPHONE NO.	EXT. NO.
WHILE YOU WERE GONE, THE ABOVE PERSON		
❏ TELEPHONED ❏ RETURNED YOUR CALL ❏ WILL CALL AGAIN ❏ PLEASE CALL	❏ CALLED IN PERSON ❏ IMMEDIATELY	MESSAGE TAKEN BY
❏ YOUR INFORMATION ❏ AS YOU REQUESTED ❏ PER CONVERSATION ❏ TYPE ___ COPIES 　❏ SINGLE SPACE 　❏ DOUBLE SPACE ❏ MAKE ___ COPIES	❏ HANDLE ❏ CALL ME ❏ SEE ME ❏ COMMENT ❏ SUPPLY INFORMATION ❏ RECOMMEND	❏ PREPARE REPLY ❏ RETURN ❏ FOR APPROVAL ❏ SIGNATURE ❏ FILE ❏ DESTROY
❏ THANK YOU!	DATE NEEDED	TIME NEEDED
COMMENTS		

5. If there are several people who work in your office, use a sign-in and sign-out sheet so that the phone attendant will know who is available. Also, persons in conference must notify the attendant when they desire not to be disturbed.

6. Maintain a log for all long-distance calls. This will serve as a checklist when the bill comes.

7. Develop a policy regarding the use of church phones for private purposes by workers or by members. What local and what long distance calls are appropriate to receive? to make?

8. If your church has a cordless phone, this can be taken when someone is on an errand in the building. If there is only one worker, the phone can be answered in the normal way without anyone being aware of where the person is. If there are several workers, the person with the cordless phone can be paged if necessary.

9. Consider the use of one of the long-distance phone services in your area. Many of them provide savings of up to forty percent over traditional rates. A prepaid calling card would be helpful for ministers to carry when out of town.

10. Limit personal calls, both incoming and outgoing, to necessary messages. Also, be careful about letting business calls turn into pleasure calls.

11. Use an answering and message telephone when there is no one in the office. Listen and respond to messages first thing upon returning.

12. Publish your church office telephone number along with the name of the church in all membership publications. List the church's name and number in the yellow pages of the phone book as well as in the white pages. In a large church, you may wish to provide and publish separate numbers for some of the offices or ministers.

Filing and Storing Records

1. Keep ready-reference materials—those items that need to be stored and used in the church office—in sturdy folders or file cabinets/containers within easy reach of workers. Categories of materials and possible filing options are given in figure 5.5.

2. Records that must be retained either for the benefit of the church or to fulfill legal obligations often are not in the ready-reference category. They must be filed and stored, but may be placed in a secure location adjacent to or near the work areas. These are materials such as bank records, historical documents, deeds, and business contracts. The usual rule is: Keep all valuable and/or historical materials in a vault or safe box, and all other records either in or near the church office. A Record Retention Schedule in figure 5.6 gives an approximate time to keep different types of materials.

3. Code all materials that come to the church office as soon as practicable. Work out a system for someone to determine what information needs to be saved and for how long. Place a code in the upper right corner, "File: ___." Items that come in bulk, such as supplies and literature, should be labeled with the person's name and location to which the items are to go.

4. Separate mail into categories: personal, church, and "to whom it may concern" items, such as catalogs and sales brochures. Handle the personal, send the church items to the appropriate person for action, and make an *immediate* decision whether to save or discard the junk mail.

5. If items will not be saved, use or circulate them as appropriate and then discard.

Figure 5.5

READY REFERENCE MATERIALS

ITEM:	FILING OPTIONS:		
	JOURNAL OR NOTEBOOK	FILE DRAWER OR SIMILAR DEVICE	COMPUTER* FILE
To-Do list	X		
Correspondence		X	
Purchasing records		X	
Leadership list	X		X
Organizational records		X	X
Membership records	X	X	X
Record of contributions	X		X
Financial reports	X	X	X
Prospect list		X	X
Sick list		X	X
Visitation list		X	X
Business meeting minutes	X	X	X
Inventory of equipment	X	X	
Personnel records—individuals		X	
Employment/personnel data		X	
Business contracts		X	
Legal data		X	

* The use of a computer compresses significantly the amount of space required as well as making the information easy to recall, tabulate, and revise. Items saved on a disk, however, should always be backed up with a spare copy. You can, of course, print copies of the information whenever desired.

Figure 5.6

RECORD RETENTION SCHEDULE

KEEP AT LEAST THREE YEARS

- Deposit records, bank statements, and processed checks
- General correspondence
- Inventory of equipment (after new one is prepared)
- Purchasing records
- Financial statements/reports to the congregation
- Organizational records (A summary should be included in the church minutes at least once a year, and in an annual denominational report.)

KEEP AT LEAST FIVE YEARS

- Insurance policies (after expiration date)
- Record of individual contributions
- Individual personnel records (after person has left employment)
- Tax records—employees
- Business contracts (maintenance and supply items/services)

KEEP PERMANENTLY

- Historical items (charter, constitution and bylaws, pictures, etc.)
- Legal items (deeds, contracts, bonds, incorporation documents, tax records, and other related items)
- Church business meeting minutes
- Audit and financial reports
- Master membership record
- Employment/personnel records
- Annual report of church activities

Some denominations provide a microfilm service to preserve church records. Contact your denominational office to inquire.

---

6. Attach copies of correspondence sent from your office to the letter being answered or the copy of the order being sent. Retain correspondence copies in two file folders. Mark one "Letters Inside" for communications within the membership, and another "Letters Outside" for others; write the beginning date underneath. When one of the files becomes bulky, remove both of them, write the ending date on each folder, and place them among the files not needed for ready reference. Prepare new file folders as indicated above.

7. Keep records of key decisions made, instructions received, actions taken, and any significant or unusual activities in which you are

involved. *This is absolutely necessary for effective administration.* Do not count on remembering the facts when something goes wrong, when someone wants to know exactly what is happening and why, or when a business sends an order and no one knows exactly what leader requested the items. For general records, write notes in your datebook or desk diary. For major actions, write notes on a sheet of paper and file in your personal records.

8. For expenditure of church funds, always follow a church-approved financial plan. Maintain either a purchase order system or a journal in which all transactions are recorded, along with person approving. For petty cash disbursements, require a cash receipt for the item signed by the person being reimbursed. For additional guidelines related to financial matters, see chapter 6.

Mailing Services

1. Establish a routine for receiving and processing incoming mail. Determine whether all mail except that marked personal will be opened and sorted by the assigned person. All mail addressed to a specific person should be placed in an agreed upon spot. Financial items such as bills and statements should be placed together for the treasurer. Non-specific mail should be processed according to established procedures.

2. If incoming mail is centrally processed, open all mail first, attach any enclosures to the enclosed letter, check to see that the letterhead has the return address information that is on the envelope (if not, staple it to the letter), stamp the first-class mail with date received, sort it, and then handle as agreed upon.

3. When there are several workers in an office, consider having a mail and message pick-up point. There should be slots or boxes for each person that can be seen easily when passing by. Normally, this location would be near the phone attendant so that messages could easily be placed in the appropriate place. Additional boxes and/or locations could be arranged for key church leaders and for employees who may work in other locations.

4. A pick-up point also is a good location for a collection box for all outgoing items. Determine the mail pickup time(s) in your area and post the time(s) by which mail must be in the box to be picked up and/or delivered to the post office.

5. Consult either with the postmaster or the customer service office of your local post office. Secure information about rates and specifications for the various classes of mail. Discuss the types and frequency

of mailings from your church, and get recommendations for how best to secure good service at the least cost. Record all information and place it along with pamphlets from the post office in a file folder.

6. Arrange the writing, editing, printing, and addressing activities for each major item mailed on a regular basis. Set the schedule so that everyone knows exactly what must be done, when, and by whom in order to get the mailing to the post office at the appointed time. A sample production schedule is included in chapter 10.

7. A postal scale will be of great assistance in determining the amount of postage to affix to letters and packages. This often saves a trip to the post office, or allows mail to be posted sooner.

8. In most churches, it is a simple matter to keep a roll of first-class stamps and a variety of other stamps in a box, replenishing when necessary. However, when there are many letters and packages mailed regularly, a postage meter is preferable. The actual cost can be determined and the postage printed on a label, just like at the post office. The amount is subtracted automatically from the amount of credit in your machine. You can even include your church's imprint on the label, if you wish. Consult your postmaster about the companies in your area offering this service.

9. Make a file for "Mail Services—Special." Secure information about special handling and next-day delivery from the post office. Get a small supply of certified and registered mail materials so that they can be prepared at your office. Find out if next-day delivery is available to and from your post office. Also call the overnight air services to determine if they pick up and deliver in your area, and the costs for letters and packages. Request a small supply of mailing envelopes. Contact a parcel service and request rates, pickup/delivery points, and schedules. Prepare the folder so that information and procedures are readily available. Make sure the person who handles the church's mail is thoroughly familiar with all options.

Communications within the Office. Effective interoffice communications make work easier. When personal contact is important, call or talk with persons directly. When this is not possible or necessary, choose one of the following methods:

1. Use an interoffice message form such as the one shown earlier in figure 5.4. Similar forms are available from any office supply store.

2. Arrange for a central mail and/or message pick-up point, such as described in the section on mailing services. The simplest device is a wooden or plastic block with one-half-inch notches, that will hold messages or envelopes. Each notch is labeled with a person's name.

The best location for this is where office workers often pass and within easy reach of the person who answers the phone.

3. If offices are equipped with computers, consider connecting them in a network. Then all interoffice communication can be sent, reviewed, and filed electronically. Consult with a computer or office supply specialist for information and costs.

4. Whenever you send an outside letter that includes information needed elsewhere in the office, instruct that a copy go to the appropriate person. This can either be indicated in the letter (c: name of recipient of copy), or it can be a *blind copy* (bc: name of recipient— placed *only* on the office copies).

5. Use NCR (no carbon required) pads for quick handwritten or typed notes. These can be standard memo forms or forms printed specially for your church. Remove the number of sheets desired, write or type on the top sheet, and you have an original and the number of copies desired. No mess, and it is fast.

6. Dictation is easier and more efficient if a recording device is used. Very rarely is dictation given personally anymore. New devices make it easier and more convenient for the person who sends information and for the person who transcribes. Devices are available that can be carried easily from office to car to home, offering a time-saving option for busy church workers. The recorded information can then be left for dictation, with the typist being able to start and stop the tape as necessary in order to prepare the desired material. Alternatively, some ministers use portable computers to prepare documents. When the material is ready, you can print out the finished copy or give the disk to an office worker for processing.

7. When asked to give a verbal message to someone in your office, especially from a member of the congregation, write it down. Then place it on the message board and forget it.

8. When preparing committee meeting minutes and other such reports, make enough extra copies to send to key staff persons. This will keep them informed with little extra effort.

9. Purchase standard office forms or develop your own for all regular information recorded and/or distributed in your office. If a suitable form is not available from an office supply store, type the form as you want it to look; leave lines and spaces where the desired information can be inserted. This form can be duplicated in your office or it can be sent to a printer. If desired, pads of your custom-designed form can be made either by the printer or in your office. Inquire at your office supply store about the way to bind forms in a tear-off pad.

10. Memos and forms that will be filed in a notebook should be duplicated on *punched* paper. Paper can be bought by the ream with holes already punched for very little extra cost.

11. All church staff members must tell the receptionist/phone attendant when they will be out or unavailable during office hours. Keep this information next to the phone.

Minutes of Business Meetings. The following procedures are helpful in maintaining an accurate accounting of important information in the life of the church. While these steps are specifically for business meeting minutes, the same process could be used for processing any records for which the church office is responsible.

1. The clerk or other authorized person should take the minutes.

2. The minutes should be prepared, typed, and reviewed for accuracy.

3. Send a copy to the presiding officer/pastor for review.

4. Minutes of the previous meeting should be read, corrected as necessary, and approved at the next regular business meeting.

5. An official copy and two photocopies should then be distributed as follows: the original to a chronological file of church business meeting records; a copy for the clerk's file; and a copy retained for ready reference in the church office.

6. Store *official* minutes in a secure, preferably fireproof location, under the care of an appointed staff member. Use them only for official purposes, such as a church audit. Minutes should be permanently bound either by the year or by several years, depending on the number of pages. If the service is available in your denomination, consider having copies made and stored in a permanent historical collection.

7. Keep the office copy of minutes in a notebook for easy use. Retain these copies on a reference shelf in the office for three years, or longer if there appears to be a need.

Membership and Organizational Records

1. Determine a scheduled time each week when all regular files are updated. A sample plan is on the next page.

2. Whenever possible, combine other tasks with the above activities. For example, when processing requests for church membership, also fill out a form that will add the person to the church mailing list, place the person's name on the prospect list for church organizations, give the minister(s) pertinent information, and notify the new member committee.

3. Evaluate the present system for handling these routine tasks. If there are not established procedures, write the exact steps that are to be

completed and review them with those who are involved. Look for ways to cut and combine steps. Then adopt the procedures that will best serve your office. Once this has been done, work can be delegated, or shared with other workers or with volunteers. The procedures become the basis for training and for determining the exact duties to be done.

4. Maintenance of membership and organizational records requires the use of standard forms and other supplies. One person should be responsible for determining the materials used regularly and maintaining an adequate supply.

5. Consult with your denominational bookstore or an office supply store to determine the best binders, holders, files, and other supplies to manage these materials. Often there are specialized devices that save much time and effort.

6. Computers provide an effective and speedy way to manage records and produce reports. Your denominational office or a theological school should be able to provide information about record management programs and suppliers.

Sample plan for updating membership and organizational records

MONDAY	Compilation of Sunday visitors Sick List Church membership requests (sent and received)
TUESDAY	Organizational files (attendance records, Visitors, new members, drops, etc.)
WEDNESDAY	Prospect file and visitation list
THURSDAY	Master membership file specialized files (newcomers list, newsletter mailing list, college students away, etc.)

CHAPTER 6

Financial Procedures
William G. Caldwell

Churches have two limited resources: money and people. Using these resources wisely requires each church to budget wisely, to subscribe the budget, and to use the funds from these limited resources in keeping with the wishes of the congregation.[1]

Research in the giving patterns of church members indicates that a minimal percentage of the membership give most of the budget money and that perhaps as many as fifty percent of the membership give nothing during a twelve-month period. The church, through its leadership, has a keen responsibility in planning effective ministry budgets and spending the tithes and offerings of the people. The highest level of integrity is called for when caring for God's money that is given through a local church.

Mission efforts and worthy programs often suffer from inadequate funding. Without financial planning, churches can be strapped with unrealistic debt, ballooning personnel costs, and rising maintenance and utility charges.

TRAINING A COMMITTEE

A Stewardship or Finance Committee, or some similar group, should be selected and trained to give vital leadership in financial matters. The committee will seek to develop distinctive Christian stewards through all areas of the church's life and work. It will endeavor to permeate all teaching, preaching, training, and mission work with biblical concepts of stewardship. This process must be developed and implemented on a year-round basis. It is obvious that church members do not automatically become distinctive Christian stewards when they come to know Christ; but they do become learners and disciples. This committee can help a church give attention to this aspect of discipleship.

Members of this committee should give evidence of being dedicated Christian stewards. They should also reflect a growing commitment to Christ. The characteristics of a distinctive steward have been described as one who makes Christ Lord, acknowledges God as owner of everything, and accepts responsibility as trustee of God's bountiful blessings. A member of the Stewardship Committee will demonstrate a redeemed life in giving, reflecting the teachings of the church in tithing or systematic giving as well as being one who manages personal money well.

Committee members should also be concerned with the growth of the church, particularly its needs and opportunities. They should be adept at informing others of these facts. Committee members should be spiritually mature persons who have the confidence of other church members. They should participate fully in the activities of the committee as well as in all stewardship functions of the church. Members of this committee should be carefully selected and elected according to the procedures of the church.

DEVELOPING A BUDGET

The best approach to budgeting is to start over each year and develop a budget based on fixed costs with variables being assigned funds in order of their priority. In a local church this plan of assessing needs and resources is called *ministry budgeting*. This is a process by which a church plans its spending around the ministries it conceives as God's will for its life. This involves the vision and mission understanding of the church. Since budgeting is an evidence of our interpretation of that will, we carefully study its processes.

Ministry budgeting is based on people. The size of a church has little to do with the ministries it performs; however, planning does. This process may be used by a church of a hundred members just as easily as it can be used by a church of a thousand members or more. The committee asks important questions:

1. What are the ministries our church will be engaged in next year to accomplish the mission God has given us?
2. How much will these ministries cost?
3. Is there a better way to get the job done?

In essence, each church needs to rediscover what it is to do, and find ways of getting that job done. Ministry budgeting is an effective way of doing the job. Guidelines for developing a budget are given in chapter 7.

PRESENTING THE BUDGET FOR CHURCH APPROVAL

Methods of presenting the budget can be changed from year to year. Using audiovisuals, panel discussion, and congregational discussion can heighten interest in the budget. Major changes in budget format, additional staff, or new buildings should be thoroughly explained and discussed until all questions have been answered. Save enough time for a discussion period.

Some churches adopt the report of the budget committee and the new church budget at the end of the discussion period while it is "fresh" on people's minds. Other churches wait several days before the vote is taken in a worship service to allow for more thought and prayer about the decision.

UNDERWRITING THE BUDGET

From the time of budget adoption and the process that will underwrite the budget, there is a time of prayer, education, and promotion. Many varied and productive plans are available to assist in this significant task.[2] Sermons will be preached, stewardship lessons will be taught in Sunday school, and tithing testimonies will be featured in the worship services. An individual commitment will be sought from each church and Sunday school member. Whether this is done through the mail or by a personal visit, it is important that everyone be given the opportunity to indicate financial support for the ministries of the church.

ACCOUNTING FOR THE BUDGET

A procedure for receiving and expending funds is critical to the integrity of the church's financial plan. Anytime money is received, at least two church members should be present to assume responsibility for these monies! Money should be counted in a place where reasonable security can be maintained. Again, at least two members should be present during the counting of the money. As soon as possible it should be deposited in the church's bank account. Under no circumstances should money remain in the church or in a home overnight.

A procedure for the accounting of church funds should follow this schedule:

- Receive monies from all sources within the church.
- Count the money, and fill out appropriate records (see figure 6.1, p. 124).
- Deposit all money.
- Post member contributions and provide each member an annual record of his or her giving.
- Record all financial transactions.
- Make a monthly report to the church.

A current practice among some churches is to secure a bond from a bonding company for each person who has fiduciary responsibility. This is a prudent business decision that all churches should follow. In no way does

Figure 6.1

COUNTING COMMITTEE REPORT

DATE: _____

BUDGET OFFERINGS	SUNDAY SCHOOL	WORSHIP SERVICE
Money in Envelopes		
Not in Envelopes		
Other		
Total		

DESIGNATED OFFERINGS		AMOUNT
Total		

Total Cash	Total checks	
Grand Total		

CASH COUNT		SUNDAY SCHOOL	WORSHIP SERVICE
Currency:	$50.00		
	20.00		
	10.00		
	5.00		
	1.00		
Change:	.50		
	.25		
	.10		
	.05		
	.01		
Total		$	$

Approved by	Date

bonding question the honesty of the person who handles church funds. It is simply good business practice.

USING PURCHASE ORDERS

Some churches control spending by using a purchase order system. When instituting such a system, it is essential that all persons in the church who might purchase for the church are made aware of the need to secure approval in advance. Vendors from whom the church might purchase items should be notified of the requirement that a purchase order must accompany all orders. The notification should include the information that after a specified date, the church will not be responsible for payment unless a purchase order has been received. The church will decide which budget accounts do not require a purchase order—such as salaries, missions, and building payment.

For purchases less than a specified amount, authorized persons can buy needed items and receive reimbursement from a petty cash fund (figure 6.2). For more costly items and those that must be ordered, a request is given to the financial secretary or the fiscal representative of the Stewardship Committee. This request may be oral or written according to church policy. (For a purchase requisition form, see figure 6.3 on p. 126). After a request is received and approved by the designated church purchasing agent, a purchase order form (figure 6.4, p. 127) is prepared and delivered. The number on the purchase order must then appear on the invoice before payment is made.

Figure 6.2

PETTY CASH SLIP

No. _____

RECEIVED OF PETTY CASH $_____

For_____

_____

Charge to budget acct. # _____

Signed_____ Date _____

Approved _____ Date _____

Figure 6.3

PURCHASE REQUISITION

Please purchase for _____
Name _____

Committee or program to be charged _____
Purpose or use _____

Deliver to_____
Notify _____
Date needed _____
Preferred vendor _____
Remarks_____

QUANTITY	DESCRIPTION	UNIT	TOTAL
		Total	

Signed _____
Approved_____
Received by_____

Figure 6.4

PURCHASE ORDER

No._____

TO [   ] SHIP TO

This number must appear on all correspondence, invoices, shipping papers and packages.

DELIVERY

DATE	REQ. NO.	TERMS	SHIP VIA	F.O.B. POINT
Quantity	Please enter our order in accordance with prices, delivery and specifications given			Price

Signed _____

Approved _____

Received by _____

Figure 6.5

CHECK REQUISITION
(NAME OF CHURCH)

Address_____Phone_____

Make Check to _____

Address_____City_____State_____Zip_____

Amount of Check $_____

Purpose of Check _____

Budget Account Number _____

Approved by _____

Pre-printed forms similar to those illustrated in this chapter are available from office supply stores. They can also be ordered with the name of your church or organization imprinted.

Checks will be drawn against the general bank account of the church when a check requisition like the sample in figure 6.5, p. 127, has been completed and authorized. Normally, payroll checks are not drawn with a check requisition. All other checks, however, should have this approval safeguard before being issued.

Many churches require two signatures on each church check. Usually the treasurer and one other member of the Stewardship or Finance Committee are authorized to sign checks.

THE ANNUAL AUDIT

There is a growing trend toward securing an annual audit conducted by an independent firm of public accountants. There are several benefits:

- credibility of the financial statement,

- assistance in developing good and meaningful financial statements and reports,

- professional advice on controls and other administrative matters, and

- compliance with legal requirements.

In addition, an experienced accountant can provide the technical assistance for establishing suitable record systems that reflect the needs of specialized church activities and simplify treasury functions. The audit establishes in-depth information provided in the financial statement.

If the church has never had an audit, the initial cost will be greater than subsequent audit costs. A base for assets and liabilities will be established and future audits will be constructed from that base. Some churches use an audit committee that reviews procedures during the time between professional audits.

DESIGNATED ACCOUNTS

Many churches have no fiscal problem with designated accounts. Churches usually seek to include all regular activities in the budget. For special purposes, however, members sometimes give funds designated for a particular cause. These funds are placed in a restricted account and used only for the specified purpose. Major difficulties and misunderstandings can be avoided by having a policy drawn by the Stewardship or Finance Committee and adopted by the church. One of the problems often faced in the absence of a policy is the giving of a gift for a specified purpose that does not fit into the church's priorities. Then the church risks losing the gift or changing its priorities. See the sample designated accounts policy in figure 6.6.

Figure 6.6

DESIGNATED ACCOUNTS POLICY

PURPOSE:

To provide procedures for the establishment, activity, and closure of a designated account.

ESTABLISHMENT

1. A designated account will be established upon a written request to the church administrator, the approval of the Finance Committee, and, if appropriate, the approval of the church.
2. The purpose of the account must be specific and consistent with the church's tax exempt purpose. It must comply with all IRS rules and regulations.
3. A minimum opening deposit of $100 is required.

ACTIVITY

1. The finance committee will be responsible for reviewing distributions to ensure compliance with the account's purpose.
2. Upon fulfillment of the purpose of the account, the account will be closed and any unused funds will be transferred to the general budget account or another account specified at the designated account's establishment.
3. When the account balance is less than $100, it will be closed, unless it has a periodically recurring purpose.
4. If the account is inactive for six months and with no immediate plans for its use, it may be closed and funds transferred to the specific account. Prior to closure, the establishing party will be notified and Finance Committee approval will be required.

CHART OF ACCOUNTS

A simple but extremely helpful device for proper budget coding is called a "chart of accounts." Each line item in the budget should have a corresponding descriptive paragraph telling what items are to be charged to that particular budget number. The Stewardship or Finance Committee prepares, evaluates, and updates the chart of accounts (see figure 6.7, p. 130).

Figure 6.7

CHART OF ACCOUNTS

Assets and Fund Balance 100
101 Cash in Bank A
102 Cash in Bank B
110 Petty Cash
120 Transfers to (from) Other Funds
190 Fund Balance
Designated Receipts 200
210 Missions
215 Organ Gifts
225 Debt Retirement
230 Other
Designated Disbursements 300
310 Missions
315 Organ Gifts
325 Debt Retirement
330 Other
Undesignated Receipts 400
410 Budget Receipts
412 Loose Offerings
Undesignated Disbursements
Missions 500
510 World Missions
520 Local Missions
530 Other Missions
Educational Ministry 600
610 Sunday School
613 Discipleship
615 Music
619 Denominational Literature
621 Vacation Bible School
625 Mission Organizations
    (Including Related Youth Groups)
630 Youth
644 Honoraria

648 Conventions and Conferences
651 Library
655 Scouts
660 Kindergarten
General Operations 700
706 Public Relations
712 Denominational Retirement
718 Insurance—Property
721 Kitchen
728 Office Supplies
735 Postage
738 Hospitality
745 Payroll Taxes
750 Utilities
756 Laundry
759 Ordinances
764 Altar Flowers
769 Employee Hospital Insurance
772 Miscellaneous
Property and Debt Retirement 800
810 Building Equipment
820 Building Maintenance
825 Office Equipment and Maint.
830 Grounds
840 Debt Retirement
Personnel Salaries; Allowances 900
910 Pastor
915 Minister of Education
920 Minister of Music
925 Church Secretary
930 Education Secretary
935 Organist
940 Nursery Coordinator
945 Nursery Assistants
950 Janitor

SPECIAL GIFTS

The Stewardship or Finance Committee will possibly have a subcommittee to seek and encourage special gifts. Because of changing tax laws and different state requirements, many church members may be unaware of tax advantages that are available to the giver. The committee should plan to inform church members of these advantages toward the end of each year. The church may also want to consult with a person who specializes in helping non-profit organizations determine the best use of non-cash items that are given to the church. Gifts that are to be sought are:

Real Estate: Opportunities for giving a home, farm, or other property will allow a federal income tax deduction for its full value, and avoid capital gains tax if the property's value has increased. Property can also be used to fund a trust that returns regular income for the life of the donor.

Memorial Gifts: Often families, respecting the wishes of deceased loved ones, request that memorials be established. Sometimes these are in the form of an endowment, where the amount given remains intact and is invested. The proceeds can then be designated for specific ministries of the church.

Gifts in Kind: Gifts in kind (jewelry, crops, livestock, works of art, coin collections, antiques, royalties, etc.) can be the perfect answer to giving interests. Mortgages, leases, or notes can be donated to the church.

Cash: If deductions are itemized on a federal income tax return, gifts of cash up to fifty percent of adjusted gross income can generally be deducted. If more than fifty percent of adjusted gross income is donated one year, the excess amount may be carried over.

Securities (stocks, bonds, mutual funds): There are three ways generally recommended for giving securities so that the gift benefits the charitable organization as well as the giver. The church should develop a policy on how these items are to be liquidated so that the proceeds can be utilized.

1. Give a security that has appreciated and qualifies for long-term, capital gains status.

2. Give the capital gains portion of an appreciated security and retain the amount of original cost.

3. Sell a depreciated security, deduct the loss, and donate the proceeds from the sale.

Life Insurance: Many people do not realize that life insurance policies or dividends paid on the policies make practical gifts. There are several ways to donate life insurance:

- Give policies no longer needed for their original purposes.

- Give a fully paid-up policy, and deduct its replacement cost.

- Give a policy on which premiums are being paid and deduct the approximate cash value, plus all future premiums paid.

A SYSTEMS APPROACH TO FINANCIAL RECORD KEEPING

Churches of all sizes are moving rapidly toward a systems approach to all record keeping, especially financial records. Personal computers are being used in smaller churches while large churches are going to more sophisticated hardware and programs.

Installing a computer will not solve all of the financial problems of a church. If good records are not in place already, adding a computer will likely compound the problem.

If a church decides to purchase a computer or upgrade present equipment, it is necessary to consider all of the needs of the church that might be impacted by such equipment. A committee composed of representatives of all areas of church life should be used to identify all possible uses. A search for software to accommodate the needs should be done prior to purchasing any equipment.

Several companies are producing software to meet the financial record-keeping needs of a church. Included in the program should be the capability to do all bookkeeping functions, individual member contributions, payroll, and monthly statements.

In addition to financial records, the computer should have the capacity to accommodate all educational organization records, membership rolls, master prospect file, and other needs identified.

CHAPTER 7

Planning and Budgeting
Bob I. Johnson

Jesus promised, "On this rock I will build my church, and the powers of death shall not prevail against it" (Matt. 16:18, RSV). In moving a church toward knowing and claiming this mind-boggling promise, planning and budgeting play strategic roles. All business and service organizations engage in these two functions. The church, however, is unique in all of the world and thus needs a specific word about how it addresses its future and utilizes its resources.

In planning and budgeting, the church will be saying something significant to itself, its community, its larger world, and ultimately to God, who birthed and sustains the church. This chapter is designed to offer you practical help in planning and budgeting. It will also seek to emphasize the impact these functions can have on the church's witness and story it seeks to tell.

PLANNING

Nothing takes the place of a good beginning in any effort, large or small. The approach you take to planning is most important in determining the outcome of such an effort. For example, if you rely solely on the planning model that studies the congregation, the geographical communities surrounding the meeting place, the resources available to that congregation for ministry, then the results will probably highlight the weaknesses, liabilities, and shortcomings of the congregation. It isn't that these things don't need to be done; however, if this is the sole approach, then the effect may be rather negative. Planning ought to help the church enhance its statement about what it wants to be and do under God.

In the first chapter, you read about ways to help a church clarify its vision and enhance its ministries. This chapter builds on that concept, showing how to provide leadership for decision-making and, then, for implementing plans. It would be helpful to consult resources on "change" along with the material in this chapter. See the bibliography for suggestions.

PRINCIPLES FOR PLANNING LEADERS

Some basic principles should undergird any planning in the context of the church, or related entity.

1. *Maintain the biblical meaning of church.* The purpose of a church is to be the people of God, a communion of saints, a called-out people in the community. The number-one requirement for an administrator is to keep clear focus on the biblical meaning of church.

Unlike other organizations the church has the undeniable promise of God that through the Holy Spirit the church will be directed and empowered for its mission. The Spirit gives power to overcome satanic forces and provides a spirit of love and self-control.

2. *Emphasize being, then focus on doing.* Danger lies in a planning process consisting primarily of setting goals and objectives, listing and choosing from alternative strategies for reaching the goals, performing the tasks, and evaluating the results. The primary danger lies in the assumption that there is an ideal to be reached and that it can be accomplished by marshaling the forces to do something. Foundational to *doing* is *being;* therefore, emphasis should be given to being God's people.

3. *Keep data in its place.* Data is important, but to base your planning solely on data that has been collected may send you off in the wrong direction. The danger lies in the fact that the more data a congregation collects, the greater the potential for confusion. This approach can also enslave local churches to the supposed inevitability of demographic trends of population growth or decline. For example, a local church may select a particular demographic trend, and on that basis justify withdrawing from active ministry efforts in certain areas.

Certainly, correlation between demographic trends and church growth exists. Some churches, however, grow in the midst of a declining population. Some churches decline in the midst of a swelling, unchurched population.

4. *Keep planning focused on the relational nature of the church.* In relation to the community, the church's task is to provide an arena where people can understand the forces affecting their lives, be confronted by the living God, and get a correct perspective on time and eternity. In short, the church must focus on its relationship to God and to people.

5. *Keep planning as a means to an end, not an end in itself.* It is fairly simple for a church to focus on lesser things and to miss the main things. A church may fall prey to an over-reliance on administrative structure,

financial planning, and the desire to eliminate risks. Planning can become an end in itself because it may be more interesting and safer than getting on with *being* the church.

Churches, however, must plan. Planning should be used to enhance mental and spiritual preparedness. It should be used to strategize actions the church should take based on the biblical purpose of the church.

6. *Major on the strengths of the church.* Strengths are present in every church and precisely so because God has empowered believers to develop them. For a church to deny its strengths for all practical purposes means that it denies God. This is not to be an ego trip because the strengths are gifts from God and as such belong to the entire congregation.

Good planning begins with helping a church proclaim its strengths because good planning begins with God. To ask, "What are our needs? What are our problems?" is to ask the wrong questions first.

7. *Base your planning on a set of stated values.* The congregation should affirm those things that are dear to it—values, in other words—and focus on these for the thrust of planning.

GUIDELINES FOR PLANNING

The principles of planning listed above should permeate the church's attitude and total process. The following guidelines are a sequential, step-by-step process that may be expanded or rearranged to suit your situation.

1. *Prepare for planning.* A key person in planning is the pastor. The pastor, in working with key leaders and the congregation as a whole, should be aware of the need and the timing for planning. The pastor is the person who knows the values of the church and expresses those values in a variety of ways. The basic philosophy and values of a church have far more to do with its achievements than do its economic resources, organizational structure, or various other aspects.

In the business world the effective companies seem to have developed cultures that have incorporated the values and practices of their great leaders, with those shared values surviving for decades after the passing of those leaders. The enduring contribution of a chief executive comes through the formation of values that guide the organization.

In preparing for planning, emphasize the church's story. Every congregation has one; it permeates the group life of the church and is the interpreter of past, present, and future. Story is the primary medium by which the identity, goals, perceptions, and strategies are communicated. Try asking "How come?" and you will probably get a story from the church's past. The story can enhance an appreciation of the rich background of the average congregation.

The local church that recounts its story gains many benefits. Narrative can identify and reinforce who and what the church is. It reveals what is important. It seems to facilitate group discussion of church life. It will reveal something of the pain in the life of the church and its needs. But most importantly, story can help the church to identify its mission and place in the world.

In preparing for planning, perhaps one way the church can be made aware of its story is to set up formal and informal group meetings in which people are allowed to share the parts of the church's story that have most influenced their lives. In a church with significant numbers of new people as well as many who have been members for many years, a time when both groups can share dreams and aspirations would be helpful. This helps people get to know each other better, understand how the church is perceived, and how they might fulfill the mission of the church.

2. *Establish purpose in planning.* By establishing purpose, I mean first of all to develop a clear statement of a church's purpose or mission. This mission statement serves as an umbrella under which the church functions in day-to-day and year-to-year ministry. Consider this example: "The mission of our church is to be a worshipping, redemptive body in Christ, whose field is the world and whose ministry includes the whole person."

A church may look at what others have adopted as samples, but each church should formulate its own unique statement. Try stating it as briefly as possible, but remember that this is a statement of purpose, not a *slogan*, such as "Family of Love." Consider displaying the statement in an appropriate place in the church building.

Such a statement should enable the church to move forward in planning its response to the future to which God is leading. If a church has no such statement at present, involve as many people as possible in the study of Scripture, history, and other church documents in writing such a statement. The pastor may find it appropriate to preach sermons on the subject. When it comes to the actual writing of a statement, a smaller group works better.

Another step in establishing purpose and direction in planning is to develop objectives. Two approaches are currently being used in relation to church objectives. In one view, objectives state the church's timeless intention to act. They are statements of ultimate ends toward which a church aims its energies. They express the congregation's understanding of the kind of church God wants it to be. Here is how one congregation wrote its mission statement.

Our objectives are to be:
1. A covenant fellowship of Christians filled with the Holy Spirit.
2. A worshiping fellowship in which God encounters people.
3. A congregation of witnesses for Christ both in this community and throughout the world.
4. A fellowship of maturing Christians whose learning results in responsible living.
5. A church that unselfishly ministers to persons in the community in Jesus' name.

Another approach makes objectives more specific. Here, objectives are stated in a sufficiently clear fashion that it is possible to know when they have been achieved. Thus, a local congregation that is effective in mission is seen as having a compelling passion for the achievement of very clear, intentional goals. In this approach, objectives should focus on specific groups with which the church wants to be on mission, like young adults or homebound elderly.

Whatever approach you take in the use of terminology, lifting the church's collective vision above the mundane through the eyes of mission objectives leads beyond yourselves. When a church is effectively on mission, that congregation is a group of persons living beyond selfish preoccupation. When this occurs, strengths are corporately developed, vision is lifted, and surges of energy make new levels of living possible.

As a part of establishing purpose in planning, keep in mind the individuals involved. Encourage members to remember that people are important. Hold up the truth that while a plan for the church is being developed, people can also grow and develop individually as Christian persons. Be aware of ministry opportunities that encourage individual growth.

Additionally, establishing purpose in planning involves a very simple but fundamental matter. What kind of planning are you doing: *long-range* (up to three years), *short-range* (up to one year), or *operational* (week by week, month by month)?

Long-range planning sets directions for up to three years, aligns major church plans with the church's statement of mission, and sequences priorities for the expenditure of resources. The purpose is not to set the future in concrete, restricting freedom and flexibility. Rather, it is to develop an informed plan that, in the congregation's best judgment, will enable the church to live out its story responsibly and courageously. Long-range planning usually begins about halfway through the current plan so that a new plan is in place before the current one expires.

Short-range, or annual, planning usually deals with working out details for up to a year. This process begins several months prior to a new year and transposes long-range plans into specific, action-oriented plans related to ongoing church programs. Short-range goals, a coordinated calendar, and budget allocations should result from this type of planning.

Operational planning is regular planning done quarterly, monthly, and weekly to implement plans. This is the type of planning regularly done in meetings of the church council or cabinet, Bible teaching council, and church staff.

3. *Involve people in long-range planning.* In most churches the church council (or cabinet) will be a basic unit already in place that can be used as a committee. The church council is normally charged with duties such as: helping the church understand its mission and define its priorities; coordinating studies of church and community needs; recommending to the church coordinated plans for ministry; and evaluating progress in the priority use of church resources.

Whatever group you choose to use should be representative of the best available human resources. These people should possess various strengths. They should be encouraged to think of the potential possessed by the church and the central fact that planning begins with God and depends on God for its completion.

Planning should be more than collecting data and/or allocating resources. It should bring out the best in everyone for the sake of the church. Planning should be forward-looking and innovative. It should encourage the emergence of new ideas, creativity, and new solutions to problems.

Use as many people as possible in the planning process. Putting it in terms of "telling the church's story," figure 7.1, provides a work sheet that can be used for people to express themselves in positive ways about the church's future.

Figure 7.1

TELLING THE CHURCH'S STORY

List the *best* things you know that have happened in the life of our church to make its story exciting.

1. _____   4. _____
   _____   _____
2. _____   5. _____
   _____   _____
3. _____   6. _____
   _____   _____

Suggest one or more possibilities for ministry the church has which can help to make its future story exciting.

1. _____   4. _____
   _____   _____
2. _____   5. _____
   _____   _____
3. _____   6. _____
   _____   _____

I am interested in being a part of the church's exciting story by participation in:

1. _____
2. _____
3. _____

(Optional)
Name:_____   Phone no. _____
Address: _____

Although warning has been given about basing one's long-range planning solely on the data collected in the community, knowing the community is important. By all means, bring into the planning process those church members who have special relationships with local government, community agencies, and businesses. Use these sources, but avoid dumping too much information on the committee at the outset. Formulate a limited number of realistic questions to collect information you believe pertinent to your church's forward look. Ask the people to collect only the information they feel is relevant to the church.

Participation in the planning process includes the church gathered to consider the finalized plans. After all the study, discussion, praying, and formalizing of plans, another important step follows: bringing the congregation together to hear the results. The way the committee presents its report is important. Advanced information should be given. Copies of the plans should be available to any who wish to see them. Clarity of presentation and information should receive high priority. Questions should be anticipated and answered during the presentation.

It should be made clear that, once adopted, long-range plans become the direction-setters for the church. People, in effect, are committing themselves to participation in the fulfillment of the approved plans. If the plans are well done, they should provide a motivational atmosphere for people to join in living out the story of the church on mission.

4. *Simplify the process.* Use four simple steps for long-range planning.

1. Assess the church's current situation.

2. Determine primary direction for the future.

3. Study strengths related to the biblical concept of church.

4. Determine major objectives/goals that will assist the church in achieving its mission.

In the first step the long-range planning committee looks at certain statistics realistically. Church consultants usually say that the average attendance at the Sunday morning worship service is an indication of the strength of the church, not Sunday school enrollment or church membership. Look realistically at participation in organizations, commitment to stewardship of time and money, attitudes about needs and opportunities for ministry, and progress during the past year.

The second step has been discussed previously in this chapter; however, an additional comment should be added. In determining primary direction, the church needs to decide such things as the maximum mission potential available in the community, the total number of people to be served in the coming three or so years, and the fundamental type of church the members want to become.

The third step has to do with a study of key strengths of the local church. This may be done by comparing the church with a predetermined list or by comparison to standards derived from biblical principles and current church-life factors. The fourth part of the process, before taking the plan to the church for adoption, is to develop strategies to help the church to reach its stated goals effectively.

The planning process will identify many specific needs and hopes toward which the church can direct ministry. It is important to be selective, however, so that human and material resources are challenged but not stretched beyond capacity. To overload a church with objectives and goals could overwhelm people and diffuse the strength of the congregation so that the church ends up helping no one with anything.

5. *Maximize the results.* One temptation following the planning process is to put the plan on the shelf or in the desk drawer while those who have worked hard on it take a rest. Make sure that proper assignments are made and that leaders of programs, councils, and committees are clear on their duties. Have regular times to evaluate progress and check up on procedures for achieving the specified goals.

Look to see if the expected results are being achieved. Are improvements being made? Are new people being reached? Is the church making better use of its resources? If the church has said it needs to reach out to single adults, is it? Is the congregation building on the strengths it already has?

A final word: Be thorough in planning the strategies of the plan. Strategies are the specific actions designed to accomplish the goals or objectives the church has chosen. You not only want to know what can go right with them, but also what can go wrong with them. This way you can work to keep the possible "wrongs" from ever happening.

BUDGETING

Budgeting is the process of allocating resources toward goals by expressing the church's dream in dollars. Budgeting is one very notable way of expressing the church's story, past, present, and most of all, what it wants to be in the future.

SET THE TONE FOR GOOD BUDGETING

Solid financial resources are required for today's effective churches. A biblical approach to stewardship undergirds the development of solid financial resources and helps persons grow in their own understanding of stewardship. Saving money and the efficient use of money do not constitute an adequate stewardship theology.

A responsible biblical approach to stewardship encourages local congregations to view stewardship as an *investment of financial resources*. It is an investment of money to (1) enlarge mission outreach in the community, (2) maximize the effectiveness of the local church, and (3) increase the number of households that contribute financially to the life and purpose of the church. It is important that the church understand that its task is not to save money or simply to spend money. The congregation must view itself as investing its funds so that the church may truly be on mission.

Setting the tone for budgeting includes worship services built around the theme of Christian stewardship. Sermon possibilities include:

- "Christian Stewardship as a Lifestyle" (Luke 12:13–21)
- "Acknowledging Our Source of Being" (Prov. 3:5–6)
- "Being Found Faithful" (Luke 22:7–23)
- "Growing Commitment to Cooperative Giving" (2 Cor. 8:1–14)
- "Trustworthy Stewards" (1 Cor. 4:2)

Setting the tone also includes developing positive attitudes for the missionary purpose of the church. Although it is not easy to maintain a worldwide view of the church's mission, such an intentional effort pays rich dividends. To develop such positive attitudes for mission support, leaders must possess deep convictions and genuine enthusiasm.

Mission support is directly related to one's attitude toward the people of the world. To believe that all people are created in the image of God is to believe that all people are important and worthy of the church's mission focus. Because it is easy for a congregation to lapse into self-centeredness, it is important that leaders consistently encourage and proclaim a world view of mission responsibility.

Cooperation and trust lie at the heart of mission education and financial support. Such attitudes grow out of fellowship, common convictions, and mutuality that involve Christians in a relationship with God and with other people. A cooperative attitude is endowed with a sense of belonging—being involved in something bigger than and beyond ourselves. An attitude of trust and cooperation is contagious and helps Christians everywhere achieve effectiveness in mission support. It validates commitment to Christ and to the concept of the priesthood of all believers.

EXAMINE THE MISSION OF THE CHURCH

This issue has been discussed in the first part of this chapter. It is mentioned here because of its importance to the church's stewardship of resources. If the church doesn't understand its purpose, then budgeting will become somewhat ambiguous at best.

Usually money follows mission. Occasionally the church may be the recipient of a large amount of money for which it has to determine purpose; however, the truth is usually the opposite. In many cases, the reason the congregation does not have enough money is that it has not effectively defined and put into practice a *mission purpose*. It may have become preoccupied with maintenance and forgotten about mission. Whenever that happens a church can usually count on diminished giving. *People want to give to mission more than they want to give to maintenance.*

Many times it is rather easy to get people to give money to build buildings. This may lead to the judgment that it's easier to build buildings than to support mission causes. The reason for this may be that the buildings are specific and concrete ways for people to see how their giving is being used.

Congregations that have been specific in stating and practicing their mission objectives tend to have much less difficulty in financing those objectives and goals. Instead of saying: "Our budget is behind. We are cutting every cost possible. Would you please help us catch up?" try saying: "Our church is seeking to reach and help many people. The money you are giving is being invested wisely in people ministries. Thanks for your giving." In summary, the church whose story includes a small mission tends to raise a small amount of money. The church whose story includes substantial mission purpose tends to raise substantially more money.

ASSESS POTENTIAL FINANCIAL RESOURCES

One of the major leadership responsibilities in church finance is to anticipate the sources of income for the church. It is important to know how much money the church might reasonably expect to receive during the period covered by a new budget.

Usually, most of a church's income will come from the undesignated gifts of members. Such gifts are given through church offering envelopes in the Sunday school and/or the worship services. A smaller proportion of total income is received as designated gifts for special causes. Each church, however, should study its giving pattern, as designated gifts may be more prominent in one church than another. Other sources of income for some churches include rental fees from facilities or parking lots, memorial gifts, interest income on money invested, trusts, wills, and capital gifts.

A church can do an analysis of the occupational groups that are present in its life and ministry. Research can then be done with the local census bureau or county planning agency concerning the average income in your region for the occupational categories that are present in the congregation. With this data, the church can make a reasonable assessment of the potential financial resources available to it—usually ten percent of the total estimated income of the congregation.

The church should be aware that, with effective financial management, any money now used for indebtedness will be available for other purposes within a few years when debt obligations are met. One such church carefully planned well in advance how it would divide its money after a loan had been paid off. Part of it went for mission purposes and another part went for needed repairs and air conditioning of its educational building.

DEVELOP THE MINISTRY BUDGET

Two primary ways to develop a budget are described on the following pages. First is a line-item approach and second, a ministry-based approach. Read the details and consider the potential for your situation; then choose the better approach.

LINE-ITEM BUDGETING

Line-item budgeting is the most common type of budget used by a church. In this kind of budget, allocation is made for each type of item where there is anticipated expenditure without regard for the particular ministry the item supports. Line-item budgeting may be done by a committee working through three important studies.

1. *What is the present situation?* This is an analysis of the church's past and present giving patterns. Look at the total undesignated gifts for each of the last five years. Determine the percentage of increase or decrease that might be expected if nothing changes.

2. *What is the potential?* Study the church's giving potential. If the potential is significantly greater than the present giving level, determine what steps would be necessary to improve financial support.

3. *Develop a proposal that will challenge the congregation.* Study the programs and budgetary needs of the church. Are there any items/areas to add or delete? What were the expenses last year? Determine the approximate amount that will provide for anticipated expenses plus some growth; compare this total with the anticipated level of support. Adjust figures for the various line items up or down to arrive at a reasonable projection of what the church will be able to do for the anticipated income.

A schedule for developing the budget is in figure 7.2, p. 146. You will need to determine any additional items that need to be scheduled and assign specific dates for the actions. See figure 7.3, p. 147, for an example of a line-item budget worksheet used by a small church.

MINISTRY-BASED BUDGETING

In this approach emphasis is placed on the fullest participation of people possible. This process involves more people than traditional budgeting by requiring a larger budget committee and extensive use of church committees and organizations. Emphasis is also given to priorities in planning. Church entities must discover needs for ministries and project solutions. In all stages, priorities are to be determined.

Understanding and purposeful giving are emphasized. In addition to the greater involvement of people, the suggested budget format communicates more clearly the ministries to be supported. Written explanations are included with each ministry area.

Eight steps are called for in the ministry-based process. The pastor, staff, and others charged with the *spending of funds* are responsible for the first two steps. The budget or finance committee will have primary responsibility for steps 3, 4, and 5. Then, as appropriate for your situation, all leaders related to the budgetary process will be involved in the final steps.

1. *Analyze ministries.* This is an appraisal of how well the church is performing its work and will be valuable to the budget committee.

2. *Propose ministry actions.* This is to include written proposals of ministries from staff members, church committees, and organizations. See

Figure 7.4, p. 148, for a sample proposal form. It calls for a description of
the ministry, why it is needed, the cause, any implications for future ministry, an alternative approach that could be used, and when the money
would be spent during the year.

3. *Evaluate ministry actions.* After all ministry-based proposals are presented in written form, the budget committee carefully and prayerfully
evaluates them in light of the church's missional purpose. Now is a good
time for this group to ask how these proposed ministries will help the
church live out the story it wishes to communicate. Priority rating must be
given to each proposal. In many instances this can be done by asking questions such as, "To what degree does this program make a contribution to
the purpose of the church?"

4. *Prepare the budget.* Now is the time to make decisions. List proposals in broad categories and begin determining the overall requirements for
supporting the proposed ministries. Make adjustments among items and
within categories according to the priorities determined in step 3.

A budget usually is organized into categories that represent the major
areas of a church's ministry, such as:

• World Missions Ministries

• Pastoral Ministries

• Educational Ministries

• Music Ministries

• Support Ministries

• Buildings and Grounds Ministries

In the simplest budgets, an amount would be specified for each of the
major categories. For most churches, however, each category is divided
into specific programs, projects, or areas of work, such as illustrated in
figure 7.5, p. 149.

While not ignoring past giving, a total amount budgeted should usually
include a challenge for growth in giving. If stewardship education is practiced and the budget clearly expresses the mission of the church in an exciting and understandable way, then members will rise to the challenge. (It
should be noted that the quality of the relationship between the pastoral
staff and the congregation affects people's response also.)

5. *Present the budget.* Interpreting the proposed ministries to the church
is an extremely important step. This is where the church members see what
their giving will help the church accomplish. Visual presentations through
slides, posters, videos, and drama can be extremely effective. Such presentations help broaden the members' view of what the church is doing and
plans to do. The budget can also be interpreted effectively through a
Budget Fair or Ministry EXPO—a festive, informal event for the entire
church family. Personal demonstrations and attractive displays depict the
various programs and ministries of the church.

In most churches, every member needs an opportunity to review the proposed budget prior to any discussion. One method of communication is by direct mail. The mailing should be accompanied by a letter of explanation and any other relevant information. A far better way to reach each home is through visitation. Visitors can deliver commitment cards, encourage members, listen to concerns, and improve understanding. In some cases, ministry needs will be discovered that were not previously known or met.

6. *Promote the budget.* Adoption of the budget will not ensure that giving will always follow. Members must be taught, encouraged, and led to make giving commitments.

7. *Report on ministry progress.* Regular budget reports should include all important financial data, but they should also become ministry progress reports. Such events as interviews, prayer periods, testimonies, visual aids, a review of plans, and reports on the number of people involved in specific ministry can be very helpful.

8. *Review and evaluate.* More than just beginning again, the entire budgeting process should be analyzed and needed changes and improvements made.

The flow in figure 7.6, p. 150, shows the process of ministry-action budgeting described above. This process requires a minimum of ten weeks and should be completed in the sequence described.

Additional figures are included for reference. See figure 7.7, p. 151, for a way of interpreting the "World Missions" section of the budget. A similar paragraph would be written to interpret each major category. Figures 7.8 and 7.9, p. 152, are other forms that may be used in this budget development process.

Figure 7.2

BUDGET PLANNING SCHEDULE

Week 1	Finance Committee distributes lists of (1) amounts spent during the last twelve months, and (2) the previous year's budget, asking committees and organizations to submit budget requests by priority and by monthly estimates.
Week 3	Committees and organizations send budget requests to the Finance Committee.
Week 4	Finance Committee meets to discuss requests and to propose a budget.
Week 6	Finance Committee and deacons meet to discuss requests and to recommend a budget to the church membership.
Week 7	Finance Committee mails proposed budget and a letter of explanation to church members.
Week 8	Church members discuss the proposed budget at a church business meeting.
Week 10	Finance Committee mails amended budget and letter of explanation to church members.
Week 11	Church members adopt the budget at a called church business meeting.
Week 12	Sunday school teachers present a lesson on stewardship.
Week 12	Finance Committee mails pledge cards and a letter of explanation to church members.
Week 13	Finance Committee sponsors Pledge Day and a commitment luncheon at the church. All choirs sing at the morning worship service.
Week 13	Finance Committee mails follow-up letters to members who did not turn in pledge cards.

Figure 7.3

BUDGET WORK SHEET

	Current Budget-19XX	Actual/Anticipated Totals This Year	Committee Requests	Proposed Budget-19XX
Undesignated Receipts	$ _____	$ _____	$ _____	$ _____
DISBURSEMENTS				
Missions				
Cooperative Program	$ _____	$ _____	$ _____	$ _____
Associational Missions	$ _____	$ _____	$ _____	$ _____
Local	$ _____	$ _____	$ _____	$ _____
Total Missions	$ _____	$ _____	$ _____	$ _____
Educational Ministry	$ _____	$ _____	$ _____	$ _____
Sunday school & Discipleship Training	$ _____	$ _____	$ _____	$ _____
Vacation Bible School	$ _____	$ _____	$ _____	$ _____
Woman's Missionary Union	$ _____	$ _____	$ _____	$ _____
Brotherhood	$ _____	$ _____	$ _____	$ _____
Youth	$ _____	$ _____	$ _____	$ _____
Total Education	$ _____	$ _____	$ _____	$ _____
Property	$ _____	$ _____	$ _____	$ _____
Debt Retirement	$ _____	$ _____	$ _____	$ _____
General Operations	$ _____	$ _____	$ _____	$ _____
Car Allowances	$ _____	$ _____	$ _____	$ _____
Conventions	$ _____	$ _____	$ _____	$ _____
Denominational Retirement	$ _____	$ _____	$ _____	$ _____
Insurance	$ _____	$ _____	$ _____	$ _____
Kitchen	$ _____	$ _____	$ _____	$ _____
Music & Equipment	$ _____	$ _____	$ _____	$ _____
Office Equipment	$ _____	$ _____	$ _____	$ _____
Postage	$ _____	$ _____	$ _____	$ _____
Church Supplies	$ _____	$ _____	$ _____	$ _____
Payroll Taxes	$ _____	$ _____	$ _____	$ _____
Utilities	$ _____	$ _____	$ _____	$ _____
Contingencies	$ _____	$ _____	$ _____	$ _____
Total General	$ _____	$ _____	$ _____	$ _____
Personnel				
Pastor	$ _____	$ _____	$ _____	$ _____
Church Secretary (part-time)	$ _____	$ _____	$ _____	$ _____
Janitor (part-time)	$ _____	$ _____	$ _____	$ _____
Total Personnel	$ _____	$ _____	$ _____	$ _____
Total Disbursements	$ _____	$ _____	$ _____	$ _____

Figure 7.4

A MINISTRY ACTION PROPOSAL

For_____   Subject _____

1. A description of proposed plan and how it relates to the church's basic
    purpose.

    _____
    _____
    _____
    _____
    _____
    _____

2. Why this ministry is needed.

    _____
    _____
    _____
    _____

3. The costs to the church (in detail).

    _____
    _____
    _____
    _____

4. What this will mean to the church in opportunities and cost in 2, 3, 5 years.

    _____
    _____
    _____
    _____

5. Alternative.

    _____
    _____
    _____

6. Alternative.

    _____
    _____
    _____
    _____

Figure 7.5

BUDGET WORK SHEET

	Current	Proposed
I. World Missions Ministries		
Cooperative Programs	$_____	$_____
Associational Missions	$_____	$_____
Direct Missions	$_____	$_____
Children's Home	$_____	$_____
Local Missions	$_____	$_____
Total	$_____	$_____
II. Pastoral Ministries		
Pastor's Salary	$_____	$_____
Housing & Utilities	$_____	$_____
Associate Pastor's Salary	$_____	$_____
Housing & Utilities	$_____	$_____
Secretary	$_____	$_____
Radio & Television	$_____	$_____
Deacon Care Program	$_____	$_____
Revival	$_____	$_____
Total	$_____	$_____
III. Education Ministries		
Minister of Education's Salary	$_____	$_____
Housing & Utilities	$_____	$_____
Secretary	$_____	$_____
Sunday school	$_____	$_____
Discipleship Training	$_____	$_____
Brotherhood	$_____	$_____
Woman's Missionary Union	$_____	$_____
Leadership Training	$_____	$_____
Total	$_____	$_____
IV. Music and Worship Ministries		
Minister of Music's Salary	$_____	$_____
Housing & Utilities	$_____	$_____
Organist's Salary	$_____	$_____
Music & Supplies	$_____	$_____
Special Programs	$_____	$_____
Worship Supplies	$_____	$_____
Total	$_____	$_____

Figure 7.6

FLOW CHART

**STEPS THAT MAKE MINISTRY-ACTION BUDGETING
A SIMPLE COMMITTEE PROCEDURE**

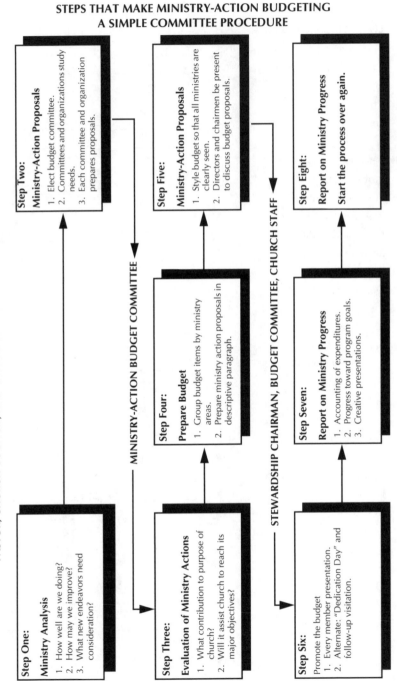

PASTOR, CHURCH COUNCIL, AND OTHERS CHARGED WITH SPENDING FUNDS

Step One:

Ministry Analysis

1. How well are we doing?
2. How may we improve?
3. What new endeavors need consideration?

Step Two:

Ministry-Action Proposals

1. Elect budget committee.
2. Committees and organizations study needs.
3. Each committee and organization prepares proposals.

MINISTRY-ACTION BUDGET COMMITTEE

Step Three:

Evaluation of Ministry Actions

1. What contribution to purpose of church?
2. Will it assist church to reach its major objectives?

Step Four:

Prepare Budget

1. Group budget items by ministry areas.
2. Prepare ministry action proposals in descriptive paragraph.

Step Five:

Ministry-Action Proposals

1. Style budget so that all ministries are clearly seen.
2. Directors and chairmen be present to discuss budget proposals.

STEWARDSHIP CHAIRMAN, BUDGET COMMITTEE, CHURCH STAFF

Step Six:

Promote the budget
1. Every member presentation.
2. Alternate: "Dedication Day" and follow-up visitation.

Step Seven:

Report on Ministry Progress

1. Accounting of expenditures.
2. Progress toward program goals.
3. Creative presentations.

Step Eight:

Report on Ministry Progress

Start the process over again.

Figure 7.7

SAMPLE BUDGET INTERPRETATION

WORLD MISSIONS MINISTRIES
FIRST CHURCH

As we interpret our part of the Great Commission, mission ministries fall into five areas:

1. Cooperative Missions give us a real part in a worldwide ministry in cooperation with others. Through Cooperative Missions, we support thousands of missionaries, hospitals, schools, and homes for children and older persons in our region and around the world.

$32,500

2. Associational missions keep us aware of the desperate needs that are closer to home and give us a real sense of participation in ministry as these needs are met.

$5,500

3. We have direct relationship with a chaplain as she ministers at the jails and institutions in our area.

$1,833

4. We have a special part in the ministry of three children's home where over 200 children are ministered to annually.

$917

5. Local benevolences are increasing due to the discovery of growing needs in our community and due to a greater emphasis for our church to become involved.

$917

OUR WORLD MISSION MINISTRY TOTAL — $41,667

Figure 7.8

BUDGET REQUEST FORM

MINISTRY PLAN AND REQUEST FOR ALLOCATION OF RESOURCES

1. Name of Ministry:_____
2. Ministry Objectives: _____
   _____

3. General Plan of Action (activity, date, responsible person, etc.):
   _____
   _____

4. Necessary Program Costs (the funds you have to have):
   Description and Amount Needed
   _____ $ _____   _____ $ _____
   _____ $ _____   _____ $ _____
   _____ $ _____   _____ $ _____
   _____ $ _____   _____ $ _____
                    Total $ _____
5. Discretionary Program Costs (what you would like to do if you had the money):

   Description   Amount   Rank
   _____ $ _____   _____
   _____ $ _____   _____
   _____ $ _____   _____
   Total $ _____

TOTAL BUDGET REQUESTS $ _____   Date _____
Requested by: _____   Position _____

_____

Figure 7.9

WORKSHEET FOR FINANCIAL SUPPORT OF THE MINISTER
(Duplicate and Use a Separate Sheet for Each Staff Member.)

		This Year	Proposed for Next Yr.
I.	Ministry-Related Expenses		
	1. Automobile Allowance	_____	_____
	2. Convention Allowance	_____	_____
	3. Book Allowance	_____	_____
	4. Continuing Education Allowance	_____	_____
	5. Hospitality Allowance	_____	_____
	TOTAL EXPENSES	_____	_____
II.	Protection Benefits		
	1. Insurance		
	a. Life	_____	_____
	b. Long-Term Disability	_____	_____
	c. Medical	_____	_____
	2. Retirement	_____	_____
	TOTAL BENEFITS	_____	_____
III.	Basic Compensation Personal Support		
	1. Cash Salary	_____	_____
	2. Housing Allowance	_____	_____
	TOTAL COMPENSATION	_____	_____

CHAPTER 8

Designing and Managing Facilities
William G. Caldwell

One of the most significant and far-reaching decisions churches ever make is the location and design of facilities in which the congregation will meet. A location that has poor visibility or accessibility will create problems for the church as it attempts to reach people. The same problems will exist if the design of the facility does not relate to the community where it is located. For these reasons it is essential that a church give careful consideration to its facilities.

Many of these considerations will relate to the need to buy, build, rent, borrow, or add space as a part of the ministry to the community. The church must be involved in feasibility studies, growth trends and patterns in the community, and demographic studies in order to determine what to do about facilities.

DETERMINING PURPOSES OF FACILITIES

The church must make some decisions about the basic use of church property before it can adequately determine its building and equipment needs. Most churches would feel that property and facilities should be used for worship, education, and fellowship. But each congregation needs to determine its own goals and then relate the use and maintenance of property and facilities to best meet those goals. The best decision relates to balance among all three areas.

Some churches would emphasize worship space needs over education space needs or vice versa, while others would give priority to fellowship. Many churches with limited resources will decide to build multipurpose space that could be utilized for all three purposes. The flexibility of space should be a key factor in determining priorities in this day of high building and financing costs.

Another consideration related to the purpose of facilities would be that of weekday use and the extent to which outside community groups would be allowed to use the facilities. A church that uses its facilities six or seven days a week will be faced with significant decisions about materials to use in construction as well as maintenance considerations. A church that is involved in sharing the use of its facilities regularly with community groups such as scouts, senior citizen groups, community interest groups, and others will need to face other considerations concerning the scheduling and maintenance requirements.

The construction of large buildings for recreational purposes has caused churches to evaluate further their purposes and objectives for ministry. The provision of such facilities calls for additional property (including outdoor recreation provisions), large financial commitments (including building and equipment plus personnel for programming and maintenance), and proper policies for the use of the facility. Even the remodeling of existing space for recreational purposes requires the same considerations.

Whatever the decision about the basic use of property and facilities, the church must develop some system of priority use for what it owns. Failure to do so may completely defeat the basic purpose of what the church is about. The instructions about planning prior to building, described in Luke 14:28–30, illustrate what happens to those who do not calculate all that is involved before beginning a project.

DESIGNING FACILITIES

The design of a church facility is determined by the purposes for which it is to be used. A careful study of several factors will enable those who oversee the project to develop an appropriate facility.

SECURE SUFFICIENT LAND

The first decision a new or an existing church will make about facilities relates to the land needed for its purposes. Various committees or task forces will assist in this process to help people relate to a vision for the church facility. A new church will be deciding where it will locate facilities from which to conduct its ministry. An existing church will be deciding if its present location is sufficient for its ministry or if it will need to move to another location because of inadequate land availability at the present site. Buying too much or too little may be poor stewardship.

A number of factors will be involved in decisions concerning site selection and the amount of land needed for the work of the church. The place where a church ministers will cause some of these factors to be inoperable. For example, an inner-city urban church in Manhattan would almost ignore parking requirements because of mass transit, but zoning requirements would be very significant.

1. *Size and shape.* Because of the many kinds of activities in which churches engage, and requirements for parking, the suggestion of a minimum size of five acres is frequently given. Another suggestion is to allow two acres for every 300 people in attendance. (This involves projecting the future growth of the church.) The best shape is a large rectangle or a square.

2. *Topography and drainage.* The land should be fairly level with a slight slope for drainage. Sites with problems in this area would require more space so that drainage could be designed properly. The cost of preparing a site for building and other uses must be considered.

3. *Easements and utilities.* An investigation must be made of the kinds of easements or other access to the property that exist. Setback requirements for buildings must also be determined. If utilities are not presently available at the site, an estimate of the cost of bringing them in must be made.

4. *Zoning requirements.* An important consideration for any site would be the zoning classification. Restrictions concerning parking provisions, building height, types of structures, and uses of buildings are items that must be investigated. An attempt to change the zoning classification after land is purchased may not be successful.

5. *Accessibility.* The location must be readily accessible to the persons the church intends to serve. It should be at the intersection of major travel arteries within a reasonable driving time of those persons. Traffic patterns during the week should be analyzed. Several entrance/exit points must be obvious. The location of buildings on the property should provide a feeling of openness and the places to enter the buildings must be prominent. Provisions for persons with disabilities are essential.

6. *Visibility.* Closely related to accessibility is the need for the location to be seen easily by the people who pass by. The often-repeated statement remains true: "If you need a sign to point people to your location, your church should be where the sign is." Signs that can convey a changing message will add to the visibility of the church.

7. *Parking.* Adequate parking is a must for most churches. Too many churches rely on street parking when provisions should be made on the property for people to park. Many cities have ordinances that require a certain number of off-street parking spaces. A church should do that much and more if it expects people to drive to the facility. The parking should be within a reasonable walking distance of the building, and it should be integrated with the landscaping to provide an attractive appearance.

Multiple services require provisions for traffic control as people are coming and going at the same time. Provisions for guest parking and parking for the disabled must be made. Churches with limited space may justify the expense of parking structures to provide sufficient parking. A good site selection would be adjacent to a good-neighbor business or office space with parking facilities not used on Sundays.

8. *Previous land use.* Environmental laws and contaminated land make this essential. The cost of clean-up can be significant.

9. *Security.* Is the land in a fairly safe area and what are the businesses or buildings nearby? Would people feel comfortable in coming to the proposed location?

SURVEY PROGRAM NEEDS

The place to begin in designing building facilities is with the program needs of the church. What needs to be done to accomplish the purpose of the church? This presupposes some basic understanding of what the work of the church is. When this is determined, then the question of programs and activities can be dealt with. All churches do not have to have every program that has ever been designed. A church will need to prioritize what it will be able to do to accomplish its purposes.

The process of surveying what the church has done in the past and what it is presently doing is necessary if the church is to plan adequately. The only way to know how to build a building is to determine what you intend to do in it.

The careful analysis of present and projected program space requirements is essential. Educational guidelines for space for learning are important here. Denominational resources should be consulted. The church will likely appoint a survey committee of competent individuals, representative of various aspects of church life, to conduct this analysis. The committee should be organized so that it will be able to study all aspects of the church life. Subcommittees should be assigned to the basic areas—education, recreation, worship, and so forth—so that they can focus on specific needs. Use questionnaires to secure information from church members concerning their ideas about church programs. Remember that adequate storage and work areas will be needed for all programs.

The entire committee should be involved in analyzing and evaluating the material developed by the subcommittees. The assimilation of the survey information should be provided in a condensed form for the church membership, along with recommendations for congregational action.

It is essential that a broad range of church members be involved in the survey process. Since the study looks at present activities as well as future possibilities, it is necessary to include as many people and ideas as possible. The decisions made concerning program needs should be based on accurate information and assessment of the work of the church. This will provide a proper basis for developing facility needs according to a priority arrangement.

DETERMINE COMMUNITY NEEDS

Another significant factor in designing facilities relates to the needs of the community in which the church is located. A part of the ministry of any church grows out of those things it intends to do to meet specific needs in the community. This may include provisions for day care for working parents, after-school care for older children, a school program, senior citizens programs, recreation programs for the community, and other types of activities that would affect the design. Public relations problems may have to be dealt with if the church is viewed as a threat to the community rather than an asset.

Many denominational offices offer a community survey instrument for churches to use in determining needs. Again, the approach to this kind of survey must be based on the understanding the church has concerning its purpose in ministry. Decisions concerning programs to meet community needs are just as vital as those concerning church needs. Sometimes they are even more crucial because of the additional funds, facilities, and personnel involved.

No church can do everything or provide every service that a particular community may need. The committee's thorough survey will provide the kind of information necessary for the congregation to decide what they can do and what must be left to others. Many programs will not require additional facilities; decisions about them can be made apart from facility considerations.

Any community ministry decision must be made deliberately after carefully considering all of the available information. Many churches have entered specific ministries without all the facts and have not been able to sustain the work. Such activities have caused churches to lose credibility in the community. Where facility additions are required, it is even more imperative that a church gather all the needed information and weigh it carefully before deciding to start a community ministry.

PRIORITIZE FACILITY NEEDS

The decisions concerning what facilities are needed must be followed by decisions concerning what should be done first. The long-range projections for community development as well as the population of the ministry area of the church must be taken into consideration. The ministry area will be determined by the reach of the church into the community and its programs of ministry. What the church does first will have a definite effect on what it does later.

Whether to build worship, educational, or recreational space first must be carefully analyzed by the committee and the congregation. The church that builds a large, permanent worship center first may never fill it up. A growing church may go through two, three, or more temporary worship centers before it decides about the permanent structure. In the meantime, facilities must be available to conduct the various ministries of the church.

Part of the consideration concerning facilities will be related to the remodeling or refurbishing of present facilities. Unless the decision is to relocate and build everything new, present structures must be looked at from the viewpoint of the feasibility of their continued use. Sometimes the decision will be to tear down and build anew in the same place. The structural soundness of existing buildings must be evaluated by structural engineers. Local building codes must be studied to determine the extent to which existing buildings must be brought into line with current codes if extensive remodeling is undertaken. In some cases, the needs can be met by simply rearranging a few walls for more functional use of a building. In other cases, the inside of the entire building will need to be torn out and new walls put in.

A long-range master plan, designed with the help of an architect and based on the priorities that the church assigns to facility needs, becomes a goal or a vision toward which the members work. Even those who may not be in complete harmony with the first stages will work at accomplishing them so that the future developments can be worked on sooner. The plan should remain flexible enough so that adjustments can be made in the future if community or ministry needs should change.

The basic purpose and objectives of the church must be evident in the way in which facility priorities are set. The special significance of church buildings makes them different from commercial buildings. Because they are dedicated to God's work, priorities must reflect those spiritual ministries of the church and the service it provides to the community. These priority decisions will be reflected in the policies regulating the use of buildings that will be considered later.

PREPARE FINANCIAL COST

The high cost of construction and high interest rates have created significant problems for churches that need to build facilities. Through the years many different kinds of financial programs for building have been used. The results have not always been good for the church. Interest payments have risen higher than missions giving. These problems point out the need for churches to plan carefully for the financing of any facility improvement.

There are tax considerations a church must include when purchasing land and improving facilities. Although churches are basically tax exempt, local taxing authorities may have regulations about land that is not yet used for church work and about certain improvements that may require tax payments. A church must investigate these possibilities early in the process of providing facilities.

Accumulating as much cash as possible before building is a must. The establishment of a building fund in an interest-bearing account is the first step to take. Encouraging people to give to the fund over and above their regular budget giving will help in increasing the giving. The use of such promotion ideas as "Double Tithing" and "Fifth-Sunday Building Fund Offering" will help. A major fund-raising activity for many churches has been the three-year pledging campaign in which people are asked to pledge and then give weekly to the building fund. Many firms as well as denominational groups have specialized in this area of fund raising for churches. Information from these groups should be sought before beginning a campaign.

How much cash should be raised before beginning construction? There are those who recommend that all of the funds should be in hand first. Others recommend a pay-as-you-go operation. Others would suggest from one-half to two-thirds of the total amount needed should be in cash. Each church will be different in terms of its needs and abilities to pay for buildings. A high interest rate, especially if the repayment is to be done over several years, could cause the total amount to be two or three times the original construction cost. A church must face the stewardship considerations of this kind of expense. There will be times when the immediacy of the building need will offset the additional cost. Waiting may mean lost opportunities.

A significant fact for the church to remember is that it is easier to raise funds for building the facility than to raise funds for debt retirement after it is completed. The continual emphasis of the effort should not be on the building itself, but on the people who will be involved and who can be reached by this effort.

The best approach is to develop a sound financial program that can be explained to the church. It will likely incorporate a cash fund-raising approach along with a feasible, limited-payment plan for financing the remainder of the costs. Such a plan should include all of the anticipated costs related to the building project: land costs and site preparation; architectural and engineering fees; construction costs; furnishing costs; and anticipated maintenance, program, and personnel costs for the use of the facility.

DEVELOP DESIGN DRAWINGS

The selection of an architect is a crucial decision for the church. Visits should be made to buildings designed by architects being considered. The one selected should be familiar with church buildings, have experience in designing church facilities, and be willing to listen to what the church has established as the needs to be met and the priorities to be followed. Some denominations can provide a list of qualified architects. The wrong decision here will further complicate an already difficult process.

The committee will need to spend time with the architect to make certain that the approach the church is taking is fully understood and that it can be implemented. Any problems should be worked out before proceeding with the project. Agreement should also be reached concerning the architect's involvement in the construction process, such as the extent of supervision to be provided.

Step One: Develop Property Utilization Plans. The best arrangement of the proposed facility along with any future buildings should be identified on the available property. It should be evident that there is enough space to provide for all that is planned on the property and that the proposal will fit the topography of the land.

Step Two: Develop Program Graphic Plans. These plans will show the allocation of the square footage of the floor space to the various age groups and programs that have been determined by the survey. The evaluation of these plans will determine if the needs that should be met are being provided for in the proposed facility. Other facilities should be visited to benefit from the development of their floor plans.

Step Three: Develop Detailed Drawings. The drawings will provide the schematic design for all the areas included in the construction: foundation, plumbing, electrical, heating and cooling, roofing, ceiling, wall and floor treatment, and so forth. This would include decisions concerning types and colors of walls and floor coverings to assure a proper "look" for the facility and good maintenance capabilities. The specifications relating to all of these components must be stated in the way the church wants the facility finished. These become the criteria on which the bids for construction are developed. Careful evaluation of these drawings and descriptions must be made.

With all of these things accomplished, along with the appropriate review and approval, the church will be able to construct a facility that will meet the ministry needs it has envisioned.

MANAGING FACILITIES

It is not enough for a church to design and construct good facilities. The church must also be in the business of managing those facilities so that the maximum benefit can be derived from their use. It is poor stewardship indeed if the facilities are not cared for and utilized in the way in which they were intended. A number of factors are related to the process of effectively managing facilities.

DEVELOP FACILITY AND EQUIPMENT USE POLICIES

Who should determine policies for the use of church facilities and equipment? Since a policy is a stated course of action that will be consistently followed, it is essential that a responsible group be involved in determining what each policy should be. Since procedures vary from church to church, the group to accomplish this will also vary. However, regardless of the group—the congregation, a church committee, an official board, or church officials—the policies should be in writing and readily available when they are needed. This would include the identification of the person or persons responsible for their application. In small churches, the pastor may have this authority; in larger churches, some other staff member may be identified. In some churches, a committee or other official may be responsible.

Since policies assist in the delegation of authority, help in reaching the goals of the church, and lead to the uniform handling of all requests, it is essential that the group developing them consider the following ideas concerning good policies:

- They should be positive in nature.
- They should be simple and easily understood.
- They should be broad, allowing flexibility.
- They should be geared toward consistent application.
- They should adequately reflect potential conflicts.
- They should be kept up-to-date.

The group will determine what policies are already in effect and will probably look at what other churches have in the way of policies. Resources listed in the bibliography will provide additional help.

A church may follow some system of priorities when developing policies. Preference in scheduling should be given to church activities rather than outside groups. Larger group activities may have priority over smaller group activities in certain facilities. Meetings that are conducted on a regular basis should be considered ahead of one-time or occasional meetings. All areas of the church facilities and equipment should be covered by policy statements. The group should consider worship areas, fellowship areas, educational areas, recreational areas, kitchen, parking areas, office equipment, and vehicles in the development of policies. Several sample policies and request forms are included (figures 8.1 through 8.4, pp. 170–172). In order to facilitate the scheduling and use of church facilities, all rooms in the buildings should be numbered. A room assignment record can then be kept and used for scheduling as well as for janitor assignments.

PLAN ENERGY MANAGEMENT MEASURES

One of the most significant stewardship responsibilities a church has is related to the wise and proper use of energy. A lack of concern and involvement of people in energy management will result in wasteful and expensive energy use. All areas of church life relate to the use of energy from the scheduling of meetings to the selection of a temperature range, to the type of lighting fixtures used, to the turning off of lights and equipment not in use.

In planning a new church facility, careful consideration should be given to energy use. The architect and Building Committee should give special attention to:

1. *Location.* The way in which the buildings are situated on the property will affect energy use. A balance should be maintained between the aesthetic view of the structures and the energy management view. Facing the building in such a way as to take advantage of the sun and using earth embankments for insulation are good stewardship.

2. *Landscaping.* The use of trees and shrubs can be advantageous from an energy-use standpoint. Careful landscape planning will result in lower utility bills. Screening the sun out in the summer and allowing the sun in during the winter can be accomplished with trees.

3. *Insulation.* Every possible part of the building should be properly insulated according to the recommended R value for the climate. This would include ceilings, walls, crawl spaces, concrete slabs, electrical outlets, outside pipes, duct work, caulking around wall openings, weather-stripping doors, thermal doors and windows, and attic and roof ventilation.

4. *Building materials.* Many building material products provide higher energy conservation. These should be considered for the building. Their use should not rule out such practical considerations as purchasing windows that may be opened when conditioned air is not required by outside temperature.

5. *Energy-efficient equipment.* The selection of heating and cooling equipment with the highest possible energy efficient ratio is a must. In addition, hot water heaters and other appliances should be selected for their energy efficiency.

Many energy-management measures can be taken in existing buildings. Some are expensive but will pay for themselves in a short time. Others should not be done because of the expense and long payback period. Some can be accomplished at virtually no cost. An Energy Management Committee can be established to develop an audit of how the church is presently using energy resources and to provide suggestions for improvement in energy management.

Here are some *no-cost* possibilities for saving energy: set back heating temperature; lower hot water temperature; set air conditioning temperature higher; shut off mechanical equipment when not in use; turn off lights when not in use; remove a bulb from multiple light fixtures when safety is not a factor; schedule meetings at the same time in facilities already cooled or heated.

Consider these *low-cost* options: caulk and weather-strip around doors and windows; repair broken windows; install higher efficiency lighting where possible; use lighter colors when redecorating; use timers or photocells on outdoor lighting; lock thermostats; check efficiency of heating and cooling systems; keep filters clean and replace when necessary. Additional suggestions will be obvious when an audit is completed.

Energy management systems are available to assist churches in the operation and control of heating and cooling equipment. Many of the companies that install these computer-controlled systems will guarantee that the energy savings realized will pay for the equipment needed. Churches building new facilities should check on the feasibility of installing this equipment during construction. Churches with existing facilities should investigate the possibility of such equipment being installed to cut down on the cost of energy being used.

PROVIDE ADEQUATE INSURANCE COVERAGE

The need for proper insurance coverage by churches has long been demonstrated. The old idea of "charitable immunity" is no longer valid for a church. Too many situations are now on record to indicate that a church is subject to the same kinds of problems that face other businesses in the insurance area. A church needs insurance to meet its stewardship and moral responsibility as well as to meet practical and emotional needs. An Insurance Committee should carefully analyze the areas of need facing a church and select insurance coverage to meet those needs.

The following categories should be covered:

1. *Personnel.* Insurance should be provided for all church employees, including staff members and other paid workers. Coverage for part-time employees should be addressed. Consideration should be given to accident and health insurance, group life insurance, disability income, worker's compensation insurance, and fidelity bonds for those who handle money. Related to these would be the provision for a retirement plan for all personnel. Leaving out any of these coverages would mean that the church might have to come up with funds to help an employee in need.

2. *Liability.* This insurance provides protection from financial loss due to suits or claims arising from accidents on the premises or away from the premises if they relate to normal church activity. This will include the operation and maintenance of church facilities, the alteration of church properties, the sale or distribution of food, church schools, and camps and other recreational activities. In addition, coverage should be provided for all vehicles owned by the church or used in the work of the church.

3. *Building and property.* This insurance should cover physical damage to any property the church owns or uses. Included in the coverage would be fire insurance for buildings and contents; extended coverage for windstorm, lightning, explosions, aircraft and motor vehicles, riots, vandalism, earthquake, flood, and special coverage for glass or other valuable property; theft and burglary; and church vehicles.

The committee should follow these guidelines for providing proper coverage.

- Cover all essential areas of risk.

- Cover the largest loss exposure first.

- Have sufficient coverage (requires an inventory of property and equipment to establish replacement cost amounts on all property).

- Seek professional help (especially with appraisals).

- Select a reputable agent and company.

- Provide coverage for special events and activities that depart from regular programs.

- Use large deductibles where possible.

- Compare premium costs regularly to get reasonable rates.
- Review coverage periodically.

Effective work in this area will assure that a church is properly insured when the need arises so that property damaged or persons injured will be adequately covered.

DEVELOP GOOD HOUSEKEEPING PROCEDURES

What does good housekeeping mean for a church? It means keeping the physical facilities clean, attractive, and in good repair as a means of providing a positive witness to the community. The appearance of the facilities will speak loudly concerning the congregation's feelings about the place that is dedicated to the worship of God, to say nothing of the need to protect the original investment made. Good housekeeping is good stewardship. A properly planned and executed preventive maintenance program will provide good upkeep on facilities and assure their ongoing usefulness to the church as well as provide a safe environment in which to meet.

In order to keep buildings and equipment prepared for service, there are three types of housekeeping and maintenance programs that must be provided. The first is *operational maintenance,* in which the custodial or maintenance staff performs the routine cleaning of facilities and the standard placement of furnishings. The second is *in-service maintenance,* in which labor and materials are provided to place into service a damaged portion of the building or a broken piece of equipment. The third is *preventive maintenance,* in which a planned program of routine service and inspection of buildings and equipment is developed to maintain service and appearance. A church should be involved in all three types for proper stewardship.

Proper organization for this type of housekeeping and maintenance program will require the use of paid personnel (full-time or part-time) as well as volunteers. The supervisory responsibility for the work, whether it is done by paid persons or volunteers, should be delegated to a responsible individual to assure its accomplishment. In a smaller church, that person may be the one in charge of a committee that has the assignment of facilities. In a larger church some staff member will be given the responsibility but will likely work in conjunction with a church committee. The use of volunteers and the employment of personnel will vary according to the size of the facility. In some larger cities, contracting services are available for operational maintenance. Investigation of these services should include references from satisfied customers. Because of the unpredictable nature of church schedules, this outside contractor approach would have to be considered carefully. It may still be necessary to have a custodian on duty for emergencies.

The person in charge would need to work in several areas to make certain that the facilities were being cared for. These would include:

- Develop inspection procedures for properties.
- Maintain an inventory of all equipment and furnishings (see last section of this chapter).
- Develop maintenance policies and procedures.
- Prepare budget recommendations for maintenance.
- Maintain records for maintenance.
- Contract for outside maintenance firms when needed.
- Develop preventive maintenance program, including forms and reports needed.
- Oversee budget expenditures and development of contingency funds for large items.
- Supervise personnel in maintenance program.

The development of forms and records is an essential part of a good housekeeping program. The ability to keep up with what has been done and what needs to be done is necessary for good facility upkeep. The proper maintenance of equipment requires a record of its use so that it can be serviced at regular intervals. The sample custodian's checklist will serve as an example of the kinds of forms which will be helpful in building maintenance (figure 8.5). Other forms could be used for weekly, monthly, and periodic assignments. The frequency of use in a specific part of the facility will determine the housekeeping requirements. Use of the same room by different groups will also complicate the procedure and will need to be planned carefully.

DEVELOP ADEQUATE LIGHTING AND SOUND SYSTEMS

Due to the nature of the activities conducted in church facilities, adequate lighting and sound systems are essential. Improper lighting can be a safety hazard as well as make it difficult for persons trying to read or study printed material. An inadequate sound system will prevent persons from hearing and understanding much of what is being said in worship services or other language group gatherings. However, providing good quality equipment without providing adequate training for those who operate the equipment is a mistake. Many times, sound problems are operator-related. One solution is to contract with the ones who install equipment also to conduct training for those who will operate it.

In most cases, adequate lighting provisions will be made at the time of building construction. When this does not happen, it becomes necessary to correct the problems with additional lighting where needed. A study should be made of the various classrooms, office areas, hallways, entrances, and restrooms as well as the worship area to determine if the lighting is sufficient. Each area will have its own needs in terms of the amount of light. A light meter can be used to determine if the required amount of footcandles of light is present in the more crucial areas. The ability to control lighting with spots and dimmers is especially helpful in worship areas. In classrooms and hallways, changing from incandescent to fluorescent fixtures will provide better lighting as well as save energy.

The acoustics of a building are also determined at the time of construction. The type of floor, wall, and ceiling materials used will affect the sound in a room. A noisy room can be deadened by placing carpet on the floor or acoustical treatment on the walls and ceiling. Other types of acoustical treatment can be used to make a "dead" room more alive. Sound systems can be installed to enable persons to hear what is being said. Unfortunately, sometimes after spending large sums of money the hearing problem still exists. The advice of experts must be sought to provide answers to acoustical problems.

Perhaps the major problem with sound treatment relates to the worship area. The problem is complicated by the need to amplify music and the speaker by using the same system. The approach with music is to make it sound like it comes from all over the room whereas the desire with a speaker is to make the voice sound like it comes from the person speaking.These two different approaches create problems for the sound system.

Proper installations will take into account the size and acoustical treatment of the building and its equipment. A number of microphone outlets will be needed for the multipurpose use of musicians and speakers. Good quality speakers can be focused to direct sound to all parts of the room. The amplifier, mixer, tape recorder, and other equipment must be of sufficient quality to provide the kind of sound reinforcement needed.

MAINTAIN SUFFICIENT HEATING AND COOLING SYSTEMS

The days of the hand fan have long since passed as an adequate means of keeping people comfortable at church. The key word is *comfort*. Whatever people have become accustomed to in their homes and in other public places regarding heating and cooling should be seen as the norm for the church facility. The installation of adequate systems for this purpose should be done in the construction of the building. Proper maintenance of the equipment will provide for its long-term use. The type of system will determine the type of maintenance that must be done. Because of construction design, some systems will need to operate year round to provide conditioned air in the facility. In buildings where windows can be opened, there likely will be several months during the year (depending on the climate) when the equipment will not need to be used.

The maintenance of this equipment requires good record keeping to enable service to be done at the proper intervals. In some instances the church maintenance personnel will be able to provide the proper service requirements. In most situations, the maintenance will need to be done by outside contractors who will provide the proper service within the appropriate time frame (see figure 8.6).

DEVELOP PROPER SECURITY MEASURES

The need for security in church facilities has been highlighted in recent years by increasing reports of vandalism, burglary, attacks on persons, arson, and other unfortunate events. No one likes to think of the church as a fortress where everything is locked up, but proper steps should be taken to protect the church property and the lives of members.

Several factors should be considered in the internal security of the buildings. A key-control policy should be established to provide for the issuing of keys to proper persons and to keep a record of keys issued (see figure 8.7). Certain areas and rooms should be locked when not in use. These areas include offices, library and media rooms, equipment rooms, kitchen, supply rooms, and the like. All equipment should be identified with the church name and control number and should be put away when not in use.

Special precautions should be taken relating to security of confidential records, computer access, and money-receiving and counting activities. Churches with weekday child care and school programs should provide training for workers relating to security precautions for children. A plan for evacuating the buildings should be developed and publicized.

Additional consideration should be given to the external security of the buildings and grounds. Doors and windows should be provided with adequate locking devices. Landscaping around the building should not block the view of windows and doors so as to provide cover for a burglar. Outside areas including the parking lots should be equipped with sufficient lighting for nighttime use. It is wise in some areas to develop parking lot patrols when people are in the building to protect vehicles from theft. A committee or special group in the church could take responsibility for providing the patrol.

Many churches have felt a need to install alarm systems for better protection of the property, especially when no one is on the premises. There are several types of systems available for the church to use. Some simply make a noise while others are tied directly to an alarm service company or to the local police or fire station. A church should carefully investigate the types of systems available before it selects the one to install.

MAINTAIN GROUNDS AND PARKING AREAS

The appearance of the church grounds and parking areas should serve as an inspiration to others in the community to improve the appearance of their own property. Similar to proper building maintenance, they serve as a testimony to the attitude of the church members concerning the place where they worship. Grounds that are not cared for may be communicating a lack of concern that is not characteristic of the church. One indication of concern is an attractive sign identifying the church and providing information about the services that can be read easily from the street.

Grassy areas around the facilities can do much to enhance their appearance amid all the brick and concrete. These areas must be fertilized, watered, and mowed regularly if they are to remain attractive. It is also helpful for them to be edged to keep a neat appearance. In some churches this responsibility is assigned to the custodial staff. Others will secure outside help for this purpose. Although professional persons may be hired, this is an excellent place to utilize youth or others in the community who can provide this service. If volunteers are used, there must be a clear understanding of the responsibilities involved or the appearance will likely suffer.

Landscaping with trees and shrubs can provide a helpful addition to the attractiveness of the facilities. Professional help will be an advantage here in the selection and care of the proper plants. The choices should be made in the interest of energy considerations as well as appearance. The plants and trees chosen should enhance the beauty of the facilities without hiding them or blocking the view of drivers entering or leaving the parking area.

Walkways and parking areas must be designed in a way that will facilitate the easy access of people to the buildings. Ramps and close-in parking should be provided for older persons and the disabled as well as guests. Covered loading and unloading areas should be considered for parents with small children and for use in inclement weather. In areas of extreme winter weather, surfaces should be treated to prevent falls.

The design of the parking areas should be planned to accommodate the maximum number of cars and still provide sufficient driveway areas. The parking angle used should be easily negotiated by all drivers. Entrances and exits should be provided in two or more locations far enough apart to prevent backup during busy traffic times. The city zoning codes must be examined and followed in determining the amount of parking to be provided.

The parking area should be surfaced to provide all-weather use. Even though more expensive to install, concrete provides a longer-lasting and more easily maintained surface. The parking spaces should be clearly marked and kept painted, so drivers will know where to park. The feasibility of parking structures should be investigated when limited land is available or when the cost of ample land for surface parking is prohibited.

As discussed earlier, sufficient lighting should be provided for all grounds and parking areas. The security factor is significant as well as the safety factor for people using the facilities. In addition, the lighting of the building or one special feature of the building such as the steeple will serve as an advertising focal point at night. All outside lights should be on a timer or a dusk-to-dawn automatic switch so that the areas are illuminated when needed. Additional lighting may be needed where outside grounds or parking areas are to be used for recreational purposes. Special lighting (as well as additional parking area) may be needed for church vehicles when stored on the parking lot.

DEVELOP PROPERTY AND EQUIPMENT INVENTORY PROCEDURE

Perhaps one of the most neglected areas in church facility management is a workable system for keeping up with property and equipment owned by the church. From the standpoint of insurance requirements (in case of fire or theft) as well as good stewardship, such a system needs to be developed and utilized. A church that must continually replace hymnals, kitchen equipment, tables, and chairs because they "disappear" is not providing a good model for its members or acting as a good steward of its resources. Taking an inventory of present equipment as well as developing a procedure for keeping up with additional purchases is required. The use of video is one means of recording all furnishings.

The Building and Grounds or Properties Committee should initiate the inventory procedure. It may be as simple as counting and listing all tables, chairs, educational furniture, kitchen equipment, and so forth or as involved as securing tags or stickers with control numbers and affixing them to every item. Whatever approach is taken, a listing of all items is necessary and a record kept as to where they are located. Policies relating to the borrowing of equipment would include a form to use in recording that information. All existing equipment should be identified as to approximate date of purchase, cost of the item, and the amount of time used in the case of motors or other items that require service.

An inventory record of all new items should be started at the time of purchase and maintained for the life of the item. Any warranty information or instructions for use should be filed in a related folder. The record form should include all information necessary for providing maintenance for the item (see figures 8.8 through 8.10, pp. 174–175). The inventory records should be maintained away from the church facility for safe keeping and to avoid possible fire loss.

Facilities that are properly designed and managed will go a long way in helping the church fulfill its mission. A lack of attention to facilities will not only handicap the church in its work; but also it may provide a negative witness to the community.

Figure 8.1
SAMPLE POLICY STATEMENTS

BUILDING USE

1. The philosophy underlying policies for building use is that all church facilities shall be used to carry out the basic purpose and mission of the church. Policies should be kept in the spirit of bringing people to Christ.

2. Use of any facility shall be done in conformity with city fire and safety ordinances. These provide for the prohibiting of smoking and overcrowding in church facilities.

3. Janitors or other building personnel shall be responsible for moving all equipment and furniture when it is necessary and for replacing it for regular meetings.

4. Regularly scheduled church meetings shall have first priority in building use. Other church-related meetings shall have second priority. Outside nonprofit organizations shall be eligible for building use when facilities are not being used by church groups and when their purpose is approved by the pastor and the Property Committee. Profit-making enterprises shall not use church facilities for any purpose.

WEDDINGS

1. The philosophy underlying policies for weddings is that a Christian emphasis be encouraged and that members relate the ceremony to Christian family commitment.

2. All weddings shall be scheduled on the master church calendar with first priority being given to church members. Non-church members shall be allowed to schedule a wedding no earlier than ninety days prior to the event to assure the church member's priority.

3. Counseling of the couple prior to the wedding is essential. The pastor or other ministers shall conduct the counseling or be advised as to the person doing so.

4. Church members are encouraged to use the pastor and church organist for the ceremony. Guest ministers shall be approved by the pastor, and guest organists shall be approved by the minister of music.

5. In keeping with the wedding philosophy, church members shall use the facilities without charge. Nonmembers shall pay a fee for facilities a week in advance according to the following schedule:

| Sanctuary | $100.00 | Fellowship Hall | $50.00 |
| Chapel | 50.00 | Kitchen | 25.00 |

6. A minimum fee of $30.00 for the services of the janitor (including rehearsal) shall be paid by all (church members and nonmembers) since the work will be extra.

7. In keeping with safety regulations, protective materials shall be used with candles, and rice shall not be used inside or outside the buildings.

8. The church wedding consultant shall work with the couple in the development of the wedding plans and the implementation of policies.

Note: Items 5 and 6 relating to charges will need to be adjusted according to church philosophy (should church members be charged?) and the current charges being made by other churches in the area.

Figure 8.2
ROOM SCHEDULING REQUEST FORM

(Submit to church office at least two weeks in advance. Form will be returned with confirmation.)

MEETING REQUEST

Date submitted _____ Requested by_____

Person responsible _____ Phone _____

Date of meeting_____ Organization_____

Type/Purpose of meeting _____

Room(s) needed_____

Time of meeting: From _____ to_____

Number expected _____ Diagram Room Arrangement on back

Standing request: Every _____ until_____

OTHER SERVICES:

Equipment needs: _____

Media needs: _____

Food service needs:

  Type of service _____

  (consult with hostess after approval)

FOR OFFICE USE:

❏ Approved and scheduled

❏ Not approved: Reason _____

  Authorized signature _____ Date_____

Figure 8.3
WEDDING REQUEST FORM

(Submit as early as possible. Non-church members no earlier than ninety days ahead of date requested.)

Date requested _____ Time _____

Bride's name _____ Church member? yes❏ no❏

Address _____

Work phone _____ Home phone _____

Groom's name _____ Church member? yes❏ no❏

Address _____

Work phone _____ Home phone_____

Minister's name _____

If guest minister: Address _____ Phone _____

Rehearsal date _____ Time _____

Room(s) required _____

Reception time _____ to_____

Room(s) required for reception _____

Organist's name _____

If guest organist: Address _____ Phone _____

Florist _____ Phone _____

Photographer _____ Phone _____

Caterer _____ Phone _____
For office use:
     ❏ Approved and scheduled
     ❏ Not approved: Reason
Authorized signature _____ Date _____
Church wedding consultant assigned _____
Phone_____

Figure 8.4
RECORD OF EQUIPMENT LOANED

ITEM BORROWED

Description: _____
Inventory number: _____ Number of items _____
Description: _____
Inventory number: _____ Number of items _____
Date borrowed: _____
     I agree to be responsible for these items away from the church property. If they are lost or damaged, I will replace them or provide funds to do so.
Signature _____

OFFICE USE ONLY:

❏ Check out approved: Signature _____
❏ Items returned; date _____
Receiver's signature _____

Figure 8.5
CUSTODIAL DAILY WORK CHECKLIST

Name of custodian _____
Area/Rooms assigned _____ Week of _____

(INITIAL TASKS WHEN COMPLETED.)

Duties	M	T	W	T	F
Dust all furniture, equipment, window sills, etc.					
Clean all glass doors					
Pick up and empty trash					
Vacuum carpets					
Clean water fountains					
Damp mop tile floors					
Clean stairwells					
Clean rest room urinals, basins, toilets					
Damp mop rest room floors					
Fill towel and toilet tissue holders					
Special assignments (see below)					
Special assignment:					

Figure 8.6
EQUIPMENT INVENTORY RECORD

Type of equipment _____

Located at _____ Inventory number _____

Description _____

Model no. _____ Cost _____

Serial no. _____ Shipping _____

Date purchased _____ Installation _____

From _____ Taxes _____

Trade-in allowed _____ Total _____

Service contract agreement date to be renewed _____

Warranty _____

REPAIRS AND MAINTENANCE

Date	Description	By	Amount

Figure 8.7
MASTER KEY ASSIGNMENT

Name	Leadership Position	Master Key No.	Issued By	Receiver's Signature	Date Returned	Received By

Figure 8.8
REPORT OF VEHICLE USE

The driver of each vehicle should complete this form at the time the vehicle is returned.

Date(s) of use _____

Group or person responsible _____

Destination _____

Reason for use _____ Acct. no. charged_____

Driver _____ Phone _____

Vehicle used: _____

Odometer reading:

    End of trip _____

    Beginning of trip _____

    Total miles _____

Maintenance needs: Please list any repair needs or conditions to be corrected that you observed on the trip.

_____

_____

Driver's signature _____ Date

Figure 8.9
INSPECTION/MAINTENANCE REPORT

PROPERTY AND BUILDING EXTERIOR

Item/Area	Inspected		Location	Condition	Action Needed	Action Performed	
	Date	By				Date	By
Church sign							
Doors/Windows							
Drains							
Exterior walls							
Lawn, shrubs							
Metal Flashing, gutters, down spouts							
Walkways							
Parking areas							
Outside equipment							

Figure 8.10
INVENTORY/INSPECTION REPORT

Room no. _____ Made by _____ Date _____

Item	Condition			Repair Needed	Recom- mendations	Number
	Good	Average	Poor			
Ceiling						
Walls						
Floor						
Lights						
Curtains						
Drapes						
Blinds						
Carpet						
Tables						
Chairs						
Piano						
Chalkboard						

CHAPTER 9

Planning Special Congregational Events
Robert D. Dale

Special congregational events put the minister's management skills—especially planning skills—on public display. These special events are common, high-profile happenings. Among the most demanding are weddings, funerals, and revivals. Each of these three events is spotlighted in this chapter as an example of and model for the administrative care that must support all types of special activities.

PLANNING WEDDINGS

Weddings are occasions when the minister wants especially to be sure everything goes according to plan. Weddings are so public and so sentimental that the wedding party, the minister, and the plan are all on display. Because churches want to avoid misunderstandings about weddings, many have developed statements of wedding policies. (For a sample wedding policy, see figure 9.1, p. 183. For related forms used to reserve facilities for weddings and other special events, see chap. 8.)

GUIDING PREMARITAL COUNSELING

Ministers often find premarital counseling unfulfilling. They feel frustrated because engaged couples usually want a ceremony, not counsel. One professional counselor friend complains that these couples are "in a state of madness." Consequently, engaged couples usually aren't at a stage of life where they are interested in making decisions; for them, the decision is already made. They want a wedding now, and they'll worry about the issues of building a married relationship later.

Rather than trying to guide a decision-making process for that which is already decided, you may want to open a discussion forum for two people who will establish one new family. A forum provides a setting in which a minister can raise basic questions about marriage and husband-wife relationships, and a couple can take advantage of that setting to make sure they have thoughtfully discussed the full range of concerns they will face in marriage.

The minister provides the setting, the questions, an objective listening ear, and some coaching in communication and conflict management processes. The couple responds with frank answers and direct conversation.

Whether you prefer more traditional counseling approaches or the forum style of premarital preparation, you may want to use some reading material to introduce issues and to prime the conversational pump. With a thought-provoking book, engaged couples and even inexperienced counselors can work together productively.

Many ministers request a minimum number of conversations with the engaged couples whose weddings they have been asked to perform as an integral part of the overall wedding planning process. Discussing the wedding ceremony itself is only one part of premarital counseling.

REHEARSING FOR THE WEDDING CEREMONY

The wedding rehearsal is a time to clarify what everyone is to do and when he or she is to do it. Rehearsals also are times to calm everyone's anxieties and to reassure them that the plan will work. Therefore, all of the wedding party and all of the officiants need to attend the rehearsal. The exact time and place should be clearly communicated to every person who is expected to take part in the rehearsal.

Some couples enlist the assistance of a bridal consultant. If so, the consultant will also attend the rehearsal and will provide an additional resource to the minister in planning for the wedding. Consultants are generally expert in the etiquette of weddings, not the content of the ceremony.

A variety of customs surround weddings and rehearsals. For example, some brides subscribe to the old superstition that it's bad luck for a bride to take any active part in the rehearsal of her wedding and prefer to use a stand-in during the rehearsal. Additionally, different denominations have varying traditions relating to weddings. The rehearsal provides the occasion for everyone to understand the traditions that apply to this particular wedding.

BEFORE THE WEDDING CEREMONY

The timing of several preceremony events can be crucial. Consider this countdown:

- *One hour before the ceremony:* The ushers arrive, put on their boutonnieres, and seat female guests by offering their right arms. If designated seating areas are preferred, the bride's section is on the left side (from the rear of the sanctuary), and the groom's section on the right.

- *Thirty minutes before the ceremony:* The organist begins playing music. If candles are used, they are lighted at this time unless the minister instructs otherwise. The groom and best man should arrive and go to the minister's study or another meeting place designated by the officiating minister.

- *During the final twenty minutes:* Some churches have facilities for all of the wedding party to use in dressing for the ceremony. If the wedding party dresses away from the church, the timing of several arrivals needs to be considered. The groom's parents arrive at the church about twenty minutes prior to the ceremony. The bride's mother arrives at the church about ten minutes before the scheduled beginning of the ceremony. The bride and her father arrive at the church just minutes before the ceremony and join the bridesmaid(s).

Immediately prior to the ceremony's beginning, an usher seats the groom's parents on the right front pew. Then, the bride's mother is seated on the left front pew where she will later be joined by the bride's father. No one is escorted to a pew after the bride's mother has been seated. Guests who arrive late must either stand or quietly seat themselves in the rear of the sanctuary. If an aisle runner is used, it should be unrolled at this time. If wedding songs are planned, the soloist should sing them just prior to the processional.

GUIDING THE CEREMONY ITSELF

The actual ceremony begins with the processional. The minister, groom, and best man take their places at the front of the center aisle. When the organist begins the wedding march, guests should follow the lead of the bride's mother. If she rises, all guests should also stand. The order of the processing group is ushers, bridesmaid(s), maid of honor, ring bearer, flower girl, and (after the organist increases the volume of the march music) the bride and her father.

Most ministers use some version of the traditional Episcopal wedding ceremony. When customized vows are preferred, the minister should guide the writing of the vows closely, be sure the vows are carefully memorized, and make a copy of the vows and carry them with her or him during the ceremony itself in case of an embarrassing lapse of memory on someone's part.

WHAT IF SOMEONE "SPEAKS NOW"?

Occasionally, a wedding ceremony develops an unexpected glitch. For instance, what are the minister's options if after asking, "If there is anybody present who has any objections to this marriage, let him or her speak up now or forever hold his peace," someone speaks up with an objection?

What if an old flame of the bride or the groom chooses the wedding as an occasion for making a public complaint? Or, what if future in-laws don't like the prospective mate their child is about to marry? Are these concerns reason enough to stop a wedding? What should you do?

According to justices of the peace, the only valid reason for halting a wedding is when the marriage wouldn't be legal. While the laws related to marriages may vary somewhat from state to state, several issues commonly constitute illegal marriages:

- If either the bride or groom has a prior undissolved marriage.

- If the parties are related to each other in a manner prohibiting marriage in that state.

- If either of the parties is under age.

- If either of the parties is judged to be incompetent or insane.

- If either of the parties is involuntarily intoxicated or drugged.

Consult a justice of the peace or an attorney in your state to see if the instances mentioned above are the law in your state or if additional causes apply also. Review the law and save yourself uncertainty and a wedding party embarrassment.

AFTER THE CEREMONY

The recessional begins the final element of the ceremony. The order of the recessional is the reverse of the order of the processional with the bride and groom exiting first and the best man escorting the bride's honor attendant. If the guests stand during the recessional, they should be seated following it until after the ushers have returned and escorted the bride's parents and then the groom's parents out of the sanctuary. The aisle runner isn't removed. If the wedding party wishes, the minister may invite the guests to the reception at the close of the ceremony.

PLANNING FUNERALS

The Bible notes that there's "a time to die" (Eccl. 3:1–2). About one percent of the American population dies each year. On the average, residents of the United States experience a bereavement because of death every six years. Funerals have always been emotionally difficult and structurally challenging services for the minister to lead. No longer, however, is death considered a dirty word in our culture. Americans are more informed about the event of death and the process of grieving.

WHY HAVE A FUNERAL?

Funerals are changing. Wakes aren't very common any more. Increasingly, families are closing caskets at funerals and even having memorial services after the burial. Do funerals have a purpose any longer?

A funeral is both a family ceremony and a community event. In the first place, funerals demonstrate the strength of our relational "credit networks." Our families and friends rally around us. Our sense of solidarity with them supports us. Second, funerals provide official, psychological farewells. This painful passage in our lives is clearly marked by the ceremony, the body, and the gathering of mourners. And, of course, funerals allow us to share our spiritual values.

THE MINISTER'S ROLE IN FUNERAL PLANNING

When a death occurs, your role as a minister is multifaceted. The family of the deceased, the polity and policies of his or her church, the funeral customs of the local area, the funeral director, and any special military or fraternal groups that may request participation must all be dealt with considerately.

In relationship to the family of the deceased, you extend your most crucial ministry. In most cases, you will likely have known and cared for the deceased previously. When the deceased has suffered some extended terminal illness, you will already have established a pattern of care and may have made some plans with the deceased concerning the funeral. When a death occurs, make a prompt, generally brief, comforting home visit and offer any assistance needed.

The funeral director generally contacts the minister who will officiate at the funeral, and together you will structure the arrangements for the service and burial. In most cases, the family of the deceased will leave the details of the funeral service to the minister. If the family requests a favorite Scripture, hymn, or element in the service, consider such appeals carefully and grant them as often as is appropriate.

Your composure at the funeral service is crucial to all of the mourners, especially the family. A brief home visit and prayer before the service, calm demeanor in the conduct of the service, firm handshakes, and sincere efforts to comfort and help will provide emotional structure and practical assistance to the deceased's family. The proof of your care of bereaved families is shown through your ongoing counsel with family members during the difficult and extended period of repairing their social network after the funeral.

No difference in your care of others should be apparent. Prominent church members, marginally participating members, and non-members should be treated alike. In fact, nonmembers may be reached for Christ and for church membership because of your—and the church's—thoughtfulness and thorough care during bereavement.

In relationship to local customs and congregational policies regarding funeral services, you should be knowledgeable and sensitive. Even if you disagree with some of these customs, don't choose a public funeral to create a test case for your views. Use other congregational settings to discuss issues and clarify church practices. Work to develop policies such as in figure 9.2, p. 185, that can be used to inform and guide members of your church.

Additionally, you should know and practice consistently the local customs regarding any fees paid to persons who assist with funerals. Be prepared to advise about appropriate fees to pay an organist, soloist, janitor, and other involved assistants. Often this information will be requested by the funeral director. In any event, ministers should never ask for a fee for conducting funerals although they may choose to accept travel expenses incurred in fulfillment of their professional responsibilities.

In relationship to previous ministers who are asked by grieving families to return to the field and to conduct funerals, the current minister should abide by the family's wishes. Anyone who returns to a previous field of service should be certain the current minister is informed. Invite the current minister to join in conducting the funeral service unless the family prefers otherwise. In any funeral in which more than one minister is officiating, all of the ministers should be fully aware of the responsibilities of each of the other officiants.

In relationship to funeral directors, you should major on spiritual and emotional assistance and leave the physical arrangements to the funeral director. While you may occasionally encounter a difficult person in the funeral home business, you will discover that most funeral directors are sensitive public servants. You may accompany grieving church members to the funeral home to make the final arrangements if members request your assistance in making decisions during difficult times.

In relationship to military or fraternal groups, you should acquaint yourself with these groups' prescribed rituals. When conducting funeral services that include these groups, carefully coordinate funeral services and graveside committals with their representatives. The Defense Department will, upon request, provide ministers with copies of its pamphlet on conducting military funerals.

PLANNING FOR REVIVALS

Revivals and similar types of meetings are a traditional means of sharing the gospel. With proper planning, they can enhance the congregation's outreach and encourage wholesome evangelism in the community. Here are the planning questions that need to be considered as a framework for pre-revival planning.

What is the purpose of our revival? The pastor and other church leaders in evangelism and ministry should guide the congregation in determining the specific purpose of their revival. Will the meeting concentrate on outreach? on building up the existing Christian fellowship? on both?

When is the revival scheduled? As far in advance as possible, the date of the revival needs to be calendared. The date may need to remain tentative until the preferred leaders can be enlisted. Care should be taken to avoid dates that compete with major community events or holidays.

Who will lead the revival? The pastor and others who may be charged with selecting the revival preacher, singer(s), and other leaders should carefully enlist persons who can best help the congregation reach its goal for the meeting. The church's minister(s), ministers of neighboring churches, and vocational evangelists provide an array of possibilities for revival personnel.

How will we organize to reach out? The church's evangelism committee (and special groups as needed) can arrange for prayer support, publicity, music, visitation, testimonies, hospitality, finance, ushers, and special emphases. In small churches, one person may be able to coordinate each of these activities.

How will we finance our revival? Misunderstandings over finances can tarnish your revival's impact quickly. Several options are used by congregations to underwrite the necessary expenses. Some churches include an item in their budgets for the total cost of their revival personnel and other expenses. Other churches use only freewill offerings. A few churches cover expenses out of their budgets, then use a love offering to show their appreciation for the preacher and singer. Whatever custom a church finds most comfortable, it should pursue its approach openly but without detracting from the revival's primary goal. If revival leaders are required to travel long distances, an advance on their expenses or a prepaid ticket is a thoughtful courtesy.

Are we involving most of our resident members in revival preparation? Prospect visitation, prayer support, and a plan for discipling every person who registers a public decision allow every member to contribute more than attendance to a revival's success. Overall involvement and careful preparation can plant the seeds for the Holy Spirit's cultivation and ripening.

PLAN, PLAN, PLAN

Special events deserve the minister's thorough efforts in planning (see figure 9.3, p. 186). You will want to remember such events for the positive results, not for what went wrong. Planning helps special events unfold in predictable stages and achieve the purpose for which they were designed.

Figure 9.1

SAMPLE WEDDING POLICY

_____ CHURCH

Your wedding is a sacred occasion and a service of Christian worship. For these reasons, the following statements will govern your plans for your wedding at this church.

CALENDAR

Careful planning is necessary for all weddings. The date of the wedding is set in consultation with the pastor. Upon your initial contact with the pastor, you will be given a Wedding Reservation Form that must be filled out and returned to the church office before the dates are entered on the church calendar. Scheduling of the facilities for weddings is on a first-come, first-served basis.

THE PASTOR

The pastor as administrator of the policy will assist you in every way possible. The pastor will discuss arrangements for pre-marital counseling with you and any other matters relating to the ceremony.

THE MUSIC

Music selected for a wedding service is a very personal and significant part of the ceremony, and individual tastes vary. At the same time, it is important to keep in mind that a church wedding is a worship service, and the music should be in keeping with the reverence that is customarily observed in worship. You should make an appointment with the minister of music immediately after applying for use of the church building. The minister of music and the church organist will give assistance in the selection of appropriate music. When you wish to invite musicians other than those on the church staff, you should consult with the minister of music regarding those you plan to invite and the selections of music to be included in this worship experience. You will be responsible for the payment of musicians.

THE RECEPTION

The fellowship hall and kitchen must be reserved through the church office. Provision is made on the Wedding Form for this arrangement. The chairperson of the Hostess Committee can share helpful information regarding this facility.

THE FLORIST

Moving of furniture will be done only by the custodian. The piano may not be moved. Dripless candles should be used. You will be responsible for repairing any damage to the property. Nails, tacks, or screws may not be put in walls, furniture, or pews. All decorations must be removed immediately after the wedding.

THE DIRECTOR

A director is needed for the wedding. The church, however, does not have a wedding director on staff. Suggestions of qualified directors will be made by the pastor at the time the Reservation Form is given to the bride.

THE PHOTOGRAPHER

Because the wedding is a sacred service of worship, flash photographs will not be taken during the processional, the ceremony, or the recessional. Video cassette recording done without high intensity lighting, however, is allowed.

THE FEES

No fee or charge shall be made for the use of the church buildings. However, a fee will be charged for the church custodian to:
1. Open and close church for rehearsal, wedding, and reception.
2. Clean before and after wedding.
3. Move furniture, if necessary.
4. Meet florist at desired times (for opening church).
5. Arrange for heating/cooling.
6. Prepare fellowship hall for reception (if used).
7. Other reasonable requests.

Fees for custodial services:

Use of Sanctuary for wedding and rehearsal — $_____

Use of Fellowship Hall for Reception — $_____ *

*This does not include washing of dishes, etc., used at reception.

Fees for musicians: responsibility of the bride.

Honorarium for minister: responsibility of the groom.

GENERAL CHURCH REGULATIONS

1. No alcoholic beverages may be served on church premises.
2. No wedding or rehearsal will be conducted when any member of the wedding party is under the influence of alcoholic beverages.
3. No rice or confetti may be thrown inside the sanctuary, foyer, fellowship hall, or anywhere in church buildings.
4. Designated rooms for the various members of the wedding party to dress will be provided.
5. The dress of the wedding party shall be in good taste for a religious ceremony.
6. Custodial fees should be paid when the Wedding Reservation Form is filed with the church office.

Figure 9.2

FUNERAL POLICIES FOR OUR CHURCH

The Christian gospel of peace, hope, and triumph is nowhere brought into sharper focus than at the death of Christians. Although we who believe in Christ sorrow at the death of persons we love, we don't "grieve as others do who have no hope. For since we believe that Jesus died and rose again, even so, through Jesus, God will bring with him those who have fallen asleep" (1 Thess. 4:13–14, RSV) The plans Christians make to face death are a testimony of faith.

Christians ought to assemble, not to mourn the dead, but to confess our faith in a living Lord. Generally, since the funeral is a service of worship, it should be held in the church building or a chapel and should itself be a witness to hope and fellowship.

On the basis of this affirmation, the statements below are offered for the guidance of our own members in the matter of funerals:

1. When a death occurs in the church family, the pastor should be called immediately. This call will give you the benefit of the pastor's solace and experience in making funeral arrangements.
2. Since a Christian funeral is a worship service, it is recommended that the funeral service be held in the church, that the congregation join in the singing of hymns of victory, thanksgiving, and fellowship, and that the pastor lead the service, drawing heavily on the comfort of the Scriptures.
3. The pastor will help the family select the hymns, Scriptures, and other elements of the funeral service to ensure the centrality of the theme of our victory over death through faith in our Savior.
4. When the funeral service is held in the church, with the physical remains present, it is recommended that public viewing of the deceased in the service be discouraged. Private or public viewing of the body may be arranged prior to the funeral service.

5. In order that worshipers may center their thoughts on the comfort and strength God provides, a memorial service may be held without the physical remains of the deceased (which may be committed to the earth prior to the service).

6. A simple casket is as appropriate as an elaborate one since the deceased's worth isn't determined by the cost of the funeral arrangements. Therefore, the church will provide a suitable cloth with which to drape the coffin for services that prefer this courtesy.

7. Families are encouraged to recommend to concerned friends the opportunity of making memorial gifts to the church or designated charities. Members of the church are reminded of the importance of acts of thoughtfulness and practical concern to the living during the grief process.

8. Because the funeral service is regarded as one appropriate function of the body of Christ, no fees of any kind are charged for the use of the church's facilities or its personnel.

Figure 9.3

SPECIAL EVENT PLANNING FORM

1. Event _____ Date _____ Time _____
2. Purpose/For _____ Approx. Attendance _____
3. Person in charge _____ Phone _____
4. Facilities needed
    _____ Auditorium (seats xxx)   ____ Nursery (ages ?_____)
    _____ Chapel (seats xx)   ____ Playground
    _____ Parlor/Bride's room   ____ Room(s) # _____
    _____ Fellowship hall   ____ Kitchen
    _____ Office reception area   ____ Parking lot
5. Equipment needed
    _____ Sound system   ____ Video player
    _____ Piano   ____ Slide projector
    _____ Chalkboard   ____ Tape recorder/player
    _____ Easel   ____ Record player
    _____ Table(s) number? _____   ____ Kitchen equipment
    _____ Chairs number? _____   ____ Other:_____
    _____ Equipment/supplies will be provided by:
    Company/Person_____ Phone_____
6. Preparation and cleanup of facilities
    Janitor needed? _____ (required for nonchurch function.)
    Payment due, if nonchurch function $ _____ Date due _____
    If church function, person in charge _____ Phone _____
7. Arrangement of facilities
    Sketch on the back of this form the room arrangement(s) desired. Show locations of tables, chairs, flower arrangements, and other items that will need to be set up.
8. Schedule and participants
    List below or attach to this sheet the schedule/agenda for this event and a list of program participants.
Person requesting _____ Date_____
Approved by _____ Date _____

CHAPTER 10

Church Publications

Bruce P. Powers

To a great extent, the personality of a church is conveyed through church publications. There is a direct relationship between how a congregation thinks and feels about its life and the content and quality of its published materials.

For example, look at your church bulletin. What story does it tell about the personality and character of your congregation? Look at the newsletters and other printed materials. Which ones make the church look best? How do they compare with the materials you see from businesses and community organizations in your town?

In this chapter you will find some ideas to improve your printed communications. Pick out the ones that appeal to you and that have possibilities for your situation. Then take a notepad and decide how to make the needed changes.

Following the administrative procedures, there is an idea section containing information on a variety of topics related to the preparation of printed materials.

GENERAL CONSIDERATIONS

1. *Be clear about your message.* Exactly what is it you are trying to communicate? The best messages are:

• concise—the writing is tight, direct, and clear.

• energetic—they are compelling, full of action verbs, and devoid of trite phrases and useless words.

- respectful—they allow the reader to interpret and make decisions, without overselling or dictating conclusions.

2. *Be clear about your target audience.* Are you speaking to insiders or to outsiders? Are you trying to communicate with an age group or with all ages? Is a message specifically for all persons in a worship service, or is it for those who are members of a Sunday school class?

3. *Follow a planned design.* Publications should not look pieced together. Look at a newsletter or bulletin. What stands out? Is this what you want to emphasize? Look at your church's material through the eyes of a stranger: What are the most important items or activities? Where would you look first, and how would you be guided through the printed messages? What would you remember? Why?

4. *Make basic information prominent.* Look at the title of your newsletter or bulletin, and the contact information. Would a stranger be able to:

- tell the full name of the church?
- address a letter to the church?
- call the church office?
- ask for the pastor or other minister by name?
- tell what the various sections or columns are about?

If a stranger would have trouble with any of these, so would many church members.

5. *Use quality paper.* What type of paper is used and what does it look like? Is it light colored, and clean and crisp-looking? Is it heavy enough so that printing on one side doesn't show through when you read the other side? Is there a good contrast between the printed material and the paper, so that reading, even in dim light, is easy?

6. *Develop editorial skills.* Who decides what goes into and prepares your church publications? Has this person developed skills in church communications, and does she/he feel good about the job being done? Consider providing some helpful resources for this person, such as those listed in the bibliography. And, when possible, encourage participation in a church publications workshop provided by your denomination or other church-related organization.

ADMINISTRATIVE GUIDELINES

The following guidelines will assist you in developing an administrative plan for your church:

1. One person on the staff should be designated as in charge of church publications. Although work might be delegated, this person would plan, organize, direct, and approve all editorial matters.

2. Develop a policy statement that describes the purpose, content, distribution, and costs for each regular publication. Have this approved by the

appropriate person/group. New publications would be approved in the same way.

3. Develop a production schedule for each regular publication. Indicate the dates by which various actions must be completed, and the person responsible if other than the editor. See figure 10.1, p. 191, for a sample production schedule.

4. Use a planning form, as illustrated in figure 10.2, p. 191, for each issue of a church publication. These forms could be prepared ahead of time for each week. A staff then could easily plan ahead for major emphases and arrange to treat themes over a series of issues. More time could be allowed for important writing assignments, and the editor could give more thought to layout and design. Such planning would enhance publications and help them serve as educational aids as well as promotional tools for church ministry.

5. Follow the same planning scheme for special brochures, promotional materials, and other related items. Plan thoroughly and far in advance of the date needed.

6. Develop a layout form for all regular publications. This will enable you to visualize materials while still in the planning stage, and it will cut down the time spent in editorial and typing work. This form is a sketch or copy of the actual publication with blanks for all items that change with each issue. In designing an issue, you place new material in the blank areas. For example, a Sunday bulletin form might include spaces for a Scripture passage, hymn titles, sermon topic, and announcements.

7. Keep a file copy of every publication. Place regular items such as bulletins and newsletters together in a binder for easy reference. Occasional items such as brochures can be filed together in a publications folder.

8. Review annually the effectiveness of church publications. This can be done by the church staff, the church council, or other authorized group of leaders. Guidelines for evaluation and suggested ways of developing an annual plan for publications are included in books listed in the bibliography.

IDEAS TO ENHANCE YOUR PUBLICATIONS

1. Design content based on the target audience. In publications designed for the total congregation, like a weekly newsletter, focus on general items such as the pastor's message, church family news, program promotion, and people features. Avoid a bunch of personal columns that have to be filled each week.

2. Space is precious; use it wisely. Information that applies to a few, such as a report to a committee, might better be sent via photocopies in an envelope.

3. Establish a news-gathering system. Determine what information is needed and how often. Enlist representatives who can gather and perhaps

write the needed articles. Determine an appropriate publication schedule, as described earlier in the chapter, and advise assistants of due dates.

4. Keep freshness in your publications. Materials that are overly predictable lose their communicating power. Try some of these ideas:

- Study books on the layout and design of church publications.

- Exchange materials with other churches by placing each other's names on your respective mailing lists.

- Collect publications that appeal to you and keep them in an idea file.

- Clip line drawings and related artwork from reading materials that will be discarded; you can use them in promotional materials. Such items also are available in printed form or on computer disks from office supply stores. Some denominations publish artwork collections designed for different seasons of the church year; check with your book store or denominational office.

- Attend a church publications workshop.

5. Become acquainted with proof-reading marks. These are used by printers and professional editors and writers to save time and to indicate specifically what is to be done when preparing a publication. Marks often used in preparing church publications are illustrated in figure 10.3, p. 192.

6. Learn the vocabulary used in dealing with church publications. Many of the words you will use are listed and defined in figure 10.4, p. 193.

7. Select a regular printshop and/or graphic designer to handle all of the publications done outside your office. Before doing this, determine the types and amounts of items normally used by the church during the year; then visit several shops. Discuss your needs, look at their products, and secure a list of prices and/or quotes. Select a firm that not only has good prices, but that can produce what you need within the time frame in which you must operate. Often you can negotiate concerning the amount of layout and design that must be done in your office and the amount that will be done by the printer/designer.

8. Develop a form sheet to use, and learn how to write press releases. Give facts: *what, who, when, where,* and *why.* Tell the most important information in the first few sentences, then give details. Print double-spaced on one side of 8 1/2" x 11" white paper. A sample form is in figure 10.5, p. 194.

9. Make an appointment to meet with each of the local editors, newscasters, and other persons responsible for deciding what news is distributed to the public. Discuss the requirements for submitting information, time schedules, and specific persons to whom you should relate. Discuss the types of information that would be printed or broadcast.

10. Be dependable. Get information together on time, in the right form, and to the right person.

11. Secure a style manual or a secretarial handbook for your office. Use this for reference whenever you are in doubt about how to communicate in

print. Check with your bookstore or denominational office to determine if a specific manual is recommended for your situation.

12. Proofread, proofread, proofread! Don't let careless mistakes make a joke of the church's image.

Figure 10.1

WEEKLY NEWSLETTER
SAMPLE PRODUCTION SCHEDULE

THURSDAY

- Determine space available and items to be considered.
- Meet with staff to plan next week.
- Complete a *Publication Planning Form* (See figure 10.2).

FRIDAY

- Compile materials.
- Write or secure commitments to prepare articles.
- Check on supplies, artwork, and other items needed.

MONDAY

- Secure all materials and complete writing/editing, using information gained from weekend activities.

TUESDAY

- Prepare camera-ready copy, or submit appropriate material to printer.
- Proofread all material!

WEDNESDAY

- Print and fold newsletter.

THURSDAY

- Label, sort, and package newsletter.
- Deliver to post office according to local requirements.

FRIDAY

- Newsletters are delivered to homes.

Figure 10.2

PUBLICATION PLANNING FORM

Title: _____ Editor: _____
Date to be listed on publication: _____
Date needed: _____ Give to whom: _____

PRODUCTION SCHEDULE

Date	Action
_____	Planning meeting with _____
_____	Make assignments for items to be written
_____	Deadline for receipt of all items
_____	Prepare copy
_____	Print, or deliver to printer
_____	Finish processing

GENERAL PLANS FOR THIS ISSUE

ARTICLES OR INFORMATION TO SECURE:

What	Person responsible	Due date
1. _____	_____	_____
2. _____	_____	_____
3. _____	_____	_____
4. _____	_____	_____
5. _____	_____	_____
6. _____	_____	_____
7. _____	_____	_____
8. _____	_____	_____

Figure 10.3

PROOFREADING MARKS

Proofreading	Mark Meaning
¶ The news is good.	Begin new paragraph
No ¶ The news is good.	No new paragraph
The news is good.	Delete (may be drawn through a letter or may be attached to a circle that encloses material to be deleted)
stet The news is good.	Leave as it was; let stand
Th^e news is good.	Insert item shown
The (is news) good.	Transpose material indicated
The#news is good.	Insert a space
The news i s good.	Take out the space; close-up
bf The news is good.	Print in boldface
The news is good.	Use italic style printing
The News is good.	Make the letter lower case
the news is good.	Make the letter a capital
[The news is good.	Move copy to end of box (may be left, right, up, or down)

Figure 10.4

CHURCH PUBLICATIONS VOCABULARY

BRUCE P. POWERS

Listed below are words often used in dealing with church publications. I have culled them through the years from workshops, courses, and working relationships with printers and publishers. Get acquainted with these terms and your ability to communicate in this field will improve greatly.

- *Art* — all illustrations, pictures, and drawings; the non-written material
- *Bleed* — an illustration that runs off the edge of a page/sheet
- *Blow-up* — an enlargement of a photograph
- *Box* — typed copy enclosed by a printed border
- *Bullet* — a solid circle of print (•), used for emphasis
- *By-line* — the author's name at the beginning of a story
- *Camera-ready copy* — finished copy and artwork pasted on a page for duplication just as it appears
- *Caps* — capital letters
- *Center spread* — two facing center pages of a publication
- *Clip-art* — artwork that can be cut out and pasted onto a master for reproduction
- *Coated paper* — type of paper with hard, smooth finish that makes pictures look better
- *Copy* — all written material
- *Copy desk* — where material is edited and given headlines before being published in a newspaper
- *Cover stock* — thick paper suitable for booklet covers
- *Credit line* — information about the source of copy or illustration
- *Crop* — to change the size or proportions of a picture
- *Deadline* — the last time to get copy in for publication
- *Dummy* — a made-up model of what the finished version will look like
- *End* — Typed at the end of a news release(--end--, also --30--)

- *Filler* — short item inserted to fill space in a publication
- *Flush* — even with the margin
- *Flyer* — an inexpensive piece of printed promotional material
- *Font* — a set of type of a particular style or design
- *Glossy* — a shiny-surface photograph
- *Graphics program* — a computer layout and design system for preparing publications
- *Layout* — Arrangement of text and artwork on a page
- *Lead* (pronounced like seed) — Opening paragraph in a news story that gives basic facts
- *Line drawing* — an illustration with solid lines and clear, non-printed areas; no shading
- *More* — When written at the bottom of a page, information is continued on the next sheet
- *Paste-up* — see Camera-ready copy
- *Point* — the unit of measure for the size of type used for printing (12-point is for average readers)
- *Proof* — first impression of set type on which corrections can be made
- *Rub-ons* — sheets of letters or artwork; put a letter where you want it, rub gently, and it transfers to the master
- *See-through ruler* — a large, transparent ruler marked with a grid; used to arrange materials on a master
- *Transfer type* — see Rub-ons
- *Trim size* — size of printed material after any necessary cutting
- *Widow* — a very short word or part of a word standing alone at the end of a paragraph of printed material

Figure 10.5

INFORMATION RELEASE

Release Date/Time _____

For Immediate Release _____

Release at Will _____

(Indicate <u>one</u> of the above.)

Church or Organization: _____

Name of Writer: _____

Position: _____

Local Address: _____

City/State/ZIP: _____

Telephone Number: _____ FAX Number: _____

SUBJECT: (STATE MAJOR FOCUS)

Begin typing here. Follow these guidelines:

- Use short paragraphs.
- Do not hyphenate words.
- Use wide margins (at least 1" on sides, top, and bottom).
- Double-space all copy.
- If a second sheet is needed, type --more-- at the bottom of the sheet before going on.
- After the first sheet, put your name, first three words from the subject, and the page number at the upper left.
- At the end of your release, type --end--.
- It is not necessary to write a headline for a news release.

CHAPTER 11

Food Services

William G. Caldwell

The extent to which a church is involved in food services will vary greatly from church to church. In some churches, there will be little or no activity relating to food, whereas other churches will have several full-time personnel and an extensive operation in food services. Regardless of the extent of the activity, a number of considerations must be made for the food service operation to be effective in a church.

DETERMINING FOOD SERVICE PURPOSES

A church must decide what it hopes to accomplish with food service activities. This decision will affect the approach taken to serving and funding meals. When it is seen as a ministry of the church, it will be used to enhance what the church is trying to do. The following purposes should be considered for a food service ministry.

ENCOURAGE FELLOWSHIP

There is something about sitting down to a meal together that encourages the fellowship and friendship of those who are involved. The informality that exists along with the amount of time it takes to eat a meal contributes to the opportunity for people to get better acquainted with one another. New members can be encouraged to participate in food service activities as a way to meet church members and to develop friendships.

SUPPORT PROGRAMS

Providing a meal is often the best way to get people to participate in some activity at the church. A regular Wednesday evening meal will encourage members to attend the prayer service and other program activities that may be scheduled at the same time. A special missions emphasis, visitation programs, training sessions, or some other ministries of the church will more likely be better attended if a meal is included.

FOSTER INVOLVEMENT

Many churches utilize volunteers in the food service operation. This provides the opportunity to involve people in the ministry of the church who might not be willing to serve in leadership roles. Adequate planning and scheduling will be necessary to make the most of volunteer involvement.

PROVIDE CONVENIENCE

The opportunity to eat at church will offer a convenient way for many individuals and families to participate in church activities. This will be especially true on weeknights when there would not be time for people to get home from work, prepare and eat a meal, and then get to the church for a meeting.

DEVELOP SPIRITUALLY

The emphasis on physical food should not overshadow the need for spiritual food. Every meal service activity should be seen as a means to helping people grow spiritually. This brings all of the purposes together. Developing a plan for outreach and fellowship helps to focus the activity of providing food. When the food service operation is seen in this light, the ministry opportunities are unlimited.

DESIGNING AN EFFICIENT CHURCH KITCHEN

The design of a kitchen will have a great deal to do with how it is used and how well it contributes to the effectiveness of the operation. Whether a church intends to serve meals from a potluck supper approach, a completely prepared and served approach, or a caterer approach, the design of the kitchen will help or hinder the process.

LOCATION

The kitchen is best located on the ground floor of the building with easy access to the outside for receiving deliveries, servicing equipment, and disposing of garbage. It must be accessible to water, sewer, electric and gas connections, and have an outside wall or ceiling access for exhaust fans. It should be near an interior corridor and directly adjacent to the dining area.

SPACE

The amount of space needed will be directly related to the type and frequency of meals served and to the number of people involved. A volunteer operation will require more kitchen space than a completely paid operation. The space should be adequate for storage and refrigeration of food, preparation and serving of meals, cooking equipment, washing and storage of dishes and utensils, and the movement of people. A room size equal to 20 to 25 percent of the dining area should be considered. It should also be large enough to allow for growth.

ARRANGEMENT

The way in which the kitchen is arranged will have a definite impact on its efficiency. If people continually get in the way of each other while trying to work, problems will exist. If the arrangement does not allow for an orderly flow of the activities relating to meal service, it will be difficult to operate effectively.

The usual arrangement is to have the preparation area in the center, with storage and dishwashing facilities to either side or at the back of the kitchen and the service area facing the dining room.

VENTILATION

Adequate ventilation is essential for a good kitchen operation. The hot, odor-filled air should be exhausted and replaced by fresh air once every two or three minutes. The exhausted air should be moved directly outside. A separate heating and cooling system for the kitchen works best when tied into the exhaust system. Filters relating to the system should be cleaned and changed regularly.

SANITATION

A church must be extremely cautious about the sanitation and health aspects of its kitchen. Even though the local health inspectors may not visit the church, county health department standards should be met by the church. The health of the people being served requires the church to be diligent in its own inspections and in the thorough cleaning of the facility. Those who work in the kitchen should have a health certificate or a food handler's certificate and should follow all the standard rules of hygiene around food. The kitchen and storage areas should be treated regularly to prevent insects and rodents from thriving. Leftover food and garbage should be removed promptly. Any outside doors or windows should be provided with screens that are maintained regularly.

EQUIPMENT

A church must recognize that the church kitchen is not a home kitchen. This will have significant bearing on the selection of equipment as well as policies for its use. The amount and type of equipment needed will be determined by the frequency of use, number of people served, and type of service utilized. For most churches, commercial or institutional equipment should be installed. If a church never plans to cook a meal, however, it would not require extensive equipment. Used equipment can frequently be obtained from local suppliers or from restaurants going out of business.

The cost of stainless steel equipment will be greater, but offers real advantages in upkeep and cleaning capabilities. The equipment should be purchased with a long-term outlook rather than the immediate cost factor. The amount of equipment secured should relate to the regular, normal activities of the kitchen. On those once-a-year occasions when more equipment is needed because of an extremely large gathering, consideration could be given to renting equipment, moving the gathering to a larger facility, or using a caterer.

WALLS AND FLOOR TREATMENT

The construction of the kitchen should take into account the heat, moisture, and sound that will be generated as well as the cleaning and maintenance needs. The surfaces should be covered with material that provides for these considerations. The sanitation of the facility will relate directly to this consideration. If proper acoustical treatment is not done, the proceedings in the dining area or other areas of the church will be limited because of the kitchen noise. As with equipment, proper construction will be more expensive, but much more effective in the long run.

OPERATING FOOD SERVICES

Designing a good church kitchen is the beginning of a good food-service ministry. Using the kitchen in the best possible way requires careful thought and planning concerning its operation. Even the best arranged and best equipped kitchen will not operate itself. Proper selection of personnel, menus, and the process of serving will determine the effectiveness of the operation.

DEVELOP POLICIES

Policies for the operation and use of the church kitchen are needed for the same reasons as any other church facility. Guidelines are needed to avoid problems and to define responsibilities. They should be protective but not restrictive and should be followed by all who use the food services. Most churches will find it helpful to have a committee to develop the policies. This may be a kitchen committee or a hostess committee or some other appropriate name. This group will consider carefully the needs of the church and the needs of the kitchen staff. The committee can also serve as a liaison between the church and the food service personnel in the implementation of policies and procedures. All aspects of the work of the kitchen and food services areas should be covered. See figures 11.1 and 11.2, pp. 203–204, for a sample policy statement and a schedule request form.

The church should also make a decision about the procedure to follow in the matter of reservations or the number of people to prepare for when a meal is served. Most churches that serve a weekly meal will be able to forecast the expected attendance on the basis of the time of year and special programs, and will not use a formal reservation system. Those who use a reservation system will have to determine the procedure for making reservations, the deadline for canceling reservations, and the procedure for collecting from those who do not attend.

In the case of banquets or other special meals, tickets should be sold or a number of plates should be guaranteed by the organization responsible. The cost of all meals should be determined in advance and paid for by those who attend. When a program organization is providing a meal for a special purpose, the food to be served and the appropriate budget account to be charged must be decided in advance.

ENLIST PERSONNEL

The selection of personnel for the food service operation is critical to its success. Most churches will use a combination of paid and volunteer help. One person (whether paid or volunteer) should be selected as the food service director. The supervisor and personnel committee should be involved in this selection. Some of the characteristics needed by this person are:

- An outgoing personality
- Ability to work in harmony with others
- Emotional maturity
- Ability to communicate
- Interest and experience in kitchen management
- Understanding of food service purposes
- Dependable and energetic

These same qualities should be looked for in other persons who will be enlisted to work.

The number of persons needed will be determined by the type of food service activity in which the church is involved. A regular, weekly meal will likely involve some paid personnel who will work every week. The food service director will plan the meals, purchase the food and supplies, and enlist and direct the persons who will be involved in cooking and serving. Volunteers can be enlisted to assist with the serving and initial cleanup. It is usually wise to use paid personnel in the dishwashing operation due to the need to maintain proper sanitation procedures as well as to recognize the limitation of asking volunteers to work after everything is over.

Helpers will usually be available from within the church membership. Utilization of youth and senior adults is a wise procedure. Enlisting volunteers from Sunday school classes, mission organizations, or other church organizations should be done for the weekly meals or the occasional banquets. Some of the tasks will require a limited amount of training, but most of the jobs to be done can be accomplished by any willing person.

DETERMINE SERVING METHODS

The arrangement of the kitchen and dining facilities will affect the ways in which food is served. This should be considered in planning a facility, but it will have to be lived with once the facility is constructed. If there is not enough room or equipment to cook a meal, then it would be unwise for a church to plan anything more than a potluck dinner. If the facility planning has allowed for different approaches to serving, then the decision can be made on the basis of the number of persons and the type of group to be served. The economics of the meal should not be the only consideration. The ages of the persons will be a factor as well as the type of group: families, children, senior adults, or others. The amount of space available and the amount of time allowed for the meal will also need to be considered since some serving methods require more space and take more time than others. The following methods should be considered:

1. *Family style.* The food is placed in bowls on the tables. Persons serve themselves. This requires enough servers to get the food to the tables while it is still hot. The cost factor is usually greater.

2. *Cafeteria.* This requires counter-serving space where food can be kept hot or cold. It offers selection, but it is not good for persons who have trouble making decisions. Cost is controlled since portions are determined by servers. It requires servers behind counter.

3. *Buffet.* This requires serving space where food can be kept hot or cold. It allows persons to serve themselves the amount they want. The cost factor is usually greater.

4. *Plate service.* Plates with food are picked up at one location. This requires enough servers to put food on the plates as people come in. It offers portion and cost control. Taking plates to the table would require more servers.

5. *Caterer.* At times it may be best to use an outside caterer to provide the meal service.

PLAN MENUS

The food service director should be responsible for planning menus in keeping with the type of meal to be served and the type of group involved. The sponsoring organization should provide input based on the cost factor as well as the occasion. Basic suggestions relating to menu selection include the following: simplify the choices; balance the menu from a nutrition standpoint; contrast textures, flavors, and colors; consider the workload and personnel available for cooking; stay within budget limitations.

The trend toward healthy eating needs to be considered in planning meals. The use of baked or broiled meats rather than fried is a good option. Reducing dietary fat can be accomplished by using skim milk instead of whole milk; using low-fat yogurt for sour cream; using cocoa instead of chocolate; and vegetable oil instead of other high-fat content oils. The desire for low-cholesterol, low-salt, high-fiber foods is valid and should be met in the planning and cooking process.

A regular Wednesday-evening meal program must also be planned from the standpoint of variety since the same people will be eating every week. Some basic items can be selected and rotated over a period of time. Seasonal items can be included when they are available. The attractiveness of the items as they appear on the plate will have a great deal to do with the taste of the food.

PURCHASE FOOD AND SUPPLIES

Because of the high cost of food, it is necessary for the food service director to shop carefully and wisely in purchasing food and supplies. If the amount purchased is large enough, institutional distributors will deliver to the church, and wholesale prices can usually be obtained. The wise food service director knows that one distributor cannot provide everything that is needed. Rather than purchase only what one distributor sells, a combination approach is better. This means buying from several distributors for a better variety of choices as well as utilizing retail outlets for some needs that a wholesaler cannot meet as well.

It is best to plan in such a way that major purchasing is done only once a week, so that the best prices are secured and time is not wasted. Quantity purchases can be made when price considerations and storage capabilities are favorable. Quality should not be sacrificed for price. Poor-quality food service will affect participation and probably cost more in the long run.

A food service director will discover over a period of time who the best distributors are and where the best deals can be made. Taking advantage of special sales is good when there will be a need for what is on sale in the immediate future. Any deliveries made to the church should be checked for quality and quantity of items ordered.

DETERMINE COSTS

All of the factors relating to the food service operation must be calculated when figuring the cost of meals and services. Many churches will provide for equipment, supplies, and labor through budget allocations and therefore only charge for the cost of food when determining a per-plate charge.

A church must decide how it will provide the cost of the food service ministry. If different charges are to be made on the basis of the organization or activity involved, the policies should identify the differences. In most cases where an outside group is involved, the church should plan to recover all of the direct costs incurred (labor, utilities, supplies, and such).

PREPARE AND COOK FOODS

All of the activity relating to food services can be a complete waste of time if the food is not prepared and cooked so that it looks and tastes good. There should also be an adequate amount of food prepared so that no one goes hungry. The menu selection must be done on the basis of the amount of time and number of personnel available for cooking. The choice of using prepared foods or cooking from ingredients will also be made on the time and personnel considerations. The higher cost of prepared foods may be offset by the cost of personnel who cook.

When more than one meal is involved, consideration must be given to oven space, refrigerator/freezer space, and utensils available for multiple use. Planning ahead will enable the food service director to be aware of upcoming situations and do some preparing and cooking ahead of time when storage facilities are available.

CLEANUP PROCEDURES

Proper and thorough cleanup is a vital part of any food service program. Decisions about leftover food should be made in advance. Sometimes items can be frozen and used later. A food service director must be just as concerned for cleaning up and putting items in their proper place as any other part of the operation. Volunteers may be effective in the initial cleanup of the dining area and in bringing the dishes to the dishwashing area, but, due to the extra time involved, it will probably be best to pay someone to do the actual washing of dishes, pots, and pans and putting them in the storage areas. Some churches have had good success in employing teenagers for this work. Adequate provisions will need to be made for getting all garbage to the outside storage area until it can be disposed of properly. Nothing should be left out in the dining or kitchen area that might be attractive to rodents and insects.

KEEP RECORDS

A competent food service director or committee will keep records of all of the activities relating to the program. A list of menus used at regular weekly meals and special banquets is essential. A cost analysis record of all meals helps to keep the program in the black and provides information for establishing the cost for meals. Written instructions to the financial secretary concerning the charges to be made to the proper budget accounts will provide information needed for budget preparation. The development of forms for these purposes helps with the record-keeping process.

SPECIAL FOOD SERVICES PROGRAMS

In addition to the regular, weekly meals in which the church may be involved, there are a number of special activities the food services ministry may consider. Each of them will have specific concerns that will have to be dealt with if they are to be successful.

WEDDINGS

Most church weddings will have food service needs. The rehearsal dinner may be held at the church, and most likely the wedding reception will be held at the church. The food service director will need to be consulted in these situations unless the church has a separate person who acts as a wedding consultant. Even when this is done, there must be communication about the use of the kitchen and serving equipment.

Policies concerning weddings need to be developed and provided to all persons anticipating a ceremony at the church. These policies should include scheduling the use of facilities, decorations, use of ministers and musicians, premarital counseling, conduct of the wedding party, charges made for the facilities and personnel, photographer and florist requirements, sound system and lighting needs, food service and receptions, use of security, and other matters.[1]

RECEPTIONS

There will be other receptions at the church given to honor staff members or others in the church membership. The church may have a committee that helps to plan such occasions. Careful planning with the food services director is necessary for these events.

BANQUETS

All kinds of banquets may be conducted at the church. Examples would include leadership banquets, Valentine banquets for youth or adults, deacons banquets, Christmas banquets, Thanksgiving banquets, youth banquets, Sunday school class or department banquets, and the like. Decisions will have to be made about the time, the cost (reservations or tickets), the decorations, the need for extra equipment or supplies, and the type of serving to be done. The food services director should always be willing to work with any group that wants to plan a banquet.

PICNICS

Many churches utilize picnics as an informal means of fellowship. Since most of these would be held away from church facilities, careful planning would have to be done by the food services director to accomplish these activities. Decisions would have to be made about securing the site, facilities available at the site, the food to be furnished by the church or the members, the supplies to be provided (including tables and chairs), and the cleanup process.

CONCLUSION

The food service ministry can be a valuable asset to the work of the church when it is conducted properly. The wise church will secure competent leadership that will plan and conduct the ministry, so that it will make a contribution toward helping the church achieve its purposes.

Figure 11.1

KITCHEN POLICIES

1. The kitchen and food services operation of the church are to be used primarily by the church and its organizations. Outside, nonprofit groups desiring to use the facilities should make a written request 30 days in advance to be considered by the Food Services Committee and director, providing there is no conflict with a scheduled church function.
2. The schedule request form shall be completed by all groups wishing to use the facilities. Written approval must be received before the facility can be used.
3. The Food Services Committee and director shall have supervision of the kitchen at all times. The director or a trained volunteer shall be present whenever the kitchen is used. Food service personnel shall have health or food handler certificates.
4. Agreements for purchasing food and supplies must be made with the director at least one week in advance of the activity to assure adequate financial arrangements are made. The number expected should be estimated and paid for. For church groups, the costs will cover the food and supplies. For outside groups, the costs will include food, supplies, labor, and an estimated amount to cover utilities and janitorial expense.
5. Keys to the kitchen and storage areas will be issued only to employed food service personnel. These areas will be kept locked when not in use to assure the security of the facilities and the safety of persons in the building.
6. Kitchen and dining room equipment to be loaned for use outside the church building will follow the equipment policy procedure in consultation with the food services director.

7. The organization sponsoring a meal shall arrange for volunteers to assist with serving and shall be responsible for arranging and decorating the dining area.
8. The Food Services Committee and director shall be responsible for maintaining an inventory of equipment and supplies and preparing a budget for additional equipment and supplies as needed.

Figure 11.2

FOOD SERVICE REQUEST FORM

Date received: _____   Date of meeting _____
Organization:_____
Type of meeting: _____   Number expected: _____
Time of meeting: From _____   to _____
Person in charge: _____   Phone _____
Area needed: _____
Type of meal service: cafeteria _____   buffet_____   plates served _____
Menu suggestions:_____
Meat(s) _____
Vegetables _____
Salads _____
Desserts _____
Drinks _____
Reception _____
Cost desired _____ :   Budget account # _____
                          (Do not write below this line.)

FOOD SERVICES OFFICE FILE

Charges: Department _____   Account _____ Amount $_____
Cleared on church calendar _____   Menu approved _____
Personnel assigned _____
Approved date _____
Summary: _____
                              Food cost $ _____
                              Supplies $ _____
                              Labor $ _____
                              Total cost $ _____
                              Per plate cost $ _____

CHAPTER 12

Legal Matters
William G. Caldwell

One of the most difficult areas for congregations today is that of the law and legal ramifications for the church. Many churches, unfortunately, act out of ignorance, a feeling of immunity, or a stance based on the separation idea that says that the church has no dealings with the state. Due to increasing litigation and legal accountability experienced among non-profit institutions, it is important that every minister and every church understand the basic legal matters that apply to the work of the church. The problem with a general overview, however, is the variance of state and local regulations concerning them. A related problem is the continual change in laws and their relationship to churches. This chapter, therefore, seeks to point out areas of concern without giving legal advice. A qualified, local attorney is the best source of detailed information.

DETERMINING NEEDS FOR LEGAL ADVICE

Every church will have need for legal advice at some point in its ministry. The need will vary according to the kinds of activities, building programs, and ministries in which the church is involved. A major consideration in this area will involve the ability to know when to seek legal help and the best approach to take when the situation calls for it.

SELECT AN ATTORNEY

A church should seek a reputable, competent attorney who will be sympathetic and understanding of the special legal needs of a church. An attorney who is a member of the congregation may not be the best choice although a Christian is preferable. The need for objectivity in legal matters could be a problem for one who is too closely related to the situation. A church should be willing to pay for the services rendered and not expect discounted or free advice. For a small fee some attorneys will serve on a retainer basis, always ready to provide the service needed. Additional charges would still be made for services rendered.

In selecting an attorney it is wise to check with other churches to discover if they have found one who has been helpful. State and local bar associations and legal aid societies may be other sources of information. The specialty of the attorney is important. Most churches will not need a person who specializes in criminal law. The more common areas of need would relate to real estate, contracts, employment, liability, and general family law.

The selection process should include an interview to allow the attorney to become familiar with the church, its leadership, and the specific areas of concern relating to legal services. The status of the church as a nonprofit entity would need to be understood by any attorney who would work with a congregation.

The church should feel free to discuss with the attorney the schedule of charges that is used for services rendered. If a retainer fee is to be used, some negotiation of the amount would be in order based on the expected time involvement and the frequency of advice needed. Once a selection has been made, there should be freedom by the church or the attorney to change or terminate the relationship if the need arises.

SITUATIONS REQUIRING LEGAL ADVICE

Numerous and rapid changes are taking place in legal matters that may have impact on the local church. At the national level the Internal Revenue Service continues to issue rulings that will affect the church. In addition, tax code changes and tax court decisions make it necessary for the church to keep up with those areas that will affect its work.

At the state level, decisions are being made concerning day-care centers and school operations that will affect those churches that offer such services.

At the local level the taxation of properties owned by a church continues to be explored. There are also many local ordinances that affect a church in its building program and the operation of church activities. Many of these situations will require the church to secure competent legal advice. Ignorance of the law will not be a valid excuse if the church is guilty of failing to abide by its legal responsibilities.

There are times when the church may be required to go to court to resolve the problem that exists. There are several considerations the church must make when this happens.

1. *Stewardship.* What is the responsibility of the church from a stewardship standpoint? If a person has attempted to swindle the church, the court may be the only place to deal with the problem. The church must analyze

the situation from the perspective of the wise and proper use of its resources.

2. *Safety.* The responsibility of the church to provide adequate safety precautions is sometimes overlooked and may result in a court case. The church must not hide behind any spiritual excuse when its negligence concerning the safety of its members and guests is involved.

3. *Fraud.* In the case of a company that has demonstrated outright fraud, the case may have to be settled in court. The church may have a responsibility to keep that company from treating others in a similar matter.

4. *Public relations.* Going to court should always be the last resort. It will be embarrassing and difficult and may have a negative effect on the image of the church in the community.

A change has come from the time when the doctrine of charitable immunity protected the church from lawsuits. More and more, the trend is toward close inspection of all nonprofit institutions—including churches—as to the ways in which they abide by the rules and regulations of society. Churches must set a good example in all those situations where they are required to do certain things—even going beyond the minimum expectations to do more than is required.

ROLE OF TRUSTEES

The work of trustees in a church will vary according to the structure within which the church operates. In most instances they will be the official group to sign papers and otherwise represent the church in legal matters. They will act as the agent of the church in transacting business.

In some cases, by vote of the congregation, the pastor acts as the agent of the church. It is important that the pastor or the trustees know and have evidence of the authority possessed in acting for the church. Entering into a contract outside that authority could result in personal liability for any loss or damage to the church or any outside party.

When acting for the church, there must be clear indication of the role of the agent on behalf of the church. A resolution passed by the church to this effect will eliminate any personal liability in the case of a dispute. Advice from an attorney can be helpful in this area. The section on incorporation provides additional information regarding this responsibility.

In some organizational structures trustees may perform additional responsibilities for the church. They may act as the Building and Grounds or Maintenance Committee, the Personnel Committee, or serve in functional areas relating to insurance and like matters. In most cases, these structures have evolved over a period of time and work well for the church using them.

RESOLVING GRIEVANCES

A church would do well to establish a procedure for dealing with disputes, disagreements, or grievances that are bound to develop in spite of the best of Christian intentions. It is tragic when such disputes must go to the court system to be resolved. Every effort should be made to settle such matters within the framework of the church structure.

Written procedures for employee grievances should include the following guidelines and be included in the policy manual.

The immediate supervisor should be the first person involved when an employee has a problem. A written record should be made of the grievance and the attempt to deal with it. Several efforts may have to be made to resolve the issue. If the difficulty cannot be dealt with at this level, then the next level of supervision should be involved. All of the records of the attempts to solve the problem should be reviewed, and additional solutions explored.

If the supervisors cannot develop a satisfactory solution, it is helpful to have some type of a committee (personnel, pastor/parish relations) made up of qualified church members who relate to personnel matters. These persons would be brought into the discussion to give greater insight into possible solutions. In some organizations they would have the final word. In others, the congregation would have to be involved or a denominational group would be called in as arbitrator if the grievance could not be resolved. Every effort should be made to deal with such matters in the church rather than securing an attorney and going to court.

UTILIZING LEGAL HELP IN SPECIFIC AREAS

There are a number of specific areas where the church will be wise to secure legal help. The extent of the help needed will be determined by the nature of the situations and the degree to which the state or county has gotten involved in the affairs of the church. Each church will have to determine for itself the extent of the need and the legal advice that may be necessary. A word of caution: This is not the place to hide your head in the sand and pretend that something will go away, especially if you pray hard enough! Issues must be dealt with and legal help will be necessary in many areas.

INCORPORATION

The effect of incorporation is to create a legal entity that the law recognizes for purposes of holding title to real estate, executing contracts, and performing all functions necessary in conducting the civil affairs of the church. It does not take away the spiritual nature or purpose of the church. While the main advantage relates to the insulation from liability for individual members, there are several other advantages to incorporation.

- The church can hold property in its own name.

- It restricts the duplication of the church's name.

- The church has continued life.

- It protects creditors.
- Certain states offer tax benefits.
- It helps the church obtain multirisk insurance.
- The church has a greater opportunity for obtaining loans.
- The church is a separate legal entity.
- It protects church members and trustees.

A church is not required to become incorporated as a nonprofit religious corporation. Each state has its own regulations concerning the status of a church as a nonprofit organization. Some states do not provide for incorporation for a church. The office of the secretary of state is the appropriate place to get information about the incorporation procedure.

The procedure will vary if the church is an independent body—a congregational-type church governed solely within itself; or a dependent body—a church governed by a hierarchical form of government, so that the church itself is a member of a larger organization.

The process usually involves the assembling of members for the specific purpose of approving the documents relating to incorporation. These will include:

- the *charter* stating the name and purpose of the organization;
- the *bylaws* that include the powers and responsibilities of the officers, the members' rights and privileges, the meetings of the body and provisions for dissolving the body; and
- the *minutes* which will detail the conduct of the meeting that approved the incorporation.

All of this information will be filed with the appropriate fee for recording the action. It may be advisable to have an attorney look over the documents to be sure they are in order.

The advantages of incorporation seem to far outweigh the potential problems of remaining a society in the eyes of the state. The advice of an attorney will be helpful in determining the proper procedure to follow for a local church.

LIABILITY

The church and the minister are not immune from legal responsibility for their actions because they are in the religion business. There is a responsibility that extends to anyone who is related to the activities of the church in terms of the care and protection of people.

A church may be called upon to provide compensation for *anyone*—members, visitors, employees, or others outside the church—when there is negligence resulting in any loss or damage. The act of negligence may result from doing or not doing something that a reasonable person would do or not do in a similar situation.

The interpretation of what is reasonable has varied from state to state and usually is decided by a judge or jury when the question of negligence reaches the courtroom. Negligence usually requires an injury caused by the defendant's conduct or lack of action. The defendant shows negligence in that the action or lack thereof shows a breach of duty in performing reasonable measures to protect against risks.

Permission slips for trips away from the church are helpful, but they cannot be used as an excuse for negligence. The church should make every effort to keep from being negligent as well as to provide adequate insurance coverage for protection from unforeseen situations. The provision of *workers compensation insurance* coverage for employees and *public liability insurance* coverage for property and vehicles in significant amounts should be maintained.

The minister as a professional also has concerns about the proper performance of responsibilities. This is evident in those acts as an agent of the church but also in those acts as a professional person, particularly in the area of counseling.

The subject of malpractice by a minister has become one of legal significance. This is due to vague interpretations of a minister's liability when advice given a counselee leads to harmful results. Again, the negligence question is open to interpretation but has become the object of suits that have been filed. Common sense precautions need to be taken.

Related to this concern is that of privileged communications between a minister and a counselee. The state laws vary as to the extent to which a minister could be required to testify concerning such communications. Almost all require reporting of child abuse situations. The main difference in some states is the conducting of formal counseling sessions as opposed to informal conversations.

The licensing of counselors by many states is an effort to provide assurance that sufficient training is being done. The minister who is not licensed should refer persons to someone who is.

TAXATION

The subject of taxation of churches is extremely complicated and open to various interpretations. The idea that a church is tax exempt does not remove the responsibility the church has for filing certain forms and for paying some taxes. It is further complicated by the differing requirements of federal, state, and local laws relating to churches.

1. *Federal taxes.* A church is usually automatically exempt from federal taxes because it is a church. A relationship with a denominational body helps. Other religious organizations must request exemption from taxes and the right to receive tax deductible contributions as a religious organization defined in *Section 501(c)(3) of the Internal Revenue Code.* (A church should have a copy of this section and the related publication on applying for exempt status.)

The Internal Revenue Service uses several characteristics to determine if a church qualifies for exemption. Among these are the following:

- a legal existence
- a formal code of doctrine
- a membership not associated with another church
- an established place of worship
- regular religious services
- an ordained ministry
- schools for training ministers

A church may have ministry programs that are not separately incorporated and are therefore recognized as units of the church. It may also have separately incorporated ministry programs that are controlled by the church and are therefore recognized as an integrated auxiliary of the church. The key words are ministry and control. A federal identification number is issued for the church to use in filing forms or other documents with the government.

2. *State taxes*. In many states, churches are exempt from paying the state sales tax on items purchased for use by the church. A tax exempt number is required in some states while others issue a refund or simply recognize the name of the church for exemption. The property tax code will also vary from state to state in terms of what is or is not exempt as church property. A church should investigate what its tax responsibilities are in the state where it is located.

3. *Local taxes*. The same variance in taxation exists at the local level. Local sales taxes and local property taxes are levied against churches in some communities. A church should not assume that all of its properties and purchases are tax exempt, but should investigate what is required and what process must be followed to obtain exemptions when they are allowed. Local authorities have attempted to levy taxes on parking lots, parsonages, excessive land, and other church property in an effort to broaden the tax base in a local community.

4. *Employment taxes*. A church is responsible like any other employer to withhold taxes from an employee's wages and to pay those taxes in a timely manner to the proper authority.

Income taxes (including state and local where applicable) must be withheld from all employees according to the tax guides provided. The exception to all employees applies to the ordained minister (and to the licensed or commissioned minister who performs substantially the same functions as the ordained minister) who is considered *self-employed* for tax purposes and files quarterly returns along with the payment of the self-employed rate of Social Security taxes. The church may withhold amounts from salary for these taxes at the request of the minister.

A newly ordained minister within the second year of ordination may file a request for an exemption (which is irrevocable) from Social Security coverage on religious principles to acceptance of Social Security benefits (or other public insurance) for services as a minister. Economic considerations for the exemption are not valid.

All other employees, whether paid by the hour, day, week, piecework, or percentage must have tax withheld. The church must keep appropriate records and file the proper forms with the employee and the taxing agencies as instructed.

Rulings on Social Security taxes also require the church to withhold the stated amount from all employee's wages and to match that amount from church funds when making the quarterly payments. Failure to do so can result in tax liens and penalties for failure to comply with the regulations. A church should consult with the state to determine if other wage and hour laws apply to the church.

5. *Unrelated-business income taxes.* A church may be subject to taxes based on business income that is not directly related to the work of the church or that the church receives from debt-financed property. The income must be from a trade or business activity that is conducted regularly. It also must not contribute importantly to accomplishing the exempt purpose of the organization.

If all of the work performed is by volunteers, it would not likely be an unrelated business. A church should carefully examine its receipts in these areas and determine if it should file the proper forms for reporting such income and pay the appropriate taxes required.

6. *Federal excise tax.* In certain cases a church may be exempt from paying the federal excise tax that is levied on certain items purchased. This is especially true for church-related schools. The proper form should be secured and filed for the exemption.

7. *Unemployment tax.* A church is usually exempt from federal and state unemployment taxes. An investigation should be made with state authorities to discover the requirement in each state. A church may be permitted to participate voluntarily in these programs in some states.

EMPLOYMENT PRACTICES

A church should establish policies relating to the employment of personnel so it will not be guilty of inconsistency in hiring practices. Legal review of these policies may be helpful. Even though churches are not required to follow the government-mandated policies regarding equal opportunity employment, every effort should be made to assure a nondiscriminatory approach in employment.

A church may want to employ only church members, but that should be a fair and consistent policy and not an excuse used only when it is convenient to keep from hiring someone else. This lack of consistency in hiring practices could result in persons feeling that they had been discriminated against since they were not hired.

Several federal laws relating to employment practices may or may not relate to churches. Some of them require a certain number of employees for the law to be effective, others apply on the basis of what the church or organization is involved in as a part of the ministry being done. Each church should look at the laws and, perhaps with legal counsel, make a decision on how they might be affected. Some of the laws to be considered include:

- Title VII, *Civil Rights Act of 1964*

- *Equal Pay Act of 1963*

- *Family and Medical Leave Act of 1993*

- *Age Discrimination in Employment Act (1967)*

- *Americans with Disabilities Act of 1990*

- *Immigration Reform and Control Act of 1986*

Since Congress is continually involved in developing legislation in this area, it is important for churches to stay abreast of changes that occur.

In addition, individual states enact legislation that may also apply to churches. There is a continuing need to be aware of how state laws may relate to the employment process.

It is also wise to take precautions in case it becomes necessary to terminate an employee. *A supervisor should carefully record any action taken to reprimand an employee and document the effort made to improve performance.* This documented record should be placed in the employee's personnel file. It is helpful if the record also includes a signed statement by the employee acknowledging the agreement to improve performance.

If repeated attempts to rectify the inadequate performance are not successful and termination becomes necessary, the records will provide sufficient information to indicate that the church was justified in its action. If a church does not follow such a process, there is a good possibility that a terminated employee could have legal grounds for a lawsuit.

WILLS AND ESTATES

The whole matter of wills and estates represents a significant area of legal concern for the church and the Christian interested in the total concept of stewardship. The advice of those trained in the field is essential for good planning because of the complex nature of government rules and state laws regulating the disposition of an estate.

Many churches have a special committee to promote the concept of making a will or establishing a trust as an act of Christian stewardship. Some churches are fortunate enough to have attorneys, bankers, or accountants who can assist church members in this area.

The advantages of estate planning must be shared with the congregation. The need to put things in order should be evident to the Christian. The desire to protect one's assets in the way an estate is settled should be of major concern. Good planning will minimize the effect of taxes and other administrative costs relating to settling the estate as well as provide for the efficient and timely distribution of property.

The making of a will is essential to the completion of estate planning. Without a will, state laws specify who benefits from the estate. By making a will, the *individual* specifies who is to benefit. The assistance of an attorney is not required in most states, but it is highly recommended. The complexity of legal terminology is such that a person may not say what needs to be said unless an attorney assists with the preparation of the will. A church can and should encourage the inclusion of Christian causes in making a will so that a person who has supported the church while living can reflect that support in the disposition of the assets of the estate. Since a will can be changed anytime prior to the death of the person, it should be reviewed and updated as changes in circumstances should dictate.

GENERAL FAMILY LAW

There are several areas of legal responsibility that the church will not face directly but may be called upon because of the involvement of church members in these matters. The church that has a day-school or child-care program will more than likely have to make some decisions concerning policies it will follow in its responsibility to children enrolled.

Perhaps the most common area of concern is that of *family violence.* This includes spouse abuse as well as child abuse. Many churches and ministers are being faced with counseling decisions as well as legal decisions relating to the reporting of such activities. Many states and communities now have laws concerning the responsibility of school officials to notify the proper authorities when there is obvious evidence of child abuse. The very nature of church work involves visits into the homes of members and prospective members; you may discover situations where abuse is apparent and must be dealt with. Some of the legal implications of these situations may call for the advice of an attorney.

The increasing occurrence of divorce has created many cases of spousal and child support that may cause difficulties for the church. Since religion is such a vital part of life, some have charged that church involvement has been the cause of alienation and separation. Wise counseling is necessary in such situations. Several well-publicized cases have presented the need for schools and child-care programs to be extremely cautious in their policies concerning the release of children to relatives or others who may not have the legal right to take the child. A formal procedure for checking children in and out may be necessary. Temporary or permanent restraining orders may have been issued by the court that the church will be involved in enforcing. A church cannot ignore its responsibilities in this area if it desires to be effective in its ministry to the community.

There may be other areas of family responsibility that will affect a church in its work. There have been situations in which court-ordered counseling has been related to the church. The activity of child adoption may involve a minister with families in the church. The problem of court-directed grandparent access may affect the church. It is not necessary that a church or its ministers become experts in these family matters as they relate to legal requirements. It is necessary, however, that a church and its ministers realize that all of these situations can and do affect their work and that legal advice be sought when it is needed.

CONTRACTS

One of the most obvious areas in which legal advice is helpful and necessary is that of making and keeping contracts. A church will have many situations when the services of an attorney will be needed to draw up, interpret, or evaluate a contract. Since a contract represents a legally binding agreement between two or more parties, it is essential that the document be accurate, clearly understood, and prepared according to legal requirements. This is necessary for the protection of the church as well as for the other parties involved.

As discussed earlier, the church acts through its authorized agent to enter into a contract. In most cases this agent would be the trustees who have been given the authority to act on behalf of the church. The trustees can only act within the authority given and cannot bind the church to contracts that have not been approved. A pastor or other minister of the church should not assume the role of agent for the church in matters of contract. If this is done outside the minister's authority, personal liability may result. Contract signing should always be indicated as being signed as an agent of the church.

Legal advice is necessary when any real estate purchase is anticipated. In many cases it is helpful to have an attorney who specializes in real estate law. It is never wise to do it yourself no matter how well meaning church members may be. The need for a title search to assure a clear title to the property, the need to examine the contract to be sure it says what it should, the need to draw up a deed that provides protection for the church, and the need to properly identify any restrictions that may apply—all point to the necessity for legal advice in real estate transactions.

Other contracts that involve major purchases or agreements lasting for more than one year should also be evaluated by an attorney. Any transaction involving an executor or agreements requiring the church to guarantee something should likewise be evaluated. Any expense the church may have to bear for these services may well be savings in the long run if it protects the church from faulty contracts or agreements.

COPYRIGHTS

There is no excuse for a church or its ministers to be ignorant of the copyright law and its application to the work of the church. A copy of the current law and forms for application for copyright registration may be obtained free of charge by writing to: *Copyright Office, Library of Congress, Washington, DC 20559.* A church is required to follow the law in its use of material belonging to other persons.

One of the first things any church should do is to go through files of educational and music materials and dispose of all copied materials that were made without permission. This would provide a good example for church members as well as remove the church from any illegal activity in this area. As the church becomes familiar with the law, it will know what practices it should follow in using copyrighted material.

Generally speaking, the church should not make copies of any material, including computer software programs and videos, when doing so would affect the sales of those materials. Exceptions are allowed for the purposes of criticism, comment, news reporting, teaching (including copies for classroom use), or for research purposes. Copyrighted musical works are also covered, but exemptions are allowed for certain types of nonprofit use. When it doubt, it is usually wise and very simple to request permission for use from the copyright holder.[1]

One area where churches should be very careful is in the reprinting of material from the church paper or bulletin of some other church. Even if the other church had received permission to use the material, it would not be right for another church to use it.

CONCLUSION

There are many circumstances in the life and work of the church in which legal advice is necessary. The wise church will secure an attorney and seek help when it is needed. The cost involved may be well worth the damages and court costs avoided or the public image preserved if proper legal procedures are not followed. Church leaders should use their positions to assure that the church is doing all it can to conduct its business in a legal and ethical manner.

CHAPTER 13

Establishing a Mission/Starting New Work

Bob I. Johnson

The idea of new work may spark many images in the minds of today's Christians. The image of a new congregation rising out of the dreams and aspirations of concerned church members is probably the first to form. New work images may also take the shape of satellite programs, special target groups of persons, and new units of work similar to or exactly like what the church has already been doing. In one sense, new work can be anything from beginning a Bible study class for a group not currently being served to the establishment of a new congregation.

The emphasis in this chapter will fall more on new congregation-type ministries; however, you should remember that beginning any new or additional ministry places more demands on a church. Both involve giving up something and gaining something when a new situation is created.

WHAT NEW WORK ALLOWS

New work allows a church to align itself with a stream of others who, through vision and purpose, have established new work in their communities and around the world. It helps a church to carry out the command of Christ as found in Matthew 28:18–20, commonly called the Great Commission.

New work allows a church to have a part in the formation of new communities or new groupings of persons within communities. New work allows the church to experiment with alternative models of congregational style and to recognize the diversity in the new institutions that may distinguish them from the sponsoring church or churches. Participating in the development of new work can also help to eliminate racism and traditionalism among the mother congregation. It also allows, and forces in some cases, the sponsoring group to relate to other churches within its denomination and even to churches in other denominations.

The creation of new work offers the church a fresh and challenging opportunity to express its own Christian faith. It forces the church to rethink its theology and its purpose, and to provide models for Christian service and ministry. It forces the church to reach out in evangelistic efforts toward persons hitherto unreached by this particular congregation. In short, it allows the church to experience faith as a verb.

BEFORE BEGINNING NEW WORK

The hopes for good results from many worthwhile projects often turn to frustration due to hasty preparation and decision making by the church. While some ideas can germinate quickly and find ready acceptance within a congregation, the case generally is that a congregation needs time to mull over significant decisions. People need to raise significant questions and then move together through a studied decision. New work falls into this kind of category. Following are several suggestions for activities for a church considering new work.

1. *Determine the mind-set and readiness for new work of the congregation.* What things are important to the congregation? What things are given emphasis in the worship services and in the printed materials published by the church? Does the church have a status quo mentality? Does the church have fellowship problems within? Or is the fellowship basically strong and healthy? Sometimes, if negative factors are present to a fairly mild degree, challenging the group to undertake new work can serve as an antidote in the situation. This is where leaders need to possess and exercise good diagnostic skills. To push a church to sponsor new work while it has unresolved internal problems may serve only to exaggerate those problems.

2. *Determine the true mission interest of the church.* The church may be a heavy contributor to mission offerings and to the denominational plan of unified giving; still, the people may not be willing to pay the price in time and money to establish a new work on sound footing. Use formal and informal ways to survey the interest and willingness of church members in becoming new spiritual parents.

3. *Get the congregation to verbalize its story and see the reason for establishing new work.* Often church members are not aware of the verbal and nonverbal cues they are communicating. Perhaps persons who have been members for a longer time and those who have been members a shorter time are not quite sure how to relate to each other in sharing their dreams and aspirations for the congregation.

One example of overcoming this problem is sponsoring one or more informal dialogues among various groups in the church. Perhaps at an evening fellowship the longer-termed members can talk about what it was like in the past, the sacrifices the founders and supporters through the years had to make, and what they need from the church as well as what they are willing to contribute to and through the church.

Newer members could be encouraged to express those things that have benefited them in the past in other churches where they have been members, what they bring in their gifts and attitudes, and what they are willing to commit of themselves to this present congregation.

Summarize some of the history of the church and point out the story the church has been telling the community by both its verbal and nonverbal expressions. Point out how the church was begun and suggest that the church may have come to a time when it needs to consider expressing itself in new and different ways.

At an appropriate point explain to the congregation that new work is being considered informally. Point out the specific needs that have given rise to the possibility of new work. Allow questions and seek to have as much information as possible to give people. Do not make commitments before the church is ready to move deliberately.

PROVIDING FOR A HEALTHY BIRTH

After working through informal discussions and study with the congregation, review all the factors with the church council or, if the church has one, a committee charged with dealing with new work. When there is a strong conviction of God's leadership among the congregation and within the council/committee, draft a formal recommendation that the church proceed to establish new work. Promote this recommendation and advise that it will be considered at a specified church business meeting. At this meeting the church should formally adopt a proposal to sponsor new work and approve procedures to guide the development.

The following steps could be presented as guidelines:

1. *Specify a committee to handle the new work.* This may be a new committee, or it could be an ongoing Church Missions Committee. Regardless, this group requires a mandate from the congregation to give positive and enthusiastic leadership to the implementation of the mission project.

Elect five to seven people who are spiritually mature, positive toward mission outreach, concerned about people, able to relate well with people who may be different, and able to analyze situations and make good decisions. Above all, they must be warmhearted, loving people who by faith can see possibilities and act when others may be immobilized.

If possible, have representatives who can give special assistance related to church educational organizations, worship services, and outreach activities. The most competent, mission-minded person should chair the committee. The pastor should, of course, be an ex officio member.

In churches working within a denomination, the committee should schedule a work session with someone in the structure charged to strategize new work. During this session, the committee will be briefed on their duties and receive information concerning possibilities for new work.

The committee (and church) should be aware that numerous ways of beginning new work have been used effectively. For example, programs such as "The Phone's for You," have been used to attract a rather large number of people to a first meeting. The calling always begins weeks before the projected date. See C. Peter Wagner's book, *Church Planting for a Greater Harvest,* listed in the resources section for more information about this and other means of beginning new work.

2. *Select the geographic area and/or people group to be targeted.* Determine the general area in consultation with appropriate others. Gather data to pinpoint specific possibilities for location and/or people group(s). From the research, make the selection for which your church will make a commitment.

3. *Prepare the church for the new work.* Develop a strong motivational climate for the new work by sharing information, discussing possibilities, and describing needs that the church will be able to meet. Inform the congregation about the location and type(s) of work that will be developed. Study ways to use gifts of the sponsoring group to energize people in the target area. Begin recruiting volunteers who can assist with surveys (both in person and by telephone), Bible studies, home visitation, worship, and fellowship activities.

4. *Cultivate the mission field.* Take a community survey to locate the unchurched and the unaffiliated persons of your denomination. Using resources from your denominational missions director, determine who the primary prospects are, where they are located, and possible strategies for establishing a trusting relationship with them.

Be alert to every opportunity for exposure and ministry. Choir concerts, fellowship Bible classes, home visitation, recreational projects, and tutoring classes are some possibilities.

5. *Begin a fellowship group.* This is the first step toward establishing an ongoing mission point. After relationships have been developed and some local support is apparent, the Missions Committee will determine the best location and target persons with whom to begin a home/office/storefront fellowship mission and/or a fellowship Bible class.

One of the laypersons could be in charge to facilitate a cooperative plan of inreach and outreach for volunteers from the sponsoring church and local participants. They would come together for fellowship, worship, Bible study, prayer, support, and planning. They would reach out into the community to identify and enlist prospects who are unchurched.

When the group is too large for one home or location, an option is to divide into two groups that can meet in different parts of the target area. When at least four such fellowship groups are functioning, a good nucleus for a congregation is underway.

Periodic rallies of the fellowship groups could be used when there are three or four groups. At first, about once a month would be adequate. Work on building fellowship, enthusiasm, and motivation for taking the message of Christ to others.

6. *Start a mission chapel.* If and when the new work is large enough and the expressed need for a central location is strong enough, begin plans for a mission chapel. You might begin with a Bible study and worship service each week at a central location, as well as continue the fellowship groups as a means of growth and community ministry.

Consider using public facilities such as a school building or community meeting hall. Other possibilities are motel conference rooms, a recreation room in someone's home, a vacant store, or even a mobile home.

Before the chapel is established, relationships with the sponsoring church must be carefully defined. Clarify finances, membership, calling of a mission pastor, and other pertinent issues. For sample guidelines, see figure 13.1, p. 223, "The Church's Relation to Its Mission."

Other items to be completed before beginning include the following:

- Enlist and train leaders for the mission chapel.

- Secure location and gain approval from the church and any other agencies that may be required.

- Publicize the chapel and encourage participation at the first service.

- Mobilize fellowship groups to prepare the location and promote participation.

- Secure needed equipment and supplies. Put out a sign if permissible.

7. *Determine the financial plan for the chapel.* If not determined earlier, specific procedures should be established to handle aid from the parent church, contributions from new-work participants, and the expenditure of funds by the leaders. Financial aid should be carefully considered, with a phaseout planned from the beginning, if possible. Stewardship education should become a part of new-work activities as persons are prepared to assume the responsibilities for their future.

As the mission develops toward maturity, the election of a treasurer and the transfer of funds to the new work account(s) may be a good training step toward constituting the new church.

Another step toward self-direction comes as the new congregation considers calling a full-time pastor to replace the interim provided by the sponsoring church. The usual guideline is that a mission congregation should delay calling someone until at least fifty percent of the pastor's support can be provided from the new congregation's offerings.

8. *Develop building plans.* When the mission has sufficient strength and stability to take on this task and when their growth and ministry require it, if not already determined, the selection of a permanent location begins.

Much time should be devoted to a study of options, raising of funds, and motivation of new-work participants. A modest, attractive, and complete first unit is the goal rather than a large facility designed to hold several times the present number. Note also that in some situations rented quarters for a longer period of several years may be necessary and/or even appropriate.

9. *Constitute the church.* The Missions Committee of the parent church should be convinced that the mission group is fully committed to the mission of Christ's church and the responsibilities of a local church for carrying out that mission in the world.

When all concerned are sure that the mission congregation is spiritually mature and sufficiently stable to become a constituted church, a date can be set to incorporate the new church.

The preparation of a church constitution and bylaws is most important and should be done two or three months before constituting.

The constituting service is usually held in cooperation with the sponsoring church, sister churches in the area, and the appropriate denominational representative(s). An organizing council is usually formed of representatives invited from sister churches. This group meets prior to the service, examines the group's request, and recommends at the appropriate time in the service that the mission be constituted into a church. A sample outline of such a service, a format for a church constitution and bylaws, and an example of a church covenant appear at the end of this chapter (see fig. 13.2 through 13.5, pp. 225–228).

WORKING FOR EFFECTIVENESS

The emphasis on church growth has naturally reminded most people of numerical growth. Numerical growth is important; however, effectiveness is more important. Resources abound to help you determine what makes an effective church. The new work should especially pay attention to the research and to the findings to aid the overall health of its existence. New churches can instill principles of effectiveness perhaps more easily than can older congregations. Generally, the distilled wisdom includes the following factors in ensuring effectiveness:

- A set of biblically based values, with a specific mission vision congruent with those values.

- An intentionally adequate ministry of pastoral care.

- A leadership team that serves to guide the church after the pattern of Jesus Christ and free the member-ministers to fulfill their ministry calling.

- Both small- and large-group opportunities for worship and study in which God is glorified and human needs are addressed.

- Adequate opportunities and encouragement for the members to express their ministries in Jesus' name.

- Adequate meeting place with as much parking as possible.

- Financial support.

The new congregation, and particularly the pastoral team, would do well to study relevant materials on beginning and sustaining ministry for effectiveness. Resources on change are essential, for example.

An effective new church will certainly be marked by an intentional ministry. The new congregation will understand what it is supposed to do and how it will go about fulfilling its purpose. As a Christian community of persons, the group will be careful that all its activities contribute to the primary task of the church. The effective congregation will operate through a planning process that includes goals and strategies that can be evaluated in terms of its purpose reflected in the New Testament. The effective congregation will institute a plan of evaluating its ministry and its opportunities.

Winning and discipling new members will be important to the effective church in its early years. Time should also be given to the effective assimilation of new members into the congregation so that the church can be one in which all members have a part and a stake in its success.

The church should be helped to have a clear image of itself that manifests itself in a specific way in its community. The church will know what it is about and each member will be able to express and defend that purpose. The effective church should work to have the strength to face the future in which surprise, excitement, and expectation can be incorporated into its life.

Figure 13.1

THE CHURCH'S RELATION TO ITS MISSION

It is important that a good relationship be maintained between the church and its mission, and this does not just happen: it must be worked for; the lines of communication must always be open.

Communications between the church and the mission will be easier and more effective if they are carried on through the Church Missions Committee representing the whole church and a group, preferably the mission's steering committee. Thus, better understandings will be developed before matters are communicated to the congregations of the church and the mission. Each will receive its communications through its own representatives who can present them in the light of the viewpoints of its people.

In reality, the mission is the church. It is simply the church meeting in a different place or satisfying a special need; it is the church, extended.

1. RELATIONSHIP

An understanding of the relationship between the church and its mission can be stated in an agreement or bylaws.

(1) The mission and the church should agree on the pastor of the mission.

(2) The mission pastor should be a member of the sponsoring church.

(3) Evangelists for mission revivals should be agreed on by the mission pastor and the pastor of the church.

2. CHURCH MEMBERSHIP

All persons who qualify for church membership should be urged to join the sponsoring church. Mission members can be received:

(1) By *baptism*. After profession of faith and request for baptism at a mission service, the person's name will be submitted to the sponsoring church for vote. Baptism is administered by someone authorized by the church.

(2) By *letter*. After a request for membership at a mission service, the person's name will be given to the church for vote and for obtaining the church letter.

(3) By *statement*. After a request to be accepted by statement at a mission service, the person's name and statement will be presented to the church.

3. BUSINESS

The mission meets for business only to recommend items of business to the sponsoring church for its consideration. All items shall be offered at least one week before the church's monthly meeting. (Items that are considered emergencies may be presented anytime.)

(1) A written report of the mission should be made to the sponsoring church at the monthly business meeting. The report is to be presented by the church Missions Committee.

(2) The Church Missions Committee and the mission nominate officers and teachers and present their names to the church for approval.

(3) The observance of the church ordinances—baptism and the Lord's Supper -should be held according to plans approved by the sponsoring church.

(4) The mission should give complaints and correspondence to the Church Missions Committee.

4. TITHES AND OFFERINGS

(1) All tithes and offerings from the mission should be kept in a separate fund and handled according to the plan designated by the sponsoring church. The use of the mission fund shall be subject to the approval of the church. The mission fund shall be used for the mission. When the mission is constituted into a church, all funds become the property of the new church.

(2) The mission is urged both to give a definite percent of its tithes and offerings through the Cooperative Program and to plan to increase this percent in future years.

(3) The mission should consider giving a proper percentage of its receipts to the associational mission program.

(4) Checks shall be signed and bills paid by the one authorized and in the way designated by the church. All checks written and all bills paid shall be reported and approved each month in the regular business meeting of the church.

(5) The mission should use the Bible and denominational curriculum materials.

(6) When both the sponsoring church and the mission feel that the mission is strong enough to organize into a New Testament church, they should express this desire to the Church Missions Committee. The Missions Committee should present this to the church for action. Plans should be made for the service.

(7) The sponsoring church should do all it can for the mission to enable it to do all it should for God. Prayer for the mission is essential. The mission should pray for, love, respect, and cooperate with the church for the mutual blessings of both.

5. PROPERTY

Property owned by the sponsoring church may be sold or transferred at the discretion of the church. It is suggested that when a mission is ready to constitute as a church, that deeds be in order so that property may be transferred without delay.

Figure 13.2

CONSTITUTING A NEW CHURCH

1. HOW TO CONSTITUTE

(1)   A Church Missions Committee, after counsel with the pastor of the sponsoring church and with the mission, recommends to the sponsoring church that the mission should be constituted into a church.

(2)   The mission and sponsoring church can receive much aid from other Baptist churches when the mission is ready to be constituted. These steps have been used.

    a. Set date to constitute.

    b. Inform and seek assistance from associational missions committee and director of associational missions.

    c. Invite neighboring Baptist churches to send representatives to form a council. Invite state director of missions.

    d. Form a council at the meeting to constitute the mission into a church by choosing a moderator and clerk. This meeting can be held before the mass meeting.

    e. Council hears reasons for the church's being constituted.

2. SERVICE OF CONSTITUTION

(1)   Devotional.
    Hymn: "*The* Church's One Foundation"
    Scripture: Matt. 16:18–19; Acts 2:41–42; 1 Cor. 12:27; Eph. 4:11–13; Col. 1:18
    Prayer

(2)   The report of the council. The council recommends to proceed with the constituting of the mission into a Baptist church.

(3)   Recommendation from the sponsoring church is read and approved by the mission congregation. The adoption of this recommendation formally constitutes the new church (see Figure 3).

(4)   Election of the officers and committees of the new church.

    a. The moderator of the council may serve as temporary moderator for the further proceedings.

    b. He should at this time hear the report of the previously appointed nominating committee. The names of church officers and committees may be presented for election.

    c. A pastor should be called according to the plan previously adopted.

(5)   If it is advisable to give the new church title to the church property, the transfer should be presented.

(6)   Incorporation is desirable and should be acted on at this time.

(7)   If the new church desires a constitution and bylaws (see Figure 4 for a worksheet), a committee should be appointed to draft them.

(8)   Worship service.

Hymn: "To God Be the Glory"
Offering
Sermon. The message should include a charge to the pastor and the people.
   The universal scope and cooperative privileges should be emphasized.
Invitation for charter members
Reception of charter members
Benediction

Charter members are greeted and commended on their new beginning by members of the council and visitors.

NOTE: A new church may want to petition an association of churches to be included in its fellowship. Some such associations provide petitioner letters for such action. The proper preparation and service for the constituting of a new church can mean much to the new fellowship in its getting a good start and in its future ministry.

Figure 13.3

RECOMMENDATION FOR CONSTITUTION

(The sponsoring church submits for adoption by the new church a recommendation prepared in advance. The following format will serve as a guide.)

Whereas we believe that there is a need for a church in this community, and

Whereas we believe we have found God's divine guidance after prayer, and

Whereas we have consulted with fellow Christians and neighboring churches, and,

Whereas we have called a council to consider this matter and the council has recommended we proceed with the constituting of the new church;

Be it therefore resolved that we do now enter upon the organization of a new church under the direction of the council composed of these members representing these churches:

Council Members	Church Represented

Be it further resolved that we adopt this as our church covenant:
   (The covenant should be included in the resolution.)

Be it further resolved that we adopt the following articles of faith:
   (to be inserted)

Be it further resolved that our name shall be the:
   (to be inserted)

Be it further resolved that these resolutions be signed by all charter members and that this document be preserved with the official church records.

Be it further resolved that this church cooperate with these denominational bodies:
(to be inserted)

Be it further resolved that our gratitude is hereby expressed to the sponsoring church and to God for divine guidance.

Witnesses on this date:

(Leave space here for signatures of charter members.)

Figure 13.4

SAMPLE FORMAT FOR CONSTITUTION AND BYLAWS

CONSTITUTION

**(A constitution reflects the basic truths and accepted patterns of interaction among members of an organization.
Write and insert statements about each item.)**

1. *Preamble*

"We declare and establish this constitution to preserve and secure the principles of our faith, and to govern the body in an orderly manner. This constitution will. . . ."

2. *Name*

"This body shall be known as the _____Church located at _____ .

3. *Purpose/Objectives*

(insert statement of purpose)

4. *Statement of Faith*

(insert statement of faith)

5. *Polity and Relationships*

(insert statement of governance and affiliations)

BYLAWS

(Bylaws are written guidelines agreed upon by members to direct the activity of the organization. Such statements focus on procedures to be followed and, as such, are more susceptible to modification as needs change than are statements in the constitution. Bylaws are designed to assist the organization in fulfilling its purpose. Items often included are statements regarding each of the following:)

1. *Membership*

2. *Organizational structures/programs of work*

3. *Officers*

4. *Committees*

5. *Meetings/special observances*

6. *Finances/organization operations manual*

7. *Amendments* (how to make changes in the *Constitution and Bylaws*)

Figure 13.5

CHURCH COVENANT

Since we have committed ourselves to Jesus Christ and have experienced the acceptance, forgiveness, and redemption of God our Creator, we covenant together as members of this church that with God's help through the guiding presence of the Holy Spirit:

We will walk together in Christian love.

We will show loving care for one another and encourage, counsel, and admonish one another.

We will assemble faithfully for worship and fellowship, and will pray earnestly for others as well as for ourselves.

We will endeavor to bring up those under our care "in the nurture and admonition of the Lord."

We will seek, by Christian example and personal effort, to win others to Christ and to encourage their growth toward Christian maturity.

We will share one another's joys and endeavor to bear one another's burdens and sorrows.

We will oppose all conduct which compromises our Christian faith and will uphold high standards of Christian morality.

We will prove the reality of our conversion by living godly, fruitful lives.

We will maintain a faithful ministry of worship, witness, education, fellowship, and service.

We will be faithful stewards of our resources and abilities in sharing the gospel with people of all nations.

As a result of this covenant relationship, we will seek earnestly to live to the glory of God who brought us out of darkness into marvelous light.

(Church Covenant of Immanuel Baptist Church, Nashville, Tennessee)

CHAPTER 14

Cooperative Relationships
Bruce P. Powers

Churches are not independent bodies. They always function in an environment of mutual support and shared ministry, with primary emphasis on faithfulness to Christ's mission. A church may be related formally to other Christian bodies, as in an association or denomination, or it may choose to function as an independent unit among Christian churches. Regardless, the commission of Christ requires that all congregations develop the best means possible to function effectively as His representatives.

CHURCH POLITY AND ORGANIZATION

Your church and denomination have a way of working together. The organization you have and the procedures you follow are called *denominational polity*. Polity is a statement of principles and guidelines that determine a Christian institution's form of government and procedures for working together. The same New Testament principles that guide local church government apply as far as possible to the practice of denominational government.

Whether rigid or flexible, clearly-defined or vague, there is an expected way of working together for the common good. To the degree that you understand and support these expectations you can guide your congregation in contributing to and drawing from the larger resources God has entrusted to us in support of the church's worldwide mission.

Most major denominations have a basic sourcebook that explains the how and why of church and denominational polity. Such books are used as resources for church leaders and as educational aids for church members. The purpose is to make Christians full participants in church and denominational activities, thereby contributing to order, effectiveness, and harmony.

It is imperative that church leaders grasp the principles by which their denomination functions. In the absence of clarity about purpose, relationships, and procedures, a church inevitably finds itself divided—either within its own house or in opposition to sister churches.

STEWARDSHIP OF RESOURCES

Effective Christian service depends on a sharing of resources. By combining spiritual and material gifts from God, churches can extend and enrich their witness in ways not possible for a single congregation. For example, most churches cannot publish their own Sunday school materials, provide homes for children or the elderly, establish a college or theological school, provide salary assistance for hundreds of ministers in pioneer missions areas, or send missionaries around the world in an orderly and systematic way.

But, by combining resources, churches can band together in enterprises that would be impossible alone. The People of God and the Body of Christ become a reality as we bring ourselves together in an overall purpose and plan.

At the same time, all bodies do not possess the same resources. Consequently, congregations that are richer must contribute a greater share while those less able will give less. And church missions and new congregations that are needy will be assisted by others—for giving and receiving are both part of the stewardship of resources.

HOW DOES THIS WORK?

Most evangelical churches follow a plan whereby local resources are shared among the home congregation and the various needs supported by the denominational group(s) with which a church is affiliated. For example, a large portion of church contributions will go toward costs incurred by the local congregation in its activities of worship, education, ministry, and proclamation.

A smaller portion will then be designated to denominational and other church-approved causes beyond the local church. The usual practice is to determine an appropriate percentage of contributions that will go to each denominational group. Then, this amount will be deducted periodically from contributions and sent to the designated body. Thus a church supports its own life as well as contributing to the larger mission of the church regionally and throughout the world.

The ways in which decisions are made about channeling contributions to various causes varies widely from denomination to denomination, and even among churches.

A denomination in which each church decides for itself what shall be contributed is greatly dependent on an accurate understanding of and commitment to denominational causes. Churches in such situations may give or not give, or adjust the amount of their contributions depending on local sentiment regarding denominational activities.

Nevertheless, among denominations that depend on voluntary cooperation, there is a general expectation that at least ten percent of local contributions will be sent to state/regional and national bodies. An additional two to four percent will be given to local causes through an association or other organization representing local churches. These contributions are intended for the use of the larger bodies according to the *polity* of the denomination.

Other denominations assign a share of the cost of cooperative activities to individual congregations. Church leaders then work out a budget that will enable the local group to meet its own needs as well as contribute its proportionate share to the common work.

BENEFITS OF COOPERATION

When churches work together, they combine their resources and channel their individual efforts into a united, systematic plan to propagate the gospel regionally, nationally, and throughout the world. Such organized efforts provide practical and efficient ways to conduct a worldwide Christian enterprise on behalf of individual churches.

At the *local/associational level,* cooperation enables churches to be involved in these and other activities:

- Starting new churches and mission points
- Sharing Christian fellowship
- Supporting one another in times of need
- Approving persons for ordination to the gospel ministry
- Determining criteria related to denominational recognition
- Assisting one another with leadership training for volunteer workers in church programs

At the *state level,* churches have opportunity to extend the functions of education, proclamation, and Christian service throughout a region. Such activities provide services to participating churches as well as an outreach ministry to unchurched persons. Depending on the availability of resources, state or regional groups might be involved in these activities:

- Developing and promoting methods and resources to assist local churches
- Developing and leading churches in state-wide ministry and outreach projects
- Providing leadership training for volunteer church leaders
- Promoting and participating in regional and global mission projects
- Receiving and distributing cooperative offerings from participating churches

- Assisting associations of churches in their work
- Publishing a newspaper to inform church members and to promote denominational causes
- Operating Christian universities, colleges, and schools
- Operating benevolent enterprises such as hospitals and homes for children and the aged
- Operating camps, assemblies, and conference centers

At the *national level,* major emphasis is placed on achieving an overall structure and design for the services and ministries required by churches in the denomination. Such activities may be developed and coordinated in one location, or they may be administered from a variety of locations. Regardless of the arrangement, the polity of the body determines policy and organization, and tells exactly how decisions are made concerning denominational causes. This information is detailed in the constitution and by-laws of the body.

Activities of a national body might include these items:

- Developing and publishing curriculum materials
- Developing and promoting financial plans to assist churches
- Operating national conference centers
- Providing theological education for ministers
- Administering home mission activities
- Administering foreign mission activities
- Developing and promoting leadership training programs
- Publishing and distributing through public means information related to the emphases and work of the denomination

LOOKING TO THE FUTURE

The future for Christian work is bright as long as cooperation is acknowledged as a basic New Testament principle. Together, churches can more nearly be the Body of Christ on mission to the world. James L. Sullivan, an astute observer of denominational relationships, suggested there is no option for a local church. For it is the lordship of Christ over the church and its mission to the world that is of utmost importance. "Even as churches defend their autonomy—their right to self-government—they ought also to defend theonomy, God's authority over them.

"A local church cannot remain fully Christian if it stays local in concept and action," says Sullivan. A church must have a burden for the whole world. There must be a delicate balance in which there can be freedom of action and at the same time cooperation in the fulfillment of the Christian mission.[1]

SECTION THREE:

How a Minister Develops Leadership and Ministry Skills

CHAPTER 15

Equipping the Saints to Serve

Judy J. Stamey

Every believer is *gifted* to serve God. Every believer is *expected* to serve God. Every believer must be given *opportunities* to serve God. An understanding of these ideas helps a church begin to develop a theology of service for its members. Throughout the Scriptures God gives instruction and challenge to every believer to become a servant. Jesus taught by example, using a life of servanthood to show followers what is expected. In Matthew 20:26–28 (NASB), Jesus teaches, "But whoever wishes to become great among you shall be your servant, and whoever wishes to be first among you shall be your slave; just as the Son of Man did not come to be served, but to serve, and to give His life a ransom for many."

DEVELOPING A THEOLOGY OF SERVICE

The Scriptures contain many passages of instruction and challenge for believers to become servants. Jesus' life of servanthood was the best example possible for disciples yesterday, today, and tomorrow. A believer's theology of service must begin with understanding the essentials in the life of Jesus and the love that motivated him to a life of service, leading eventually to the cross. When this understanding is clear, believers can live a full and meaningful Christian life that will reflect the lordship of Jesus and inspire others to seek to know how Jesus can change their lives.

A church leader's theology of service can be greatly broadened by passages in Scripture that give specific instructions on providing training for new believers and help them to experience a growth and understanding of their commitment that will lead to a life of service motivated by a love for God. Ephesians 4:12 (NASB) clearly communicates the responsibility of "equipping the saints for the work of service, to the building up of the body of Christ." Too often churches see themselves as non-profit organizations that depend upon a core group of volunteers to accomplish the goals. However, a church has much greater potential than any other organization because God has said that every follower is gifted and has a responsibility to serve. If the church believes this, a great deal of energy must be spent in helping individuals discover the gifts and/or interests that can be used in Christian service.

Church leaders must decide that it is not their job to motivate lay members to serve but rather to help them grow in understanding why they must serve and what joy comes from serving. Sometimes, church leaders are apologetic for asking a member to take a job, and they allow the person to think that it would be doing them a favor to accept. The theology of servanthood is clearly defined in the Word of God when Paul says in Ephesians 2:10 (NASB) that, "We are His workmanship, created in Christ Jesus for good works." This puts our personal persuasiveness in perspective and helps the church leader to know that to allow someone to take a position just to help is not biblical.

In James 1:22 the challenge is for believers to prove themselves as doers of the Word and not merely hearers. James asked the question, If a man says he has faith, but he has not works, can that faith save him? Church staff members often become so excited about sharing the gift of salvation that they fail to communicate that work and service are expected and natural responses for every believer. The theology of service can be defined for a new Christian as love for God in action.

DISCOVERING SPIRITUAL GIFTS IS ESSENTIAL TO SERVICE

The Holy Spirit endows the members of Christ's Body with the gifts required for healthy life and service in the world.

The Bible clearly says that God has given gifts to each. 1 Peter 4:10 (NASB) says, "As each one has received a special gift, employ it in serving one another, as good stewards of the manifold grace of God." Ephesians 4:16 says, "The whole body, being fitted and held together by that which every joint supplies, according to the proper working of each individual part, causes the growth of the body for the building up of itself in love" (NASB). Other passages in 1 Corinthians 12:4–7 describe the variety of gifts and how they all are given to manifest the spirit for the common good and in 1 Corinthians 1:6–7 (NASB) there is assurance that "as the testimony concerning Christ was confirmed in you, so that you are not lacking in any gift, awaiting eagerly the revelation of our Lord Jesus Christ."

The church is blessed because God has given every believer a gift that can be used to help the church to be healthy and accomplish its mission. It is God's plan that everyone should become a volunteer—a *servant*. Therefore, it is vital that church leaders seek to provide opportunities for the membership to discover the gifts with which God has so richly blessed them. In most churches this would need to be an ongoing activity where members and new members are invited to participate and experience the joy of discovering where they are best able to contribute to the life and work of the church.

There are many resources available in Christian book stores that address the subject of spiritual gifts. Some are designed for groups, while others are designed for a one-on-one teaching and discovery time. Resources have been designed to help church leaders do a better job and to lead the congregation to actualize its mission by putting a greater emphasis on helping every member to find a place of service.

Another way to build awareness is occasionally to provide devotions at church leadership meetings about the gifts that God has given to us and how the church can provide each of us a place to use those gifts. Leaders can also encourage members to participate in completing an interest survey that has been designed to point them to service possibilities. A sample "Service Interest Form" is shown in figure 15.1, p. 244.

A church leader must continue to dream of serving a church where every member senses a call to use his or her gifts to serve the Lord and build up the Body of Christ. This dream may never become a reality, but church leaders must never lose sight of the accountability for being faithful to provide opportunities for every believer to discover gifts and use them in service.

ESTABLISHING QUALIFICATIONS FOR SERVICE

How do you know that a person is right for the job? The only measuring stick for knowing this is the list of qualifications that the church has endorsed and clearly expects from every person who serves. The following qualifications are examples of what a church may expect from its volunteers.

RELATIONSHIP TO GOD AND THE CHURCH

This is probably the most significant qualification for enlisting someone to serve in the church. When a person works because he or she wants to serve and please the Lord, that person will be much more effective than one who serves just to receive personal satisfaction or to fill an ego need. This means that the person in charge of enlisting will need to spend adequate time with potential volunteers to learn about their desires and commitment level. This qualification often requires more time than one is willing to give. But if patience is exercised and we allow God to give an affirmation that this person is right for the job, the results will provide greater success and longer tenure among workers.

It is important to remember that when a person says "I am called" to do a job, that the one in charge of enlisting also needs to feel that this person is called to do the job. Many times we enlist the wrong people because we fail to spend the time to discover what has motivated a person to serve.

Questions to ask: What does their life say to the church? Are they faithful in attendance in the programs of the church? Are they faithful in worship attendance? Do they contribute to the financial support of the church? How long have they been members of the church? These are only a few questions that can help the leader to determine if persons have the foundation needed to do a particular job.

GOOD REPUTATION

Many times people will say, using Scripture, "By their fruits you shall know them!" when they are trying to point out that a person says one thing and does another. The Bible does teach that we are known by our fruits and it is the fruits we bear that create a person's reputation. Many times a person will not be able to serve in certain positions until the reputation problems have been resolved.

First Timothy 3 emphasizes that one who serves should be a person "above reproach." This is just another way of saying the person's reputation should be as good on the inside of the church as on the outside. You can trust this person explicitly.

COOPERATIVE ATTITUDE AND TEAM PLAYER

This qualification means that a person has the ability to relate to and work well with others. When a woman tells you that she would rather work alone, this may be a "red flag" to mean that this person does not work well on a team. If this is the case, you would need to evaluate how important it is for the person in this position to be a team player and to cooperate with a group of fellow workers. Attitudes are often very difficult to change; therefore, it is very important before enlisting a person to know the feelings related to authority, schedules, and evaluations.

Team spirit is vital in most areas of service, which means that members must become interdependent and share the overall success of the work being done. When team members are committed to the idea that working together is important, more effective decisions will be made. When a person works on a team, no one is left out on a limb alone. Everyone is there to share the victory or the loss. Support is felt because you are a team.

A WILLING LEARNER

Every position requires training. Recruitment is not the end, but the beginning. The volunteer must understand how each position fits into the overall purpose of the church. The provision of training may involve many approaches and the potential worker needs to be made aware of the expectations of the church.

When these qualifications are used as a guideline to understanding an individual, you will have a much keener awareness of whether this is a person who could serve with you as an effective volunteer. In some cases, you may see potential in persons, but feel that they need to be involved in additional discipleship training, such as doctrinal or denominational studies. It is important that you work with them to provide the attention and training that is necessary for future positions of service. Members can also be encouraged to serve as apprentices in areas in which they are interested in working.

Other qualifications may need to be developed as they relate directly to the job being considered; for example: Is there a minimum age for serving in the preschool area? Does a person need experience to do this job? Can a husband and wife work in the same department? These and other qualifications may need to be discussed before beginning the enlistment process.

ENLISTING FOR SERVICE

Enlistment procedures vary from church to church; therefore it is important to know how people are enlisted in each organization. The most important question to ask is, "What guidelines are used to consider who is qualified to serve?" The answer to this question may lead to a training session for the purpose of formulating a set of guidelines that will aid the church in enlisting the right persons in all areas of service. The main principle for a church to understand is that when a person is properly enlisted, performance will be at a much higher level than when one is not. Another benefit from proper enlistment is that the person will most likely take a personal pride in doing a good job.

Proper enlistment begins with the person doing the enlisting. This person must understand the need for the position, the goals, the tasks, and how the job is to be evaluated. The leader will then be ready to make an appointment with the person being considered to discuss the position.

It is very important that this meeting be "face to face" and in a place where there will be little or no interruptions. The setting for the interview is very important. The first part of the meeting should focus on the service opportunity that is available. The leader's attitude should convey to the person that the position is important and that it contributes to the on-going work of the church.

During the course of the discussion, the leader should go over the *job description*, pointing out the specific assignments and how one is evaluated. It is extremely important that every service opportunity include a written job description that can be given to the individual being considered.

If you do not have one for all volunteer positions, it would be wise to delay the enlisting process until they have been written, following the sample job description outlined in figure 15.2. When positions are the same, such as on committees, the same job description will be used. The important part of writing a job description is to tailor it to meet the requirements of your church. Samples of what other churches use can assist in the writing, but your church's job descriptions should reflect what your church expects. This will help members understand the job being considered and the helps that are available to assist in achieving the assigned tasks.

It is not unusual for persons to turn down a position after reviewing the job description. They recognize immediately that they will not be able to perform the tasks in an acceptable manner. The person enlisting should respond with appreciation for their honesty and feel blessed that someone did not take the position knowing that they would not be able to do it.

If someone being interviewed does not respond to the expectations in the job description, it would be appropriate to ask, "Do you believe that you would be able to give the time and effort needed to do the tasks listed on the job description?" If the answer is positive, you will be able to continue the interview process. If it is negative, or there is a lot of hesitation, it may be best to thank the person for his or her time and encourage the person to let you know if interest develops later.

If both parties feel positive at this point, continue the interview by discussing expectations related to training. The leader needs to explain what has been planned for the year and how important it is for the volunteer to be involved. There needs to be an agreement from the potential worker that participation in these planned training activities will be a priority.

Training may include explaining to those who serve in the preschool, children, youth, and special education departments that the church requires all workers in these areas to read a set of guidelines adopted by the church and sign an agreement to observe the safeguards listed. These guidelines are in addition to the job descriptions that were reviewed earlier. Even though an agreement of this nature may not be required by law, a church would be wise to consider its use, since many child-abuse cases are being reported in schools, day-care ministries, and churches. The sample set of guidelines in figure 15.3, p. 246, may be adapted and used by your church.

Following the job-description review and discussion, and the completion of agreement forms, the next important part of the interview is the presentation of the available resources. It is important to point out required resources, such as a curriculum that must be used in a teaching program of the church. The leader must not assume that the one being enlisted knows these special requirements. Other resources that must be reviewed are budget allocations, budget procedures, room assignments, and supplies. These items are very important because they enable the worker to do a much better job.

PROVIDING TRAINING FOR THOSE WHO SERVE

Every worker must be given an opportunity to learn how service in a position contributes to the work of the church. When one has been trained to understand the importance of the job and has committed to it, the specific tasks will make much better sense. A well-planned training program can reduce conflict and misunderstandings in the organization.

The purpose of training is to help the person succeed. Each position will dictate what should be required to accomplish this. Training may range from a brief orientation to involvement in many training events throughout the year. The important thing is to decide what you need to provide to keep the worker focused, motivated, and productive.

Leaders must think of training as an ongoing responsibility that begins when the person agrees to do the job. This means giving new workers an opportunity to talk about the specific tasks on the job description and how they intend to accomplish them. Ask them if they have any questions about expectations, scheduling, deadlines, or any other matters that tell you how they plan to begin the new assignment.

Listening skills are very important at this juncture. If you hear a comment about their intentions to do something differently from what has been done before, it is important that you affirm their intended changes or guide them back to the traditional methods, explaining why those have to be the best way. This informal aspect of training helps the worker to understand that while there is freedom to do a good job, there is also responsibility to discuss change with the leader before doing it.

Formal training is also important and should be planned well in advance of the enlistment time. This gives the leader an opportunity to discuss what is being planned and how it will help workers do a better job. It is very important that people know ahead of time what is expected in the way of training, so their commitment to the job includes training.

The schedule of training must also fit people's needs. Whether it is set for a week night, a Sunday afternoon or a weekend, this should be determined by what time is best for the workers.

Every training tool a leader provides should be thoroughly examined and evaluated before asking a worker to invest time in it. Too often people have left a meeting, watched a video, or read a book that was supposed to help them to do a better job, and felt that the activity was a complete waste of time. When this occurs, workers quickly develop the attitude that training is not important. One bad experience for workers will require a lot of encouragement from the leader for them to be motivated to participate in future training events.

Leaders have a vast selection of training tools available to train workers in their specific areas of service, such as those listed in figure 15.4, p. 247. Again, the key to selecting the best training tools is to determine how they will make a contribution to the person's job.

With more options than ever, it is important to choose the training tools that you know can be used most effectively in your church. It is the leader's responsibility to select the ones that will effectively train the workers and also make them feel that the time invested was worthwhile.

EVALUATING WORKERS

When a person accepts a position of service, the responsibility of the leader increases. The leader is called to equip workers to become effective and enjoy their contribution of service. When a worker fails to serve in an acceptable manner, the leader may also feel a sense of failure. Before the worker can be evaluated, the *leader's* role must be evaluated. A leader can expect a favorable worker evaluation if the answers to the following questions can be answered in a positive manner:

1. *Was the worker properly enlisted?* This includes meeting personally with the worker, discussing job-description requirements, and clarifying expectations about training opportunities and accountability. And don't overlook the importance of praying together.

2. *Is the job description current?* Can a person understand what is expected and how to do it in an acceptable manner? Job descriptions should be reviewed annually, making changes or deletions, to assure the worker of a reliable guide.

3. *Have training opportunities been provided throughout the year?* Were the commitments met that were discussed in the enlistment interview? Many times problems of performance arise because of failure to provide adequate training.

4. Have regular follow-up meetings been provided for the worker and leader? Time for meeting together is vital to developing workers. These meetings reflect the accountability relationship that was discussed in the enlistment time.

If the leader feels that there are certain areas of weakness related to any of these areas, it is important to discuss them with the worker and to decide what corrections can and will be made. Many times workers do a good job regardless of how well the leader enlisted them; however, when a worker's performance is poor because the leader did not do a good job of enlisting, it becomes vital that these issues be discussed thoroughly before a worker is allowed to resign.

A worker evaluation provides a time to discuss the assigned tasks, how well the worker is accomplishing the tasks, and what improvements can be made. It gives the worker and leader an opportunity to work out and agree upon goals for improvement. An evaluation helps the worker to know how important the job is in relationship to the work of the whole church. It also is a time for the leader to express appreciation for specific things that the worker has done exceptionally well. The leader should always conclude the meeting with words of encouragement and prayer.

Occasionally, a leader enlists someone who does not do the job he or she was enlisted to do. This is very disappointing for the leader and many times creates problems because the work needs to be done. The question the leader must address is: *Is replacement worth the cost?*

The answer to this question will depend upon the leader's experience during the evaluation. Did the worker express hostility, complacency, or a negative attitude? If this person is terminated, how much will it hinder the work of the church? Do you sense that replacing this person will damage the person's spiritual development? How many people will be affected, and will they leave the church?

If the leader believes that replacing this person will have a long-lasting negative response, it may be more beneficial to wait until the next time the church nominates and elects people to serve in various positions. If this approach is not possible, the leader may have to decide that it is best to ask for the person's resignation. When a person for some reason—like stubbornness—refuses to resign, your only option may be to begin the steps of termination. This is probably one of the most difficult tasks for a leader. Use the following steps if termination is necessary:

Step 1: Prepare for a meeting with the individual. Prayer is vital. It will give the leader strength to do what must be done, and—it is hoped—give understanding to the one who must be terminated. In addition to prayer, the leader must write down specific reasons and dates that indicate poor performance. The meeting will be very weak without proper documentation.

Step 2: Inform the pastor and proper screening committee. Every case will be unique. The leader will need to decide if the pastor or a member of the screening committee should be present when the worker is confronted about the problems. In either case, it is very important to make these people aware of the situation. Occasionally, the worker will become upset and feel a need to go to the pastor or the proper committee. If they are aware of the problems, and are supportive of what you have done, then they will affirm your decision.

Step 3: Arrange to meet in a place of few or no interruptions. The environment is very important for a meeting of this nature. In most cases, it would probably be best to meet at the church in an office or conference room. A controlled environment helps prevent possible embarrassment that you or the person might experience if interrupted by others.

Step 4: Clear your mind about what is to take place. Face-to-face encounters like this are the most difficult and require the leader to be prepared to address the problem directly. The leader should begin the session by stating the purpose—to discuss the contribution of the worker. A time of prayer will be helpful as the leader and worker ask God to guide them in this meeting to enhance the work of the Lord and of the church. The leader is then ready to present to the worker the problems that have been documented. It is important to allow the worker to respond to each one as it is presented.

The leader should listen well in order to respond in a caring way. However, the task of terminating the worker has not changed. Be sure to affirm the worker by pointing out the positive qualities that you believe will lead to a better and happier place of service.

If the worker does not resign, be prepared to indicate that the committee or council in charge feels that it will be best for the organization to terminate the worker from the position of service. Explain that this decision was made after much prayer and evaluation, and they, along with you, feel that it is best for the individual and the church.

Conclude by thanking the person for meeting with you and then, if appropriate, pray again. If the person has potential in another area of work, you could suggest the possibility of seeking God's leadership about other opportunities for service.

Step 5: After the meeting, check on the individual periodically. It is only in caring genuinely for people that we can effectively terminate an individual who is not doing the job. This kind of respect for people will enable the leader to continue building a relationship that helps the person discover and commit to another place of service. The spiritual challenge for the leader is to follow the example of Jesus who never gave up on people.

There are no easy answers to dealing with workers who are ineffective. Because equipping believers to grow spiritually and serve the Lord is at the heart of our calling, terminating someone is probably the most difficult duty we face. The task will not be easy, and hopefully will rarely be necessary. However, leaders must always stay focused on the understanding that God will provide the strength, wisdom, and courage required to do what is best for an individual and for the church.

SUPPORTING THOSE WHO SERVE

Support means:

- Someone cares.
- Someone is there to help you when the going gets tough.

- Someone is praying for you.
- Someone appreciates the contribution you are making to the church and the work of the Lord.

Support lends strength and encouragement to those who are trying to do their very best to serve. When or if support is neglected, those serving may feel that their contribution is being taken for granted. The only way to avoid this is for every leader to make the responsibility of affirming as much a part of his or her job as enlisting, training, and evaluating.

Support from the leader does more than just give recognition. It affirms that the job is important; it offers motivation to the worker to continue to do a good job. Most of all, it helps the worker to know that the work and the workers are appreciated.

Support means having a listening ear. Workers must be given the opportunity to talk about their work and discuss the various concerns related to their jobs. The leader must develop a sensitivity to knowing when this is a need for a worker. Often, when a worker is talking, there is an underlying need to hear how the leader feels things are going.

Support means taking the time to affirm those who serve. There are many ways to do this. Figures 15.5 and 15.6, p. 248, give ways a leader may affirm and guide the work of others. It is important to choose ways of affirmation that will be most meaningful to the individual. A leader who is a strong advocate for and supporter of workers is usually one who is also appreciated; people feel good about being on the same team.

Support means the leader prays for and with workers. It is so important for every person to know that the work he or she is doing is for the glory of the Lord, and that prayer is essential to doing an effective job.

Support from the leader is vital, but the leader should never neglect to remind workers that they are a team and that their ultimate goal is to serve God in such a manner that someday they will hear the words from Matthew 25:21: "Well done, good and faithful servant; . . . enter into the joy of your master" (RSV).

Figure 15.1
SERVICE INTEREST FORM

Name _____

Address (home) _____

Address (bus.) _____

Phone (home)_____ (bus.) _____

Employer _____

Type of business _____

Position in company _____

Age: 17–25 ☐ 26–35 ☐ 36–55 ☐ Over 55 ☐

Birthday _____

Marital status _____

Spouse's name _____

Formerly served as an ___elder?___ deacon?

Please list educational experience:

What kind of service would you be interested in?

Hours available to serve:

Monday ___   Friday ___

Tuesday ___   Saturday ___

Wednesday ___   Sunday ___

Thursday ___

PLEASE CHECK INTERESTS/SKILLS/HOBBIES

___ Acting	___ Food Services/Cooking	___ Public Relations
___ Animals	___ Fund Raising	___ Public Speaking
___ Art Work	___ Graphic Arts	___ Puppetry
___ Bible Studies	___ Greeter	___ Radio/Television/Film
___ Bridge	___ Handbells	___ Reading
___ Budgeting	___ Horticulture/Gardening	___ Receptionist
___ Calligraphy	___ Hunting/Fishing	___ Recreation
___ Child Care	___ Instrumentalist	___ Research/Archives
___ Choir	___ Interior Design	___ Scouting
___ Clowns	___ Job Placement	___ Senior Citizens
___ Community Ministries	___ Languages:	___ Set Design
___ Computers	___ French	___ Sewing
___ Construction	___ German	___ Singing
___ Costume Design	___ Spanish	___ Small Group Leader
___ Counseling	___ Other	___ Song Leader
___ Crafts	___ Library	___ Stage Lighting
___ CPR/First Aid	___ Mail-outs	___ Statistical Analysis
___ Dance	___ Mechanic	___ Surveying/Polling
___ Education	___ Misc. Repairs	___ Telephoning
___ Preschool	___ Organist	___ Tellers
___ Children	___ Narration	___ Transportation/Driving
___ Youth	___ Photography	___ Travel
___ Day School	___ Pianist	___ Tutoring
___ Vacation Bible School	___ Prayer Room	___ Typing/Secretarial
___ Electrician	___ Printing/Typesetting	___ Ushers
___ Exercise/Aerobics	___ Prison Ministries	___ Visitation
___ Financial/Estate Planning	___ Public Address Systems	___ Woodworking/Carpentry
___ Flower Arranging	___ Programs for Disabled	___ Writing

Figure 15.2

GUIDELINES FOR WRITING JOB DESCRIPTIONS FOR VOLUNTEERS

TITLE OF POSITION:

SUPERVISOR:

PURPOSE:

DUTIES:

1.

2.

3.

4.

EXPECTATIONS:

1.

2.

3.

4.

Figure 15.3

SAMPLE GUIDELINES FOR PRESCHOOL, CHILDREN, YOUTH, AND SPECIAL EDUCATION WORKERS

PURPOSE:

The disturbing and traumatic rise of physical and sexual abuse of children has claimed the attention of our nation and society. Unfortunately, churches who have children's programs are not insulated from this alarming trend. The following policies have been established in response to this trend and reflect our commitment to provide protective care of all preschoolers, children, youth, and special education pupils attending any sessions at the church or any church-sponsored programs or activities.

GENERAL:

1. Individuals who have been convicted of either sexual or physical abuse should not volunteer to serve or seek employment in any church-sponsored activity or program for preschoolers, children, youth, or special education pupils.
2. Adult survivors of childhood sexual or physical abuse need the love and acceptance of this church family. Individuals who have such a history should discuss their desire to work with preschoolers, children, youth, or special education pupils with one of the pastoral staff prior to engaging in any volunteer service.
3. Volunteers in the preschool, children, youth, or special education areas are required to be members of this church, and must be approved by appropriate church personnel before they may begin working directly with pupils in these areas.
4. Workers will be expected to observe the "two-person" rule. This means that when working in the preschool, children, youth, or special education areas, workers should avoid one-on-one situations with pupils.
5. All paid and volunteer workers should immediately report to the age-appropriate minister, church administrator, minister of education, or minister of music any behaviors or other incidents that seem abusive or inappropriate. The age-appropriate minister, church administrator, minister of education, or minister of music is responsible for making sure that appropriate actions are taken.
6. From time to time opportunities for training in the prevention and recognition of the sexual abuse of children will be provided by the various ministry areas of our church. Paid and volunteer workers in these areas are expected to participate in the sessions.
7. A criminal records check will be run on all new preschool, children, youth, and special education paid and volunteer workers. The criminal records check may also be run on all current paid and volunteer workers in these areas. Criminal records checks may be re-run periodically.
8. Have you ever been arrested for, charged with, under probation for, convicted of, or pleaded guilty or *nolo contendre* to (a) any sexual or physical abuse, (b) molestation, or (c) any felony crime or any action prohibited by the Texas Family Code (or similar code or statute in any state)?

     ___Yes (Please describe on a separate sheet of paper.)

     ___ No
9. If you were personally a victim of child abuse, we require that you make this information known, prior to your beginning service, to the minister under whose leadership you will serve (if you prefer, you may discuss this with the

pastor, minister of youth, minister of children, minister of preschool, minister of education, minister of music, or church counselor). You understand and agree that this information is being provided for the purpose of determining the suitability of those who will be allowed to work with the church's preschoolers, children, youth, or disabled. Admitting you were a victim will not automatically disqualify you from service. This information may be discussed with the pastor or one or more ministers, but will be kept confidential.

I have read the above policy and agree to observe the safeguards listed.

Signature_____ Date _____

Please print name _____

Figure 15.4

CHOOSING THE BEST TRAINING TOOL

I. MEETINGS. Time should be well planned with a written agenda. It is important to communicate to the worker in advance the purpose of the meeting and how long it will last. Every meeting should begin on time, follow an agenda, and end on time.

II. BOOKS. Choose books that are up to date and will help the person understand the role of a position and how the position enhances the work of the church. Point out specific chapters that will be most beneficial to their position.

III. VIDEOS. More and more videos are being published for training. Check your denominational office to see what may be available to you with a small purchase or rental cost. Be sure to review the video before giving it to the worker for training. You may develop a written guide for workers to use while viewing the tape.

IV. CONVENTIONS AND RETREAT CENTERS. Request conference schedules many months in advance to determine what may be available for your workers. Give the workers a copy of the schedule with your comments about what sessions would be helpful in their job. When a leader encourages workers to attend, there should be a strong feeling about what the conference has to offer to help the workers do a better job.

V. GUEST LECTURERS. Choose very carefully. If you have not heard a person speak before, take the time to interview others who have. When you extend an invitation to a speaker, write down what you are hoping to accomplish and go over it with the person and ask if they feel comfortable with the challenge. Give the speaker a schedule and emphasize how important it is to honor it.

VI. OBSERVATION. Many times it is better for someone to see how another person is doing the same job. The leader should choose a class or situation that best models the position of the worker and work out a period of observation for the new worker with the one being observed. An observation questionnaire for the person to complete during each session is a good tool to use for follow-up discussion between the leader and the worker.

Figure 15.5

25 WAYS TO RECOGNIZE WORKERS

1. Smile.
2. Be open to suggestions.
3. Reimburse assignment-related expenses.
4. Ask for a report.
5. Send a birthday card.
6. Recognize personal needs and problems.
7. Keep challenging them.
8. Provide good pre-service training.
9. Help develop self-confidence.
10. Take time to explain fully.
11. Enable them to grow on the job.
12. Create pleasant surroundings.
13. Take time to talk.
14. Provide expenses for special training conferences or workshops.
15. Write "thank-you" notes.
16. Invite participation in formulating policies.
17. Celebrate outstanding projects and achievements.
18. Provide useful equipment in good working condition.
19. Plan social events.
20. Provide opportunities for conferences and evaluation.
21. Plan a "recognition edition" of the church newsletter.
22. Adequately orient.
23. Be familiar with the details of assignments.
24. Say thank you.
25. Greet by name.

Figure 15.6

WORKERS WILL DO BETTER WORK WHEN THEY KNOW:

1. They will be given regular supervision.
2. What is expected of them.
3. To whom they are responsible.
4. They are making a contribution to the cause of Christ and their church.
5. They will be furnished the needed physical resources.
6. There will be opportunities for training.
7. There are standards for measuring performance.
8. There will be support and affirmation.

CHAPTER 16

Staff Relationships

William G. Caldwell

The development of good staff relationships should be of primary concern when a church has several people working together in staff leadership. These relationships will involve all paid staff members to some extent. This is especially true when a team approach is taken. In addition, those who provide ministerial leadership will desire closer relationships with each other as a means of becoming more effective in their work.

Many staff members will have certain feelings about their relationships with others, whether in reference to a specific staff member or to the group as a whole. These feelings should indicate that things are good and getting better, rather than bad and getting worse. However, it is necessary to work on relationships. They don't just get better by themselves. The following suggestions are provided to help staff members work on relationships.

IMPROVING CHURCH-STAFF RELATIONSHIPS

If a church staff is defined as a group of Christian persons, called by God, who willingly agree with God, a local congregation, and one another to live out their vocational task as they guide a church in its mission, then feelings about staff relationships become extremely important. All members of the staff must be committed to improving relationships.

CONCEPTS

There are four highly significant concepts about building relationships among staff members:
1. It is a mandatory activity.
2. It is a continuing activity.

3. It is to be done with God, with a church, and with other staff members.

4. It involves shared responsibility and shared authority.

Each of these concepts also has a significant corollary for all staff members:

1. It should be both encouraged and engaged in by all.

2. It should begin during one's pre-staff experiences and continue throughout one's time in a position.

3. It should encompass all three parties—God, church, other staff members.

4. It should include both dimensions—responsibility and authority.

The choice is not whether to have relationships. The choice is what kind of relationships we will have!

COMMITMENTS

Without commitment on the part of all staff members, good relationships will not be developed. It is imperative, at the beginning of their work together, that staff members are clear about their working relationships with each other and their agreements with the church about their work. If staff members do not work at the task of clearly defining their commitments and expectations with each other and the church, then significant misunderstandings, conflicts, and unhappiness will develop.

DEVELOPING EXPECTATIONS

Staff ministers do not serve very long on a church staff before becoming aware that the expectations that are held by church members, other staff members, and they themselves about their role and function are numerous, varied, and often conflicting. While some expectations are apparent to everyone—perhaps even specified in writing—and others may be evident enough to be "sensed" by a perceptive staff minister, many may be unknown (or "hidden") to a particular staff minister. When expectations clash or are not met, problems arise in staff relationships.

For the optimal potential in staff relationships to be realized, there must be a clear agreement between a staff member's personal expectations, the expectations of church members, and the expectations of other staff members. The testimony of scores of staff ministers is that where there is not a clear understanding by all parties of the expectations of each party, there is apt to be misunderstanding. This is especially true when inadequate effort is made by a staff member to clarify these expectations during the process of joining a staff as well as during the period of service.

Because clarity of expectations among all parties is prerequisite to healthy staff relationships, it is appropriate for each party to ask the question: What are the common understandings that we must have in order to work together most redemptively?

COMMON EXPECTATIONS

Although a church staff is likely to have access to many documents that provide information on how the staff is to work together, it would help if every church provided for its staff at least one document in which the general expectations of staff work are clearly stated. It should be perceived as the standard agreement common to all staff members. It should be the primary reference document which guides the church staff in their work together. The following information is presented as it might appear in a sample document. You could adapt this for your situation and use it as the staff manual in your church.

BASIC PRINCIPLES TO GUIDE A STAFF IN THEIR PLANNING AND WORKING TOGETHER

Spiritual

1. All staff members love the Lord, love the church, love one another, and behave like Christians.

2. All staff members are predisposed to joy.

3. There is among all staff members a spirit of humility and submission.

4. All staff members maintain a daily devotional time, and during this time they intercede in prayer for all other staff members.

The Scripture on which these spiritual principles are based is Galatians 5, which speaks of the "fruit" of the Spirit rather than the "fruits" of the Spirit: "The fruit of the Spirit is love," and it is manifested in "joy, peace, longsuffering, gentleness, goodness, faith, meekness, temperance" (vv. 22–23). For the church staff, joy is love's strength; peace is love's security; long-suffering is love's patience; gentleness is love's conduct; goodness is love's character; faith is love's confidence; meekness is love's humility; and temperance is love's victory. Every staff member—without exception—should be committed without reservation to the faithful practice of these spiritual guidelines.

Administrative

1. The staff is a shared ministry leadership team, and there can be only one chief of staff.

2. There is ongoing attention given to building relationships in order to ensure clarity in policies and guidelines.

3. There are regular staff meetings with adequate time devoted to both short-range and long-range planning.

These guidelines affirm the validity and necessity of the ministry of each staff member. Ministry that is to be united in effort and objective but divided in responsibility is to be expected. The pastor is acknowledged as having the church-assigned responsibility of leading the team. While diversity of function among staff members is recognized and accepted, wholeness and unity in the ministries of all staff members is affirmed. There is a commitment to expending whatever time and energy it takes to ensure that all staff members have clear understandings of expectations and ample opportunity to participate in all planning processes affecting their work and ministries.

Practical

1. Each is loyal to the Lord and one another, and all are loyal to the church.

2. Each staff member is encouraged to think and function as a "full" minister and a team member.

3. There is good communication—especially when there is a problem.

4. Relationships are also built on a personal level.

An understanding must be developed concerning the practical ways in which expectations are worked out with each staff-member. This requires that each staff member must have a good self-image and be able to relate well to others who are equal in their team responsibilities. The personal involvement with one another and family members outside of work assignments is an essential part of this understanding.

These guidelines provide for great latitude in the responsible use of freedom in exercising one's ministry to the fullest extent possible. A high level of trust, openness, relationship, interdependence, and maturity among staff members is assumed.

SPECIAL EXPECTATIONS

In contrast to standard expectations that all staff members and the congregation hold in common, there is a need to clarify the agreements, understandings, and expectations that are unique for each staff member. These special expectations include:

* How will you be supported?

* What will be your job?

* How will you work with others?

Although these will vary from situation to situation, each of them will be developed in some form. In the simplest form they will be informal working agreements, determined primarily by tradition and the ways in which various people mesh in their personality and work styles.

In more developed forms, there will be church-approved statements concerning how the congregation expects staff members to work together and specific job descriptions for each position. (These were presented earlier in chap. 4.) Staff members will learn to work intentionally on the issues that will bring them together into an effective ministry team.

HOW WILL YOU BE SUPPORTED?

An agreement that specifies the resources provided by a church for maintaining a minister's services should be written. Its purpose is to (1) clarify the personnel policies of a church as they relate to a specific staff minister and (2) clarify the financial resources provided by a church for that minister.

This agreement is usually negotiated with the Personnel Committee, the Finance Committee, and/or a Search Committee, and approved by the church. Churches without these committees will develop their own process for establishing this agreement.

Thorough negotiation should take place at the outset of one's ministry in a church. There will never be another time as opportune as this for negotiation of this agreement. A staff minister should use this opportunity wisely to ensure that an equitable salary (including housing), benefits, and other provisions are made for adequate support. There should be an annual opportunity for discussion of selected contents in the agreement with the Personnel Committee and/or the Finance Committee.

Information about any or all of the following may be included in the agreement: employment policies and procedures (interviewing, calling, moving expenses); salary (arrangements, administration, review); office and equipment; travel reimbursement; basic work schedule; vacations; holidays; sick leave; time off for personal reasons; personal/professional development; sabbatical/study leave; advancement; grievances; insurance; retirement plan/pension; dismissal policy and procedures; release/resignation.

A checklist (figure 16.1, p. 256) may be used for purposes of clarity. A written letter (figure 16.2, p. 258) should be provided to assure that no misunderstanding happens. Ministers and churches will have to decide what happens if there is a disagreement about the provisions being made.

WHAT WILL BE YOUR JOB?

A written agreement specifies the functional responsibilities assigned by a church to a specific staff minister. The purpose of such a statement is to clarify what the church expects a specific staff minister to do. It answers the question: *What is my work responsibility?* It focuses almost exclusively on the relationship a staff minister has with the church. This type of agreement is typically called a job description.

The channels for negotiating a job description are usually the same as the ones mentioned earlier. However, for certain staff members, such as a minister of music, additional opportunities may be available through a specialized group or committee. Staff ministers with multiple responsibilities because of combined jobs will need to have clear information concerning how the duties will be handled.

The discussion of a job description should be done at the outset of one's acceptance of a position. Schedule adequate time for this discussion. Many sessions with various persons/groups may be necessary. An opportunity for review of a staff member's job description with a church should be provided annually through the personnel evaluation process.

A staff member's job description with a church should be much more than just an organized listing of duties and responsibilities—as important as that is. It should be based on the vision that a staff minister and the church have for that person's overall ministry. Sample descriptions of the duties usually expected of staff ministers are included in chapter 4.

HOW WILL YOU WORK WITH OTHERS?

Staff members must understand how they are involved with other staff members. The focus is more on knowing how one functions in a team relationship rather than on what one does; more on knowing how one does the work than on what is achieved. Its purpose is to clarify: the quality of relationship that now exists; the perceptions each minister has about how to work with every other person on the staff; and how in their working together the quality of relationship between and among staff members can be significantly strengthened.

As with the other types of agreements, much attention should be given at the outset of one's ministry to understanding relationships with colleagues. This understanding, however, requires continuing work on a regular basis. Rule of thumb: Touch base with other staff ministers as often as possible—not because you have to, but because you want to! When staff members both solemnly and joyfully enter into a relationship with one another, the outcome is a better relationship and a clearer understanding of how they can most effectively work together and enjoy the Lord's work.

Each person's understanding of self and others in the areas of value system; self-image; the goal, nature, and work of staff ministry; church expectations of staff members; leadership style; and church personnel policies and procedures must be dealt with for effective ministry results. These and other issues considered significant by staff ministers should be a part of the content to be discussed. It is unlikely that all of these issues will ever be discussed fully, and they need not be discussed in any particular sequence. However, none of them should be avoided or ignored in building relationships with staff members.

EVALUATING MINISTRY RELATIONSHIPS

Each minister must accept personal responsibility for ministry by taking the initiative in purposefully directing one's life as much as possible rather than simply allowing it to be determined by past and present pressures. It is a proactive—in contrast to a reactive—ministry stance. But ministers who work together must also develop processes for evaluating how they are working together. The use of some instruments that have been designed for relating to others may be helpful. Staff groups may want to consider Life Orientations (Communication Styles), Performax, Bi-Polar, Taylor-Johnson Temperament Analysis, or other such instruments for this purpose.

USING STAFF MEETINGS PRODUCTIVELY

The most effective approach to evaluating relationships can come as a part of a regular, weekly staff meeting. Amid the time allowed for prayer and Bible study, calendar coordination, problem solving, and reporting, there should be time allowed for evaluating and building relationships. Any discussion of conflicts over scheduling, finances, or use of volunteers should include a frank evaluation of relationships that exist among and between staff members. Only as relationships improve can there possibly be any effective and productive resolution of conflicts.

All staff members must be involved in the regular staff meetings. They should remain as long as the agenda calls for their participation. This procedure will usually mean that support staff members will return to their work after the first several agenda items. It is possible that some time may be given to relationship building before they are dismissed. Of necessity, the ministerial leadership staff members who remain for program and ministry planning and evaluation will want to be involved in strengthening their relationships with one another.

USING RETREAT SETTINGS

The logical expansion of the staff meeting for relationship building is a staff retreat. Three main differences in the two allow for this to happen. One is the time factor—much more time is available in a retreat setting. The second is the location—being away from the office reduces the possibility of interruptions and distractions. The third is fellowship—the possibility for increased fellowship is provided on a retreat. Scheduling a retreat every six months would be helpful.

A retreat setting does not have to mean going to an expensive property. It will help if recreational opportunities are available and time can be allowed for these activities. The main need is to get away and to have sufficient time to work on relationships. This might be accomplished in a meeting room at a neighboring church, or in a conference room at a local hotel, or at a church member's vacation home. Each staff member will need to make a commitment to use the time provided to strengthen relationships with other staff members.

EVALUATING CONSTANTLY

Meetings are not enough. It is essential that regular evaluation of relationships takes place. There must be involvement on a one-to-one basis between staff members. Honest communication about facts and feelings must take place. Potential and actual conflicts must be dealt with in terms of improving relationships. Turf protecting and importance of ministries must be discussed in light of how the staff works together to accomplish the mission of the church. One of the purposes of performance analysis is to determine how effectively staff members work with each other—the peer group.[1]

The results of evaluating relationships will be seen in more satisfied, joyful staff members who remain in a position for a longer period of time; but more importantly, much more effective work will be done in leading the church toward its vision and the accomplishment of its mission.

Figure 16.1

CHECK LIST FOR CLARITY IN A CALL

		YES	NO
1.	Church moves/provides moving expenses?	___	___
2.	Church provides housing?	___	___
	If yes, in what form?		
	Church-owned house _____		
	Housing allowance _____	___	___
3.	Church provides utilities or allowance?	___	___
4.	Church assists in purchasing home?	___	___
	If yes, indicate the following: Provides down payment as gift or loan in the amount of $___ at an interest rate of ___% to be repaid at $___ monthly. Amount loaned to be paid in full within _____ days of termination. (Any gift or loan amount forgiven must be treated as added income.)		
5.	Monthly salary to begin $_____ with review for increase at the end of: _____ months Recommendation for increase to be made by committee.	___	___
6.	Monthly travel expenses reimbursed? If yes, in the amount of ___cents per mile for travel on church business.	___	___
7.	Church provides insurance coverage? If yes, how much?_____ Health $_____ Life $_____	___	___
8.	Church provides reimbursement for ministry expenses? If yes, up to what annual amount? $_____	___	___
9.	Church provides weekly days off? If yes, number of days _____	___	___
10.	Church provides annual paid vacation? If yes, _____ number of weeks first year; second year and thereafter _____	___	___
11.	Is necessary supply paid by church for vacation absences?	___	___
12.	Church provides time off to assist other churches with meetings? How many weeks?_____	___	___

13. Church provides time and expenses to attend denominational conventions?
How much?_____   ____ ____

14. Is necessary supply paid by church for these absences?   ____ ____

15. Church provides time off for death of family members?   ____ ____
If yes, how much time?_____

16. Church provides time off for illness?   ____ ____
If yes, amount of time annually_____

17. Are salary and benefits paid during time of illness?   ____ ____
For how long?_____

18. Necessary supply paid by church?   ____ ____
For how long?_____

19. Church provides annual physical examination?   ____ ____

20. Pastor is designated as supervisor of other staff?   ____ ____
If no, who is designated and for which staff members?_____

21. Time off is provided for study leave and professional development?   ____ ____
If yes, how much time annually?_____

22. Does church pay cost of job-related training?   ____ ____

23. Does church provide retirement benefit?   ____ ____
If yes, what amount?_____

24. _____   ____ ____

25. _____   ____ ____

Figure 16.2

SPECIFIC AGREEMENTS
(THESE WILL VARY FROM CHURCH TO CHURCH)

ANNUAL FINANCIAL ARRANGEMENTS

1. **VOCATIONAL COMPENSATION**
   Basic Salary: to be paid $_____
   Housing Allowance $_____
   Utilities Allowance $_____
       Total $_____

2. **PROTECTION COVERAGES** _____ % of
   Retirement Plans _____
       Vocational Compensation
   Family Health Insurance
   Life Insurance
   Disability Insurance
   Worker's Compensation
       Total $_____

3. **REIMBURSEMENT OF PROFESSIONAL EXPENSES**
   Travel _____ cents a mile
   Conventions and Meetings
   Professional Dues
   Entertainment/Hospitality
   Books
   Other ministry expenses
       Total $_____

4. **ANY OTHER CONSIDERATIONS***
   Christmas Bonus or Cash Gift
   Social Security Tax Allowance
       Total $_____

5. **RELOCATION COSTS***
   Commercial mover
   Transportation
   Motel/Meals
   House down payment
       Total $_____

*Will be added to W-2 Form.

ANNUAL TIME ARRANGEMENT

The church acknowledges that a minister's work cannot be rigidly regulated because of the nature of ministry. Crisis situations and emergencies along with meetings and a heavy schedule may alter the schedule and sometimes necessitate arranging work and leisure at different hours.

Despite weekend work and evening obligations, a minister must find some time to spend with the family and for personal needs.

    $_____

1. Day(s) a week off _____
2. Weeks for vacation _____
3. List holidays _____
4. Study-leave time _____
5. Sunday absences _____
6. Total number of Sundays for church-paid supplies _____
   Vacation time _____
   Conventions or conferences _____
   Study leave _____
   Other engagements _____
7. Sick leave arrangements _____
8. Any other arrangements _____
   _____

CHAPTER 17

The Minister's Personal Life
Robert D. Dale

What does it take to live happily and healthily in our hectic world? One formula for effective professional functioning includes a partner who loves you, a vocation that challenges you, and five friends whose faces light up when they meet you. Add your personal faith in Christ to these three factors—a mate, a calling, and a tribe of encouragers—and you have the raw material for managing the personal dimensions of your professional ministry.

Ministry requires effective support-system management. Why? Because ministry is a stressful, wear-and-tear calling and because ministry is a vocation of attrition for ministers and their families. The give, give, give of caring for others causes some ministers to give out and others to give up.

We who minister must receive in order to give to others. Thankfully, the Christian faith has rich resources for ministerial support: prayer, the Holy Spirit, and the fellowship of other believers. Building on these resources, three major aspects of managing personal dimensions of ministry will be spotlighted in this chapter: family relationships, career development, and support system design.

ENRICHING YOUR MARRIAGE AND FAMILY LIVING

Ministers are reminded by biblical instruction to be responsible managers of their marriage and family relationships. When discussing the minister's qualifiers and disqualifiers, the apostle Paul links home management with church management (1 Tim. 3:5). To fail in family relationships is to be disqualified as a church leader.

When family living is viewed as a lifelong process, managing household relationships becomes an ongoing practice of updating our promises and vows to our family members. Consider the stages of a family and the recommitments that are basic for each phase.

1. *The happily ever-after family.* Newlyweds view family life simply: We love each other—and that's all there is to it. Life is a romantic fantasy of roses and rainbows.

Then the "I never knews" begin to be discovered. New and disappointing revelations come to light: the early-morning grouch, the inability to balance a checkbook, the irritating habits. The "I never knews" reveal the essential double-edged nature of relational growth and raise up several occasions for the renewing of promises:

- Building a new family unit separate from the two families of origin
- Developing a mutual partnership
- Learning to disagree agreeably
- Accepting personality differences as growth opportunities, not as threats, flaws, or faults

2. *The "making-ends-meet" family.* Two-paycheck families make up the majority of American households. In fact, for many families, two incomes are a necessity rather than an option. Ministers increasingly are finding that making ends meet is a state of life instead of a passing stage. Several important promises need to be considered for these families:

- Keeping work from becoming a wedge between family relationships
- Avoiding letting jobs become the primary at-home topic of conversation
- Developing a joint plan for managing incomes

3. *The "bundle-of-joy" family.* Parenthood creates family in its fullest sense. Especially when the child has been planned and prayed for, births of babies are really blessed events. Conversely, the introduction of new babies into the family circle creates strains—loss of schedule flexibility, added expenses, care responsibilities, and potential neglect of the primary husband-wife relationship. These challenges suggest some additional updating of vows:

- Seeing children as unique persons, not rivals or substitutes
- Developing a parenting style appropriate to your current family situation
- Keeping the husband-wife relationship strong as a base for family health and effective parenting

4. *The "expanding-world" family.* This stage is a blossoming phase for both parents and children. Adults are putting down roots and investing in their careers. Children are entering school and developing a circle of friends beyond the family. New commitments also confront this family:

- Facing power struggles as the family's interests diversify

- Resisting the child-centered family and consequent neglect of the fundamental husband-wife relationship

- Coping with deadening routines

5. *The "breaking-away" family.* Teenagers have a habit of storming the family fortress in their attempt to grow up and develop their own personalities. At this stage of family life, a double bind often develops between children's adolescent search for identity and direction and parents' "middlescent" search for identity and direction. Both generations face similar struggles simultaneously. A range of renewed promises present themselves to this family:

- Admitting that some tension is natural in families

- Adjusting discipline approaches as teens become more responsible decision makers

- Resisting the temptation to become pals with children and go through a second childhood

- Creating family boundaries with flexibility enough to provide children with both protection and freedom

- Preparing the husband-wife relationship for the empty-nest stage

6. *The "untying-the-apron-strings" family.* Launching children into their own independent lives is both exciting and frightening. Excitement arises from watching our parental influences and emotional investment in our children being tested in others' lives. Fright frequently emerges in the discomfort of letting children go and seeing the family circle shrink. Parents who have focused exclusively on child rearing may especially feel the trauma of losing their identity when they launch their children. Becoming obsolete looms large on these families' horizons. Crucial new promises face these families, too:

- Passing the torch to younger generations gracefully

- Coping with the loss of children's dependency and facing the evidences of aging

- Seeing children as only one aspect of our legacy to the world

7. *The "empty-nest" family.* This is a husband-and-wife family again. The real test of this family stage is the health of the spouses' relationship. Grandparenthood opens a new and generally more relaxed dimension of parenting. Painfully, the empty nest can refill as children return temporarily after economic or relational losses and as aged parents become dependent on their adult children. Three generations are learning to relate to one another in new ways during this stage. A number of recommitment opportunities emerge at this stage.

- Concentrating on spouse rather than children

- Becoming in-laws
- Nurturing another generation as grandparents
- Assisting aging parents

8. *The "three generations" family.* Many families experience intergenerational relationships "sandwiching" three generations. In reality, Grandma alone is the third generation in many families. Grandmothers who have lived traditional life-styles are confronted with an unfamiliar role—putting themselves first. Another rare role some members of the third generation face is great-grandparenthood. Several decisions call for updating promises for three-generation families:

- Affirming the present when you have so much past
- Freeing and encouraging children and grandchildren to live their own lives
- Identifying with grandchildren without isolating the generation in between

Each stage of family living takes on its own texture and challenges. The test of healthy families is how well they recognize the stage they're in and how completely they update their faith and coping actions to their current stage.

HANDLING FAMILY STRESS

The minister's family is both a great resource and a heavy responsibility. Parenting is an increasingly demanding role. Some family counselors refer to parent burnout, the condition of trying to be superdad or supermom with only ordinary resources. Burned-out parents feel tired, depleted, numb, angry, and blue. Stressed families are not fun for either parents or children. Mothers may be a bit more apt to burn out than fathers, especially if teens are in the home.

Parents are waking up to the magnitude of stress modern teens face. Suicide, for example, is the second highest cause of death among teenagers, following accidents. The incidence of teen suicide has nearly doubled during the past decade. What are the primary teen stresses?

- Peer pressure
- Personal appearance
- Parental expectations
- College and career decisions

Being Adolescent: Conflict and Growth in the Teenage Years, a study of teenagers' activities, private thoughts, and emotional ups and downs, yields some interesting findings. Teens use forty-two hours weekly in leisure activities and thirty-eight hours in schooling. Teens spend 19 percent of their time with other family members; less than 5 percent of their time is spent alone with one or both parents. Dramatic mood swings of only fifteen minutes in duration are normal. Contemporary parents apparently need to devote more time and patience to their parenting efforts.

Preteen children also experience stress. These stresses arise from a variety of primary sources:

- School performance
- Too little playtime
- Parental unemployment
- Minimal contact with grandparents and extended family
- Peer pressure
- Too much responsibility too soon
- Lack of discipline
- Excessive television viewing

These stresses frequently affect children's health.

Warning signs of stress in children are similar to many normal ailments. However, physicians agree that when at least five of the symptoms listed below persist for an extended period, a child is showing high levels of stress.[1]

- Bed-wetting
- Chronic complaining
- Compulsive ear tugging or hair pulling
- Cruel behavior toward people or pets
- Poor grades
- Feeling afraid or upset without being able to identify the source
- Depression
- Aches or pains
- Sudden crying
- Extreme nervousness and worrying
- Listlessness or loss of interest
- Poor eating and sleeping habits
- Difficulty getting along with friends, siblings
- Alcohol or drug use
- Nightmares
- Nervous tics, twitches, or muscle spasms
- Lying

HOW TO HELP

Steps can be taken to help your family cope with its stressors. For example, you can:

- Talk about pressures. After all, two (or more) heads are better than one when families face their stresses.

- Escape for a while. Everyone needs a break from togetherness occasionally, particularly when family relationships are already strained and nerves frayed. Give each other some space and read a book or take a walk.

- Exercise away some pent-up energy and frustration. Jog, swim, or enjoy a family outing.

- Talk to someone outside the family circle. Friends, fellow ministers, or a counselor can help put pressures into healthier perspective.

- Serve others. Get your mind off yourself.

- Create a private place for yourself. Prayer and meditation are recognized methods for reducing stress.

- Use figure 17.2, p. 276, from later in this chapter as a measuring stick to see how much change and stress have accumulated.

CHARTING YOUR CAREER SPAN

Just as your marriage and family move through stages, so your calling of ministry can be charted and examined as a developmental process.[2] Think of ministry spanning five phases.

1. *Entrance into ministry.* The secular work world claims that a worker's first professional job is crucial. It helps shape the worker's outlook about that particular vocation, about success and failure, and about his or her fit with that type of job. The same is apparently true for ministry as vocation, too. For some, the work is exciting. For others, it is overwhelming and bewildering. The first three or four years of full-time ministry mold our feelings about working with people.

2. *Advancement and stabilization.* Now essentially committed to ministry, the still-young minister faces the "make or break" element of career spans. Identity and skills begin to mesh comfortably.

3. *Maintenance.* Thoroughly into the career of ministry by this time, ministers may begin to feel some pressure not to rock the career boat.

4. *Decline.* The point of no return in work is being approached now. The minister must resist the attitude of "a job is a job is a job."

5. *Retirement.* Giving up work is difficult for most workers. But this transition is even more traumatic for many ministers who lose professional identity as well as vocational status.

PLANNING FOR CAREER GROWTH

The calling of ministry is a dynamic career; it grows and stretches the minister as God opens new frontiers to us. Some of the new opportunities are positive and exciting. Other situations are more uncomfortable and crisis-oriented.

Three predictable crises in a minister's career have been identified. The first predictable crisis in ministry tends to occur about three to five years out of seminary. In this crisis the realities of congregational leadership collide with the idealism of youth and academic life. To overstate the issue, the young minister feels the internal tension between a head full of theology and a bellyful of people. Application of theological and biblical insights to the real world of caring for people is a basic challenge for young ministers.

A second crisis emerges about midlife. Typically, young adults invest their energies in a variety of enterprises: work, family, advancement, and individual concerns. Life and ministry begin to feel frazzled around the edges. The challenge of midlife is to put all of our career eggs into one basket and regain a focus in our professional lives. As the apostle Paul said at midlife, "This one thing I do" (Phil. 3:13).

Predictably, a third crisis develops as retirement nears. Many ministers find laying down the mantle of ministry as difficult as it was to take up at our experience of calling. Older ministers are overlooked for new ministry opportunities. As an energetic minister friend reported to me, "A Pastor Search Committee visited my church, heard me preach, and enjoyed an animated luncheon conversation with my wife and me. They spoke of a visit to their church field, so we could get acquainted with their ministry opportunities. Then, they asked me how old I am. When I replied, '62,' the conversation tailed off. They said their good-byes. I haven't heard a word from them since." Preretirement and retirement are difficult emotional, financial, and leadership transitions to face.

These crises are prime times to consider career assessment. Contact the denominational office or a theological school in your area to secure recommendations. The network of career assessment centers across the United States coordinated by the Career Development Council headquarters in Lancaster, Pennsylvania, is one organization that provides counseling support for ministers.

DISCOVERING THE STAGES IN A MINISTER'S CAREER CYCLE

Life and our careers move through a series of important stages. Each new stage builds on the former stages, profiting from the lessons learned earlier or being blocked by other lessons that haven't been incorporated. These stages, while natural and fairly predictable, are fueled primarily by our decisions.[3]

Novice adults enter the work world from their late teens to about age thirty. Novices experience some suspension of expectations. Five basic issues confront the novice: (1) What dream or life goal will I structure my life around? (2) Which career will I pursue? (3) Who will become my mate? (4) Who will become my mentor? (5) Who will become my lasting friends? Vocational issues underlie and color all five of these concerns.

Novice adults in ministry can take several positive steps to meet the challenge of this stage in ministry.

- Study the life of Christ as a model—especially His vision of the kingdom of God.

- Allow your sense of calling to grow. Ministry directions often require some time and experience before they emerge clearly and finally. Jesus, Paul, Luther, and Wesley were all mature persons before they launched the ministries for which we remember them.

- Recognize that ministry involves "paying the rent" of varied expectations. Some members will expect what's within your power to perform. Others will expect the magical and unrealistic of you.

- Accept the guidance of experienced adults. Mentors can often sense our best potential even before we see it ourselves.

- Cultivate professional relationships from seminary and early ministry experiences. These friendships are apt to sustain you personally and professionally during the rest of your ministry.

- Choose a ministry style that's comfortable for you. Let your own unique approach emerge over time rather than adopting someone else's style wholesale.

Junior adults settle down as they enter their thirties. Junior adults begin to stand on their own two feet; they aren't still novices, but they aren't senior adults either. They are junior adults—in between and deserve mentoring.

Junior adults face four challenges: (1) Junior adults put down roots. During the late twenties or about thirty, adults examine their life structure and, if it has served well, they get serious about life. (2) Junior adults focus on career advancement. They pursue a dream and try to become craftsmen. (3) Junior adults recognize and concentrate on meeting real needs. They begin to take some time to cultivate emotional and spiritual gardens. (4) Junior adults grow more independent. They put away the childish ways of earlier days (1 Cor. 13:11) and ready themselves to become mentors in their own right.

A number of actions can be taken by junior adults to move them purposefully forward.

- Develop a strong ministry-support system. You can find several strategies to consider in strengthening your support network later in this chapter.

- Renew your marriage and family relationships. Keep in mind that no relationship flourishes on autopilot. Don't neglect these precious relationships; heed the suggestions mentioned earlier in this chapter.

- Plan for continuing education. Reading plans, seminars, and similar resources help us keep our ministry skills sharp.

- Cultivate your devotional life.

- Guard your physical and mental health. Discipline in diet, exercise, and stress management are wise actions.

- Establish family financial planning practices now. Saving now for college and retirement keeps more of your options open for the future.

Midlife adults slow down for a major life and career evaluation sometime after age thirty-five. For the first time, they sense they are approaching "old." They discover that aging is rarely fun—especially in a youth-worshiping culture.

1. Midlife adults examine the structures of their lives. This "time out" to review life's progress is often referred to as midlife crisis.

2. Midlife adults often revise their life dream. "Middlescence," midlife's echo of adolescence, raises two teenage questions again: Who am I? What will I do with my life? These issues are raised when we feel "plateaued" and stuck, feel that we peaked too soon, or feel that we've failed in some significant way.

3. Midlife adults are threatened by obsolescence. The deadline decade, ages thirty-five to forty-five, causes them to feel a sense of urgency and to ask, "If not now, when?"

4. Midlife adults try to create a personal and professional legacy. Symbolically, ministers work to make themselves immortal by living on through children, building programs, publications, and persons whom they have mentored.

5. Midlife adults watch the home nest empty.

6. Midlife adults face obvious physical and emotional changes.

7. Midlife adults move toward senior status.

Numerous possibilities are open to ministers at the midlife stage:

- Create and maintain supportive relationships. Our friends often sustain us during difficult days.

- Continue to be involved in marriage and family enrichment activities.

- Research midlife issues to lessen the anxiety of the unknown.
- Consider career assessment if you seriously question your fitness or ability to serve effectively in ministry posts.
- Stay fresh devotionally.
- Get regular exercise.
- Become a mentor for the next generation of ministers.
- Clarify your ministry priorities.
- Recommit yourself to lifelong learning. Many midlife ministers investigate Doctor of Ministry programs as a structured approach to continuing education.

Senior adults approach their fifties and sixties feeling the double-edged nature of aging: mellowing because purpose and meaning in life have been discovered, or becoming more brittle, bitter, and angry about growing older. Senior adults are approaching membership in America's largest minority—retirees.

Thus, senior adults deal with several basic life and career transitions. (1) Senior adults transfer hope to the younger generation. To illustrate, aging Elijah gave his mantle to the younger Elisha. (2) Senior adults cope with fixed income. This situation is made even more difficult because fewer than one half of Americans under fifty-five have made any financial plans for retirement. (3) Senior adults face the erosion of health and vigor. (4) Senior adults accept followship. They may find freedom in an elder-statesman role. (5) Senior adults may accept an expanded mission in life.

Numerous strategies are available to senior adults for moving through the transition to retirement:

- Plan for retirement. Some psychologists claim that vacations are miniretirements; our reactions to vacationing provide clues to how we'll retire.
- Stay green above the ears. Keep on learning.
- Exercise. Medical doctors prescribe walking because they describe our thigh muscles as substitute hearts.
- Take the risks of new ministries. Now may be the time in your life to start a new church or write a book. You've done so much else that the risks are low.
- Don't become angry that churches tend to value energy more than experience. The greying of America is working in the direction of raising the status of older ministers.
- Work smarter, not harder. You know some shortcuts now. Use them and save energy.

- Remember the difference between self-concern, a necessity for us as we age, and self-absorption, an unattractive trait in persons of any generation.

- Keep in perspective that ministry is an attitude as well as a role. Caleb at eighty-five asked for the toughest task in the conquest of the Promised Land; he was aging, but he retained an exciting "can do" attitude about life and work (Josh. 14).

- Families and career opportunities are important aspects of managing our personal lives. Basic to guiding our own lives, additionally, is the strength of our support network.

BALANCING YOUR SUPPORT NETWORK

Support networks generally contain at least five ingredients: soul mates, lifelong learning, spiritual coaching, mentoring, and physical fitness. Each of these five ingredients suggests ways ministers have arranged for ministry support. Each ingredient is crucial; none is complete by itself. Some ministers, however, rely on one or two ingredients to the virtual exclusion of the others. All five ingredients, when balanced according to personal and professional needs, provide resourceful support for your ministry.[4]

Ingredient #1 in an effective support system is your network of friends. Ministry support is people-to-people relating. That's where our friends in Christ fit in. Friendly soul mates believe in us, pray for us, provide listening ears, share objective feedback amid our questions and struggles, and lend us a shoulder to cry on. Soul mates help us repair the frazzled edges of our lives. Intimate encouragers from our family and friendship circle help us recharge our spiritual and emotional batteries after we drain ourselves by constantly caring for others, helping in crisis situations, and standing with others amid the general wear and tear of ministry.

Jesus, our Savior and model, chose twelve persons to minister with him and *to be with him* (Mark 3:14). Our network of friends provides us with similar vital assistance:

- Offsetting isolation

- Learning to be a "helpee"

- Encouraging us

- Exploring problems

- Helping face our weaknesses and owning our gifts.

Ingredient #2 in your support network is a portable seminary. Support for ministry is fresh ideas and lifelong learning.

Some ministers take a "union card" approach to education and assume that a seminary degree provides all of the information and training the minister will ever need. That mind-set cuts the minister off from new insights and overlooks what professional education means. The term *seminary* literally means seedbed. Seminaries are greenhouses where seeds are sprouted before they are transplanted into the world. A seminary is a starting point, not a finishing school. A plan of continuing education and ongoing growth, therefore, keeps us "green above the ears."

Our portable seminary lends us support in deepening our convictions and expanding our ideas. Book clubs, loan libraries of theological books and tapes, and idea-sharing groups are basic learning resources. Idea groups help us trade, test, and organize our thoughts. Some groups structure themselves to review books and read formal papers on topics of mutual interest. Most are less formal in their organization.

Because two (or more) heads are better than one, our portable seminary allows us several possibilities:

• Brainstorming ideas

• Exchanging newsletters, clippings, and resource lists

• Evaluating new approaches

• Analyzing books, literature, and programs

Ingredient #3 in your balanced support system is your spiritual coach. Ministry calls for the constant growth of our faith. One way many Christian groups have traditionally encouraged spiritual development is through the enlistment of a spiritual coach.

A spiritual coach is a person who helps you set, evaluate, and celebrate the milestones in your spiritual development. Almost always a one-to-one relationship, spiritual coaching requires maturity from the coach and commitment by the novice.

Disciplined spiritual growth takes advantage of a variety of resources. A spiritual coach helps us use all the avenues of development available to us:

• Studying the Bible

• Praying and confessing our sins

• Contemplating and using silence

• Reading the devotional classics and biographies of spiritual giants

• Fasting and other forms of self-discipline

• Fellowshipping with other Christian pilgrims

Ingredient #4 in your support network is mentoring. A mentor in ministry is a model, sponsor, advisor, and ally. Our mentors believe in us. They are ordinarily older ministers who have already reached some goal in ministry to which we still aspire. Our mentors see our potential and nurture the promise they see in us.

Mentor relationships are common in the pages of the Bible: Abraham for Lot; Elijah for Elisha; Saul for David; Barnabas for Paul and John Mark; Paul for Silas and Timothy. These biblical mentorships, like modern instances of mentoring, are intense and sometimes, therefore, end pain-fully. Being effectively mentored strengthens us for solid ministry now and for becoming a mentor for others in the future.

Mentoring brings a range of valuable resources to us:

- Apprenticing in our craft

- Evaluating professional progress

- "Learning the ropes" of ministry

- Modeling how-to-do acts of ministry

- Mapping a route of advancement

Ministry is an on-the-job-training vocation, for the most part. A mentor provides a key link in our ministry-support network by placing a mantle of confidence on us.

Ingredient #5 in your support system is your physical health. The apos-tle Paul described our bodies as temples of God (1 Cor. 3:16). Public speaking is considered the most fearsome activity humans indulge in. Someone has estimated that a twenty-minute sermon is as physically taxing as eight hours of moderate labor. Vigorous health provides us the energy to engage in strenuous ministry.

Regular exercise and dietary discipline yields several important divi-dends:

- Maintaining health

- Looking fit

- Feeling good

- Increasing energy levels

CHECKING FOR BALANCE

Balanced support is necessary for healthy and effective ministry. Emo-tional support is aided by our network of friends. Practical ideas for min-istry grow out of our portable seminary. Development of our religious life is assisted by our spiritual coach. Professional growth is encouraged by our mentors. Physical fitness occurs when we treat our bodies like God's tem-ples.

When one or two elements of support are stressed primarily or exclu-sively, our support network becomes somewhat unbalanced. A complete system of support can be visualized as a wheel (see figure 17.1). Like a wheel, symmetry is essential for balance in our ministry-support resources. And balance is a critical clue to the strength of our support net-works.

MANAGING PERSONAL AND PROFESSIONAL STRESS

Stress accounts for the best-selling prescription drugs in the United States. According to family physicians, two of every three office visits are stress related. Ironically, our lifestyles are making us sick.

Stress is the "wear and tear of life,"[5] according to Hans Selye, the father of stress research. Stress is triggered by life changes that demand we adapt. A "ready response" is created by stress: adrenaline pumps, blood sugar levels soar, circulation to our extremities lessens to reduce blood loss in case of injury. (The last fact explains why our hands and feet feel cold and clammy when we get nervous.) The ready response is vital when we're in a real emergency situation. But if our lifestyle keeps us revved up too much of the time, we catch "hurry-up sickness" and wear out too fast. Then stress becomes distress, or bad stress. Interestingly, some folks react especially well to stress and are described as hardy personalities.

Stress-free living is both impossible and unattractive. The complete lack of stress is death. Studies suggest that life needs some stress to spice it up. Moderate stress, then, becomes "eustress," or good stress.

Several clues serve as early warnings of stress. This range of detection symptoms provides helpful signals for our self-care.

- Physical—fatigue, headaches, backaches, sleep disorders, chronic illness, hypertension, ulcers

- Psychological—boredom, irritability, defensive behaviors, anxiety, depression

- Behavioral—overeating, compulsive use of prescription or illicit drugs, drinking and/or smoking too much, temper tantrums, withdrawal from social contacts, escapist behaviors

- Occupational—job dissatisfaction, decreased work productivity, tardiness and absenteeism, sloppy decision making, sense of helplessness.

Our natural "fight or flight" response, when constantly switched on, supercharges us and keeps us stuck in overdrive. The powerful chemicals triggered by stress combine to place unrelenting strain on our weakest organs. Our "reward" may be heart attacks, ulcers, diabetes, cancer, high blood pressure, suicide, and other physical or emotional breakdowns.

Some jobs are more stressful than others. Traditionally, we've thought policemen, surgeons, coaches, and air traffic controllers occupied the most stressful work positions. However, two factors combine in the most stressful jobs: high demands from people and low control over those demands. In reality, the toughest jobs belong to cooks, waiters, cashiers, telephone operators, and assembly-line workers. And ministers? Yes—when high demand and low control factors become especially prominent in our work.

Two mental health researchers, Thomas H. Holmes and Richard H. Rahe, have devised and refined a now widely-used instrument, the social readjustment rating scale, to measure stress. These men have listed and ranked the forty-two common life changes they discovered to be precursors of illness. Strangely enough, an outstanding achievement was found to be as stressful as some dreaded catastrophe. Their basic finding was clear: change causes stress. For an indication of your personal level of accumulated stress, see figure 17.2.

Stress management has grown into a multimillion-dollar-a-year industry in America. Professional help, while useful, isn't always required. Some personal strategies for coping with stress make our lives more manageable:

- Read up on stress and stress management. Understand the problem.

- Exercise. Change pace. Rest.

- Adjust diet. Eat balanced meals. Stop drinking caffeine and other stimulants. Lose weight. Reduce sugar and salt intake.

- Slow the pace of change. Approach decisions, career moves, and major projects deliberately. When large-scale events are completed, don't stop all activity abruptly. Live life as a process, not a series of sudden starts and stops.

- Cultivate your social support network. All of us need encouragers. Families and friends are particularly crucial in managing stress.

AVOIDING BURNOUT

When ministers worship their work, work at their play, and play at their worship, they burn out personally and professionally. Misplaced priorities trigger burnout. Satisfaction in ministry wanes when we become messianic. Inflexible overresponsibleness opens the door to disillusionment in ministry.

The minister who is "most likely to succeed" in the burnout process is the idealist who pursues an unattainable goal, like setting out to bring in the Kingdom single-handedly by Thursday. Our good intentions, verve, and extreme optimism can consume us and leave us spiritually arid and psychologically depleted. Godly persons don't have to carry their burdens along like the godless do.

As mentioned above, the most likely candidates for burning out (1) work with people and (2) have a low degree of control over their jobs. As a career, ministry may be more stressful than medicine, law enforcement, coaching, and air traffic control. Why? Because ministers deal with many situations in which their degree of control is low.

Four career stages indicate the process of dampening idealism. The burnout cycle repeats itself but can be recognized and successfully confronted.[6]

Enthusiasm is stage one. Most ministers zero in on new tasks with fervor, hope, and tunnel vision. Typically, we overinvest in the new—jobs, relationships, and challenges. When idealism collides with reality, we may find ourselves blue, disillusioned, and unsure of our resources for coping.

Stagnation is stage two. The thrill of the job is dulled. Idealism tilts toward concern for days off, income, and evaluating performance. Dealing with isolation and intangible results wears on us. We still do the job, but the job does less for us.

Frustration is stage three. Powerlessness, red tape, and little leverage for change cause us to feel fatigued, irritable, and pessimistic. Because we wonder if we have any say in our own life's direction, we allow our frustration to set off a cycle of questioning our own effectiveness.

Apathy is stage four. We feel trapped. We must work, so we adopt an "a-job-is-a-job-is-a-job" attitude. We withdraw from our tasks emotionally and do only what's absolutely necessary. Security becomes our goal. Otherwise, we just go through the motions. Apathy is the bottom of the barrel, but isn't the end of the story. We can light the fire again after burning out.

Self-care for the caregivers is the key to recovering from burnout. While churches and other Christian institutions help ministers cope with depletion and disillusionment, the recovery and preventive processes are set in motion by ministers themselves. Four families of growth strategies are available:

1. *Boundary marking.* Creating clear boundaries deflects burnout in ministry. Several boundaries need to be marked off and contrasted: call to ministry and basic identity, personal life and professional life, self and others, work and play, and possible goals and unrealistic expectations.

2. *Monitoring.* Tracking our feelings, patterns of ailments, and sense of spiritual depletion helps us confront the burnout process. Ministry is a vocation of attrition. When we give, give, give without renewal, we may give out and give up. Keeping tabs on where we are helps us avoid burnout.

3. *Replenishing.* Ministers need a backlog of encouraging relationships and accessible resources to offset burnout. Visualize your support system for replenishment as a cube. The cube's front face is your devotional disciplines and sense of relationship to God. The back face of the cube represents your family's encouragement. The cube's top face is your professional network's available relationships and continuing education resources. The bottom face of the cube symbolizes your local congregation or institution's atmosphere of encouragement. The cube's right face points to your network of peers in ministry. Finally, the left face of the support cube notes the link ministers have with other helping professionals in the community and their insights into and resources for refreshing our vocational batteries. All six aspects of encouragement are needed for full and balanced support.

4. *Providing safety valves.* In spite of our best efforts, burnout can still sneak up on us. Real friends, spiritual revitalization, a healthy sense of humor, physical exercise routines, and medical assistance provide primary back-up resources for recouping from burnout.

When response and reward remain at a minimum after idealism and effort have been kept at a maximum, burnout is a likely possibility. Ministers can begin the rebuilding process by taking some self-care actions. Then, with our batteries recharged again, we can minister effectively and give freely.

SELF-MANAGEMENT: A KEY ISSUE

Managing your personal life is crucial. In fact, it's commanded for the Christian. Jesus' great commandment reminds us to love God totally and to love our neighbor as we love ourselves (Matt. 22:36–40). By implication, if we're to care for others, we must take care of ourselves.

Figure 17.1

BALANCED SUPPORT SYSTEM

Figure 17.2

HOLMES AND RAHE STRESS CHART

Think back over the past year. How many of the events have occurred in your life? Check them on the list below.

RANK EVENT   VALUE YOUR SCORE

	RANK EVENT	VALUE	SCORE
1.	Death of spouse	100	____
2.	Divorce	73	____
3.	Marital separation	65	____
4.	Jail term	63	____
5.	Death of close family member	63	____
6.	Personal injury or illness	53	____
7.	Marriage	50	____
8.	Fired from work	47	____
9.	Marital reconciliation	45	____
10.	Retirement	45	____
11.	Change in family member's health	44	____
12.	Pregnancy	40	____
13.	Sex difficulties	39	____
14.	Addition to family	39	____
15.	Business readjustment	39	____
16.	Change in financial status	38	____
17.	Death of close friend	37	____
18.	Change in number of marital arguments	35	____
19.	Mortgage or loan over $10,000	31	____
20.	Foreclosure of mortgage or loan	30	____
21.	Change in work responsibilities	29	____
22.	Son or daughter leaving home	29	____
23.	Trouble with in-laws	29	____
24.	Outstanding personal achievement	28	____
25.	Spouse begins or starts work	26	____
26.	Starting or finishing school	26	____
27.	Change in living conditions	25	____
28.	Revision of personal habits	24	____
29.	Trouble with boss	23	____
30.	Change in work hours, conditions	20	____
31.	Change in residence	20	____
32.	Change in schools	20	____
33.	Change in recreational habits	19	____
34.	Change in church activities	19	____
35.	Change in social activities	18	____
36.	Mortgage or loan under $10,000	16	____
37.	Change in sleeping habits	16	____
38.	Change in number of family gatherings	15	____
39.	Change in eating habits	15	____
40.	Vacation	13	____
41.	Christmas season	12	____
42.	Minor violation of the law	11	____
	TOTAL		____

Add up your total score. (Be sure to multiply individual event values by the number of their occurrences.)

Here's how to understand your score. A total of 150 or less gives you a 37 percent susceptibility to disease during the next two years, 150 to 300 points a 51 percent chance, and over 300 points an 80 percent possibility of health difficulties.

Practicing preventive or management measures can help you deal with your stress level.

CHAPTER 18

Being the Pastor
in a Small-Membership Church

Bob I. Johnson

There are more churches with only one staff minister than any other kind. Such a church calls and/or receives you as pastor because they feel you can lead the church to be the kind of church they ought (or want) to be. A vital question is then, "How do I lead the church not only so that the people sense fulfillment, but also so that God is pleased?" This chapter is intended to help answer that question.[1]

GETTING STARTED

Although it is not possible here to provide comprehensive coverage on how to lead a congregation as the only remunerated staff member, it is possible to say some things that will make life for you and the congregation more fulfilling. Every congregation exhibits unique characteristics; however, common factors do exist in most if not all such situations. One surely is that there are always starting points you can look for as an opportunity to impact ministry for good. When your tenure begins as pastor is one of those times.

One approach is to make as many needed changes as possible in the first year, or *honeymoon* time. That doesn't work too well in marriage, and with few exceptions, it doesn't hold true in churches. Most situations call for the steady, long-term process of change—the exception being a church with a history of failure and/or turmoil that calls a pastor specifically to make rapid changes. Even then, watch out!

ASSESS THE SITUATION

Ask questions. Is it a newer parish? An older congregation? Rural? Urban? Does it have a history of destructive conflict (not all conflict is bad)? Have pastors served long or short tenures? How does the church view and how do you view authority for pastoral leadership? What are the capabilities and commitment of lay leaders? What are the resources available? Does it appear the church needs to remodel existing buildings and/or provide new space? What are other congregations in the area like; and how effective are their ministries?

Has the church done formal planning? If so, what were the results? How does the church make decisions, budget its resources, nominate and choose its official leaders? Who are the power brokers? Are they among the elected leaders? And after a number of other questions one can pose, ask, "Who am I? Can I be the person to lead this congregation, with all that implies, to be the people of God on mission for God?"

GET YOUR BEARINGS

Usually, to begin a formal planning agenda immediately is not the next step to take. Take advantage of the informality of the smaller congregation and talk to people and groups about what the church is like and what it ought to be doing to fulfill its calling from God. Emphasize that as pastor you want to lead the church to be the church God wants it to be, and to help its members grow. Remember that the church has chosen you because it believed you were right for the church. Ask for suggestions on how to be the most effective pastor you can be.

TAKE A BASIC APPROACH

As people make suggestions for your leadership, listen without comment. There will be time for you to respond. When meeting with a small group or the entire congregation, set up a chalkboard or attach large sheets of paper to the wall and write the suggestions in brief form. At this point, receive each one as though it has equal value with all the others. This will encourage people to believe that you want to hear what they have to say.

When suggestions cease, you may want to mention any items omitted that you think are important for consideration. Then look at the list and say something like, "Thank you. It looks like we have several things that you feel are important . . . more than we can get done any time soon. We will need to decide which one(s) we do first."

Point out how the items relate to the church's ministry. It may be appropriate to ask the group to choose the top two or three items for priority attention. Or it may be better to determine if there is one need or emphasis that seems to have stronger support to serve as a lead ministry emphasis. An example is the children's ministry. To lead with one emphasis doesn't mean that others will not get attention. It simply means that the church will address other ministries as they relate to the lead ministry. This approach may be especially helpful where unhealthy conflict or other troubles have prevailed by focusing on something where there is strong agreement.

Within the context of such an exercise, it is appropriate to introduce the concept of dreaming. The people should be encouraged to think back to the original dream of the founders if it is an older church, and to re-dream that dream in the context of today's ministry.

With this basic approach to planning, you may be able to take members a step at a time toward longer-range planning. In the beginning stages of this effort, the leader can focus on the church's self-image. One way to do this is to ask the people to respond to questions such as these:

- What does our church do well?

- What are our strengths?

- What are the good things about our church that are on the community grapevine?

- What things about our church would you *like* to be on the community grapevine?

It is not suggested here that you focus on a *strengths versus weakness* assessment. People too easily know the weaknesses. Focus on the strengths, and the weaknesses will be addressed. When a congregation expands its strengths, the church becomes more effective in mission. The companion truth is that when a church becomes taken up with weaknesses, the church begins to lose the strengths it has.

Retain the information you have gathered for future use. Allow this information to come alive and help tell the story of the church. Study it for your own thinking about which steps should be taken next. Use it in preaching to show the strengths and challenges of the church.

MOVING AHEAD

Moving ahead implies, among other things, staying connected to the church's past. Indeed, in many single-staff churches, people are usually much more attached to the past than pointed to the future. Ignoring or fighting this attachment always means trouble for a pastoral leader. To overcome a preoccupation with the past and to use it for good, celebrate it and learn to tie new ministries to the helpful aspects of that past. Where possible, show how changes are true to these traditions of the church.

USE A LEADERS GROUP

If the church already has a council or cabinet consisting of leaders of programs and major committees, use it as the base of planning and support of the overall ministry. If no such group exists, either formally organize one with church approval (or permission) or simply meet with such people on an informal basis. In a very small church where few qualified people are available for council and committee assignments, consider the following suggestion. Form one task team. Decide on the major areas of ministry such as worship, Bible study, youth ministry, stewardship, and outreach and missions. Bring together a leader from each of these areas to form a group. The leadership of the group depends on the matters to be discussed. When Bible study is the focus, then the Bible study leader is the chairperson of the group, and everyone else serves on the Bible Study Committee. The same would be true for the other major areas. This group then, under the leadership of the pastor, could serve as a church council to coordinate the entire ministry of the church.

CHOOSE THE CURRICULUM RESOURCES

Remember, the *curriculum* of the church is all that the church does to carry out its commission to be the church. *Curriculum resources* are the Bible, lesson guides, audiovisual materials, and other items used to assist the church in fulfilling its commission.

As the pastoral leader you will need to be involved in selecting curriculum resources, even as you are involved in helping the church to determine its curriculum. Study what the church says it wants to be and do. Gather information from denominational offices and other desirable sources about curriculum materials that fit your church. Ask for samples for this study.

Use the *leaders group* mentioned above or another appropriate group to assess current curriculum materials that are being used. Make recommendations for the church decision-making process to act upon if changes are desired. Once adopted for use, provide interpretation sessions on how to use curriculum materials. Keep reading the materials on a regular basis after adoption to assure their relevance to the church's needs.

MOBILIZE THE WORKERS

The minister must remember the pithy words of the person who said, "Pastor, we will do anything you can get us to do." Like it or not, this statement places the burden of leadership on the single-staff minister. It also implies that there are people who will share ministry responsibilities if they are properly recruited, trained, and supported.

People want to know where they are being led. Therefore, as a leader one should know what is to be accomplished and how to accomplish it. Once these issues are established, it is time to recruit persons for ministry positions.

Recruiting. In some cases the pastor is the person best suited to recruit workers. Recruiting requires special skills as well as prayer and patience. Be sensitive to each person's needs. Some nominees need all the facts about the potential ministry you are asking them to consider. Others are interested mostly in how it will help those involved. Still others like to be a part of a team effort, and provide and receive support from team members. Also, some are primarily more attracted by the challenge of the task. Be sensitive to personal preferences.

With appropriate sensitivity to personal preferences, refer to the following suggestions for face-to-face contact with persons to be recruited:

1. *Schedule a time that is convenient to the person.* Avoid asking someone to make a serious decision hurriedly or in a place that is not conducive to thoughtful consideration of your request.

2. *Recruit in the atmosphere of prayer.* Pray for the person to be asked to serve and for yourself, especially for yourself if the person does not respond positively.

3. *Explain clearly the ministry task you are asking the person to accept.* Include what is expected, the potential joys and heartaches, the resources available, the names of others with whom the person will work closely, and the potential for personal growth.

4. *Furnish printed information to leave with the person.* This may include a brief list of things he or she is expected to do, resources available, copies of helpful materials, and any pertinent church document(s).

5. *Allow the person adequate time to think and pray before giving a decision.* Ask the potential leader if a week is enough time to make a decision. Suggest that you will call in a few days to make another appointment to receive the decision.

6. *Complete the task as promised.* Call in a few days to see if additional information is needed and to make an appointment to receive the decision. If the answer is negative, thank the person for his or her consideration and leave open the possibility of other service. If the person responds positively, provide any further information needed and review information already provided.

Developing workers. The pastor may get some help from outside sources, such as denominational training events, but most of the development of volunteer workers will be the responsibility of the pastor. This is a biblical role as indicated by Ephesians 4:11ff. Pastors and teachers are to equip the saints for the work of the ministry.

First Peter 2:9 describes all Christians as ministers, or priests. Every member of the faith family through Jesus Christ is to do the work of the church. A primary task for the equipping pastor is to ingrain this biblical role of ministry in the minds of the people.

Also, the concept of 1 Peter 4:10 is vital to the worker's identity. This verse reminds us that all spiritual gifts are to be used in serving one another, and not to be exploited for self. Remember that for many people, the best use of their gifts does not always parallel the way they earn their paychecks. The most creative expression of their gifts may be in and through volunteer ministry.

As pastoral leader, you probably have more training in Bible knowledge than do the volunteers with whom you work. Helping them to grow in such knowledge can be one of your most challenging and rewarding tasks. Provide systematic Bible study where you deal with the knotty theological and biblical problems as well as with biblical material that is easier to interpret. If such study is led by someone the workers trust, they can handle more than one might suppose. Make sure you are trustworthy and then go for it!

Workers need someone to walk with them and be available to provide guidance as they do their tasks. As the pastor, you may even have to take the leadership in a ministry for a period of time while providing in-service training for a newly recruited worker and potential leader.

Take the youth ministry as an example. As a younger minister you may have served as a youth leader and can offer expertise no one else in the church possesses. You may find that the best way you can spend some of your time is to work in the youth ministry until you can train someone to take the leadership.

Workers need to know how to handle problems and conflict. You can offer classes or seminars on how to minister at such times before those times come. People need to know that problems will arise and conflict will occur. Teach them that not all conflict is bad and that it may occur because of a difference over how the church can best do its work. When people care deeply about something, they will disagree about what is best. Sharpen your own skills and knowledge about problem solving and conflict management. Then teach volunteers about them.

Volunteers want to know how they are doing with their work. Provide some specific time for workers to tell how they are feeling about it. Encourage questions. Ask questions. Offer assistance and give encouragement. Watch for signs of stress and/or dropout. Do prevention. Show that you genuinely care for them. A follow-up note in which you can give substantive evaluation as well as encouragement is always fitting.

Moving ahead requires *recognition* and *celebration*. How do you show recognition as the single-staff minister? It is best to be specific. Handwritten notes are effective. Praise in front of others when possible is also appropriate. Recognize achievement and service during a worship service or at another church gathering if you are careful about certain points. Be consistent, factual, and Christian in the practice of public praise.

Memorable accomplishments, both small and large, can be celebrated with great profit for the entire church as well as the individual workers. You and your church should know how best to celebrate. Decide specific criteria about celebration that at the same time you plan for ministry with a council or committee. However you decide to celebrate, let it be intentional and consistent, but not superficial.

CONCLUDE A MINISTRY

Concluding a ministry depends to a large extent on the conditions present. In the usual closure, celebration and a focus on the future can be mixed with the tears of departure to help strengthen all involved. If conditions are unpleasant, however, negotiation may be the best approach.

As the departing minister, you seek to leave the church poised for life and ministry without you. That means you either do not start ministries that cannot survive without you, or you make sure new ministries have leaders in place and can succeed after you are gone (this usually requires a few years).

Seek to leave all the aspects of the church in a healthier state than when you arrived. Remember that the church belongs to God, and you are a steward of the local expression of that divinely ordained institution.

FOR THE ENTIRE JOURNEY

Certain matters are vital all along the way. Remember, people do not want to be managed; they want to be led. If you want to manage someone, manage yourself. You must manage your time and resources. Use a pocket calendar or notebook. Record major events first, such as conferences, revival meetings, and family commitments. Then schedule other events and appointments according to priority. Jotting down specifics is a vital behavior. There is a Chinese proverb that says: *The faintest ink endures longer than the strongest memory.* Learning to impose a disciplined approach to memoranda will offend few people and accomplish more.

Here are basic guidelines to enhance your ministry:

1. Communicate clearly and persistently.
2. Learn what needs to be accomplished and pursue that.
3. Make your agenda decent and open.
4. Be willing to take risks because success is not assured.
5. Keep a calendar and publicize events well ahead.
6. Follow good business practices consistent with Christian principles.
7. Communicate clearly and persistently.
8. Know the difference between leading and pushing.
9. Be willing to share the power.
10. Develop your own personal ministry so as to be more than just a "professional" minister.
11. Learn and use good telephone manners.
12. Guard study and prayer times, and let the people know when those times are.
13. Guard and practice quality family time, even if you are a family of one.
14. Practice good communication.
15. Relate to fellow ministers in a mutually helpful way. Consider forming a support group for study and mutual counsel.

16. View every person as one for whom Christ died, and therefore as the object of the church's ministry.

17. Ask for specific help from people who can provide it.

18. Make prayer, Bible study, and spiritual direction priorities in your ministry.

19. Discover, reinforce, and practice the importance of Christian education in the life of your congregation.

20. Learn good writing skills and practice them.

21. Be a loving and caring human being.

22. Keep your promises.

23. Make a lifetime goal of being a skilled servant leader after the pattern of Jesus Christ.

Be secure in your calling. The calling to be the only paid staff person is indeed a challenging one. It isn't impossible, however. Success depends on many things. Be as wise as a serpent and as harmless as a dove. Remember that according to Romans 8:28, God is at work in everything, both good and bad (though God doesn't author the bad) to bring about good for those called for God's purpose. You are linked with a powerful partner in your ministry—and that ensures the foundation for ministry.

CHAPTER 19

Getting Started in a New Ministry
Bruce P. Powers

Getting started in a new position is not difficult. However, getting off to a good start that will forge a productive partnership requires effort by the new minister and by a knowledgeable person in the church.

There are three phases to getting started: *making the transition* (at least four weeks before arriving), *getting oriented* (about one week of intense orientation and four weeks follow-up), and *developing a data base* (about three months).

PHASE ONE: MAKING THE TRANSITION

The first phase requires at least four weeks before moving to a new position. This time is used for the new person and for the church to get all their affairs in order so that from the first day both parties can give themselves unreservedly to each other.

For the church. This phase allows time for getting the person's office ready; approving financial arrangements; agreeing on housing matters; and making plans for welcoming, orientation, and so forth.

For the new minister. All responsibilities to a previous congregation or job must be terminated or clearly agreed on with the new church. All personal business needing to be resolved should be cleared prior to the move. Study information from the new church, such as church history, constitution and bylaws, and organizational structure. Acquaint yourself with information about staff members and key volunteer leaders. Write brief notes to these people expressing your anticipation in working with them. And don't forget those professional colleagues who care for you; send them a note about your move and give your new address.

PHASE TWO: GETTING ORIENTED

The purpose of this phase is to get the new person acquainted with the persons, facilities, procedures, and ministries of the church and with the leaders and resources of the community. This requires about one week of intense orientation and three to four weeks of follow-up activities.

For the church. The responsibility for orientation of new staff members definitely belongs to the church. Usually the orientation can be conducted by persons closely involved with various areas of the church's life, but the overall schedule should be planned and directed by the supervisor of the new person. In the case of a new pastor, the orientation would be planned and offered by an appropriate lay leader, such as the chairperson of the personnel committee or of the deacons. Although much of this information will have been discussed during interviews, it is helpful to make a complete review.

Here are things that should be included. Naturally, adjustments would be necessary depending on the level of experience and the background of the individual.

- Introduce staff members and tour the facilities.

- Tell how the staff is organized and how the various programs and ministries are administered.

- Describe the church's programs, ministries, calendar of events, and schedule of services; interpret the personality of the congregation; review the church's history.

- Review how the church operates through its deacons, church council, committees, and so on.

- Explain employee benefits, personnel policies, salary plan, pay dates, work hours, holidays, and other pertinent items.

- Review and discuss job expectations and office protocol.

- Tour the community. Introduce the new person to the director of missions and other local ministers as well as to important business contacts with whom he or she will work, such as the postmaster, printer, bank officials, and social service representatives. Visit the church's mission(s), if any. Have an informal staff luncheon to allow the new person to get better acquainted with co-workers.

The intense orientation of the first week gradually subsides as the new person settles into a daily work routine. The orientation continues, however, at the initiative of the new staff person. For example, get-acquainted and orientation meetings with church program leaders, committees, and appearances at church functions should have high priority.

For the new minister. Check signals once a week with the person(s) responsible for your initial orientation. Clarify any impressions about the work and expectations of the church. Ask if you are missing anything. Look ahead to other responsibilities that might slip up on you, such as Vacation Bible School, budget projections for a new church year, or an annual revival. Find out what has been done in the past, what has been planned (if anything), and suggestions about what must be done and when.

Plan a schedule for visiting in the homes of church families. Ask if there are some priorities for these initial visits, the reasons, and what might be expected. For example, a key leader may not have been favorably impressed with your coming to the church and may need reassuring.

You will see many needs, but don't try to remake the church into an ideal situation during these early months. Rather, find what is good and affirm the people. Get acquainted with them and the way in which this unique congregation lives and functions. Withhold for a while your judgments and your ideas for significant changes. Right now, you must earn the congregation's trust and come to understand and appreciate the people, the organization, the facilities, and the community as they are. Once you truly love and have become a part of them, you will be in a much better position to help the congregation deal with shortcomings.

PHASE THREE: DEVELOPING A DATA BASE

The third phase of getting started is an extension of the basic orientation begun in phase two. During this time, the new minister develops the knowledge and secures the information that will guide his or her planning and strategy for this place of service. This phase requires about three months.

For the church. As the new minister develops a data base, more information may be needed than was obtained during orientation. Cooperate by furnishing pertinent data and/or referring the minister to persons knowledgeable about the needed information.

For the new minister. This third phase is a professional way of equipping yourself to provide the most effective ministry in a church. The data base you assemble informs every decision in your ministry and becomes the foundation for effective church administration. In the absence of such information, decisions for planning, organizing, staffing, budgeting, and evaluating will be based on emotion and personal opinion—an approach to leadership that tends to create conflict.

Use the following items to guide the collection and development of information that will assist you and your congregation in making good decisions about your future together.

CHURCH MINISTRY DATA BASE

I. General
   1. Name and address of church
   2. Constitution and bylaws

3. Incorporation and other legal data

II. History
   1. The church's history: its beginnings, major developments, and changes
   2. Significant events and personalities

III. The Church's Community
   1. The church's location, history, socio-economic situation, population trends, business and industry, educational resources, civic and social life, and such
   2. The church's immediate community
   3. How has the community situation affected the church's programs and ministry?
   4. How is the church seeking to meet the challenge of its community?

IV. Membership
   1. Active membership in church and in organizations
   2. Inactive membership in church and in organizations
   3. How has church and organizational membership varied numerically each year for the last fifteen years?
   4. Demographic data on church membership (including age profile, location of residences, etc.)
   5. The church's targeted area(s) for outreach

V. Grouping and Grading
   1. How are organizations set up and graded (age, sex, etc.)?
   2. How are decisions made to start new units/classes/groups?
   3. How are decisions made to merge or disband organizations or units?

VI. Curriculum
   1. How does the church select organizational resources and curriculum materials?
   2. What resources and curriculum materials are approved or recommended for use in the various organizations/units?
   3. What process is used to coordinate selecting, purchasing, and distributing church materials?

VII. Cooperative Ministries
   1. How does the church participate in the work of the association? the state and regional groups? national and international bodies?
   2. How does the church cooperate with secular community organizations (such as schools and clubs) and with other local religious organizations?

VIII. Building and Equipment
   1. Survey of church property

2. Architectural drawing of facilities
3. Appraised value of church property and outstanding debts
4. Inventory of equipment available for church use
5. Plan for supervision/servicing of building and equipment
6. Floor plan of church facilities, with dimensions of each room, furniture and equipment in each, current assignment, and schedule for use

IX. Finance

1. Church budget
2. Stewardship plan (planning and supporting the budget)
3. Total annual income and expenditures for the last ten years
4. Administrative plan for receipt and disbursement of funds

X. Records and Reports

1. What kinds of records (membership, attendance, activities, etc.) are kept? Who keeps them? Where? For how long?
2. What information is reported? To whom? When?

XI. Communications

1. Administrative plan for church communications
2. How is the church's ministry interpreted to the public?

XII. Outreach and Ministry

1. How are members being trained and motivated to share their witness on the job and in the community?
2. What are the general attitudes related to evangelism? to missions? to Christian service projects?
3. What specific approaches are used (or have been used) to reach non-Christians in the community? church visitors?
4. How does the church receive and assimilate new members?
5. How are benevolence funds received and distributed?

XIII. Leadership and Administration

1. What style of leadership does the congregation expect?
2. What are the principles, policies, and procedures that guide church administration?
3. How are volunteer leaders recruited, trained, nominated, and elected?

XIV. Organization

1. Diagram each program and organization (show the relation of each group to the overall program, and the lines of responsibility and authority now in operation).
2. What are the reporting and coordinating responsibilities for each member of the ministerial staff?

3. What informal working relationships are important? With whom? Under what conditions?

XV. Planning, Coordinating, and Evaluating

1. By whom and when are planning, coordinating, and evaluating done for the church? for church programs? for the staff?
2. How is the work of the church evaluated? the work of church programs? the work of staff members?
3. What are the appeal procedures in case of disagreement among groups or persons in the congregation or on the church staff?

BUILDING A MINISTRY TEAM

Shared ministry is more than a concept; it is a biblical imperative. Simply going through the steps described in "Making the Transition," "Getting Oriented," and "Developing a Data Base" will not ensure an effective start. These activities must be undergirded by an intense desire to become part of a ministry team. This approach includes developing a work-family commitment to caring about, sharing with, and supporting one another in common tasks.

In addition to calendar-work and regular planning, staff meetings should include time specifically for (1) reviewing personal needs and job pressures, (2) clarifying perceptions of how staff members are relating to one another, and (3) sharing in fellowship and worship. This approach will enhance the team concept and will make routine work more enjoyable.

These ideas for getting started are a way to move into an effective and personally satisfying ministry. By following these suggestions, you will have the knowledge, skills, and support system that will prepare you, your staff colleagues, and the congregation for exciting years together!

CHAPTER 20

Finding Fulfillment in Ministry

Bruce P. Powers

The best approach to getting and keeping a ministry position—and *enjoying* it—is twofold: (1) perform job responsibilities at a level acceptable in your church, and (2) meet your *personal* needs at a level acceptable to you and your loved ones. One approach cannot be emphasized to the neglect of the other! The manner in which job responsibilities and personal needs mesh is the clearest indicator of future job success.

The starting point is effective job performance. Life is made up of a lot of things you have to do. I call this *paying the rent.*[1] For example, in keeping myself fit to live and work with, there are certain things I must do. I must bathe, brush my teeth, keep my body healthy and my mind reasonably alert, and maintain a wholesome outlook on life.

Look at your job. What are the minimum job expectations that will make you and others feel good about your work? This list of expectations is what I mean by things you have to do to *pay the rent.* To whom are you responsible? The deacons? personnel committee? pastor or other minister? church business administrator? Their expectations are a large part of paying the rent.

Paying the rent is a two-dimensional activity; that is, you can approach the same work in two entirely different ways. One leads to satisfaction, and the other leads to dissatisfaction.

As shown in figure 20.1, the reaction to any dimension of life begins with a choice of active response or passive response. From that point, the direction is set. We may progress slowly or rapidly, but the potential is limited by the choice of an active or passive response.

One way of viewing this concept is that each route begins with the way in which we respond to *paying the rent*. An active response puts me in control of my life. A passive response is surrender.

"But isn't the minister to give away his or her life?" you ask. Yes, if that is the active choice to achieve the desired results of your life. But, no, if it is a passive surrender because you are immobilized and cannot deal with the pressures and tugs of priorities in your life. Results are achieved by active ministers.

But beware! There often is a major misunderstanding about paying the rent. Some active persons get trapped by paying the rent and paying the rent and paying the rent. They never stop to calculate what is appropriate in light of their personal needs; they overpay in one area while draining themselves in other areas.

The appropriate choice is to calculate the rent (something many of us never do), then pay the rent perhaps 110 percent. Beyond that, channel energy and resources into other areas that are important to you. After calculating the rent, if you have difficulties with paying the cost, or if you are unwilling to pay the cost, you have four options![2]

OPTIONS IN GETTING AND KEEPING A POSITION

When matching personal needs and job potential, you always have at least four options for a job and even for your profession:

1. Stay and accept the situation,
2. Leave or get out of the situation,
3. Change yourself, or
4. Change the situation/organization.

The first option is the "grin-and-bear-it" approach. This approach sometimes is a conscious choice, but more often it is the result of a passive ministry stance. We gradually lose drive, and survival becomes the primary concern. The "grin-and-bear-it" approach is a yielding, no-decision stance, halfway between retreating and advancing.

The second option—*leave*—is always a viable choice. Whenever one's basic values are threatened and alternatives are exhausted, resigning may be the only route that preserves personal integrity. This option must be distinguished from forced termination, which might be a consequence of the first option. Leaving by your choice is an aggressive action designed to assist you in meeting personal needs and values.

The third option—*change yourself*—is designed to help you bring your values and skills more in line with the needs of others. This option assumes that you have some areas in your life in which you can become more tolerant and harmonious; and as situations change, you can make your share of adjustments related to common tasks.

The fourth option is to *change the situation or the organization*. Under certain circumstances, you might choose to implement change in order to accommodate better your needs and values. This choice must be made on the basis of the cost to you personally as well as to the church. This option assumes that you will make changes that improve your status while helping or at least not harming the institution.

So, in the face of any problem, you always have these four options. Each is acceptable if you look logically and sincerely for the best answer for all involved.

My particular bias is a combination of the third and fourth options—a combination of changing myself and the situation. This, in my judgment, is the basis for an effective, long-term tenure in a local church.

CHOOSING A STRATEGY

Option 1—Grin and bear it. If this strategy is preferred, such as surviving in a position until retirement, do not take major initiatives. Rather, focus on maintaining existing work and good interpersonal relationships.

Determine what has to be done and at what performance level. Then do your best to meet these minimum expectations. When asked to do something, make no promises unless you will follow through. Work out a schedule for the time you are able and willing to give, then try to maintain it.

Maintain supportive relationships wherever possible. Expand the time you are with people of the congregation, going with them and being with them in as many church activities as possible. Do not respond directly to criticism. Counsel with a trusted friend or with your spouse.

Option 2—Leave. In many ways, this decision is the most difficult to make. It involves leaving a known situation for the unknown, which may turn out to be worse. Yet, this option may be the best choice under intolerable circumstances.

This option should include an accurate assessment of the issues leading to separation. If you have not made a thorough assessment before decision, do this before moving to a new situation. Try to answer these questions: What are my values? What are the job possibilities? What are my life circumstances? What changes must be made?

When facing a change, plan ahead. If you are convinced that a move is necessary, negotiate with the person(s) to whom you are responsible for a phase-out period. This phase-out period is a time, usually three to six months, during which you fulfill your job duties while seeking another position. The church avoids conflict, and you have a support system while seeking new work.

Consult with your family, trusted friends, and a mentor or denominational leader who helps with ministry transitions. Then contact your school's placement office, a state or regional placement consultant, and professional colleagues who might recommend you. Prepare a résumé that accurately tells the benefits you could provide a church.

If you have been fired abruptly or have been out of work for some time, consider attending a vocational guidance workshop, a career assessment program, or seeking personal counseling. Ask the persons mentioned above for advice about vocational assessment or write the editor of this book for recommendations. The address is at the front of the "Resources" section in the back of the book.

Follow-through is essential for this option, so focus on personal assessment concerning your job skills and personal needs. What was out-of-balance that caused the termination? Searching and redirection are necessary; otherwise, termination may happen again.

Option 3—Change yourself. This choice requires knowing job requirements and developing and/or improving needed skills. How do you do this? Review basic textbooks such as this one and the *Christian Education Handbook*.[3] Seek feedback about your job performance and interpersonal skills. Find areas of weakness and make plans to improve.

Option 4—Change the situation/organization. Although a person sometimes seeks to change a situation for selfish reasons, most are sincerely seeking to help the church become more effective.

If you believe your motives are pure and the job and working relationships are the problem, you may seek to change the situation to make it more compatible with your perception of what is needed. This approach involves a high degree of risk and an assumption that if it is good for you it is good for the congregation (which may not be so!). If you are not successful, you will need to switch to one of the previous options.

GUIDING PRINCIPLES

1. Remember, you *always* have four options. The best way is to assess who you are and what a position requires, then make your own decisions about the future. The most harmful situation for you and for a church is for *them* to make the decision.

2. The pastor may not always be right, but the pastor is the person to whom the congregation looks for overall leadership. If you are not the pastor, you always are subject to the pastor's perception of whether you are *paying the rent.* If you are the pastor, remember that the congregation and/or the official representatives of your church or denomination will make the judgment. If you disagree, you must negotiate, keeping in mind your four options.

3. Before accepting any new position, explore all facets of the situation. Know to whom you will report, and get a clear understanding of the expectations for the job—as listed in the job description and as interpreted by those who would evaluate your work.

4. Don't oversell yourself. When considering a job, we too often say "Yes, I can do this; I can do that!" as the people name off all the high expectations they have.

The church also can oversell itself to you. The result often is discouragement and disillusionment for them and for you. Be realistic, set achievable goals, and make good decisions that will serve you and the church well not only now but also in the future.

5. Maintain your *anchor points*. Amid change and increasing pressure, try to keep some points stable. Maintain your recreation times with family and friends, keep your body healthy, and protect your worship and study time.

6. Make a plan and follow it. Where or what do you want to be five years from now? Describe these goals on the right-third of a large sheet of paper. On the left-third, list where or what you are now. In the middle, list the steps that you need to take to achieve your goal(s). This step is the beginning of your plan for the future. Now look at your present situation and evaluate your four options. *Make plans for tomorrow!*

Figure 20.1

RESPONSE PATTERN TO PAYING THE RENT

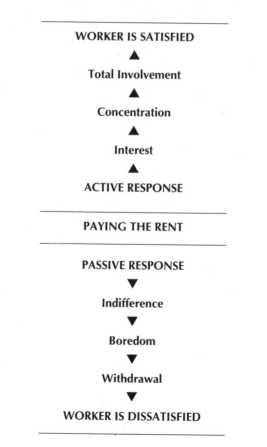

WORKER IS SATISFIED

▲

Total Involvement

▲

Concentration

▲

Interest

▲

ACTIVE RESPONSE

PAYING THE RENT

PASSIVE RESPONSE

▼

Indifference

▼

Boredom

▼

Withdrawal

▼

WORKER IS DISSATISFIED

Resources for Church Administration

The items below are provided as references for additional information and study. This list includes a variety of resources from religious and secular publishers that relate to the three sections of the book. Readers will need to determine the appropriate applications consistent with the Christian leadership and biblical guidelines presented in this text.

For an up-to-date list of resources, write the editor:

Dr. Bruce P. Powers
Campbell University Divinity School
P.O. Drawer 4050
Buies Creek, NC 27506

SECTION ONE:
HOW A MINISTER RELATES
TO ORGANIZATIONS AND TO PEOPLE

Ashley, William C., and James L. Morrison. *Anticipatory Management*. Leesburg, Va.: Issue Action Publications, 1995.

Cohen, Allan R. *The Portable MBA in Management*. New York: John Wiley and Sons, 1993.

Conger, Jay A., and Associates. *Spirit at Work*. San Francisco: Jossey-Bass, 1994.

Dale, Robert D. *Leading Edge: Leadership Strategies from the New Testament*. Nashville: Abingdon, 1996.

———. *To Dream Again*. Nashville: Broadman Press, 1981

Drucker, Peter F. *Managing in a Time of Great Change*. New York: Truman Talley/Dutton, 1995.

Gangel, Kenneth O., and Samuel L. Canine. *Communication and Conflict Management in Churches and Christian Organizations*. Nashville: Broadman and Holman, 1992.

Kouzes, James M., and Barry Z. Posner. *The Leadership Challenge*. San Francisco: Jossey-Bass, 1995.

Malony, H. Newton, Jr. *Win-Win Relationships*. Nashville: Broadman and Holman, 1995.

Martin, Glen, and Gary McIntosh. *The Issachar Factor*. Nashville: Broadman and Holman, 1994.

McLaughlin, Curtis P. *The Management of Nonprofit Organizations*. New York: John Wiley and Sons, 1986.

Powers, Bruce P. *Christian Leadership*. Nashville: Broadman Press, 1977.

————, ed. *Christian Education Handbook, Revised*. Nashville: Broadman and Holman, 1996.

Rush, Myron. *Management: A Biblical Approach*. Wheaton, Ill.: Victor Books, 1983.

Sheffield, James A. *Church Officer and Committee Guidebook*. Nashville: Convention Press, 1976.

Smith, Douglas K. *Taking Charge of Change*. Reading, Mass.: Addison-Wesley, 1996.

Stacker, Joe R. and Bruce Grubbs. *Shared Ministry*. Nashville: Convention Press, 1985.

Tapscott, Don. *The Digital Economy*. New York: McGraw-Hill, 1996.

Tidsworth, Floyd, Jr. *Life Cycle of a New Congregation*. Nashville: Broadman and Holman, 1993.

Tidwell, Charles A. *Church Administration*. Nashville: Broadman Press, 1985.

Tjosvold, Dean, and Mary M. Tjosvold *Psychology for Leaders*. New York: John Wiley, 1995.

SECTION TWO:
HOW A MINISTER PERFORMS
ADMINISTRATIVE RESPONSIBILITIES

Ashley, William C., and James L. Morrison. *Anticipatory Management*. Issue Action Publications, 1995.

Anderton, T. Lee. *Church Property/Building Guidebook*. Nashville: Convention Press, 1980.

Bender, Henry E., and Evelyn Eichel. *Performance Appraisal*. New York: AMACOM, 1984.

Bloss, Julie. *The Church Guide to Employment Law*. Matthews, N.C.: Christian Ministry Resources, 1993.

Brown, Richard, and Melva Cook. *Special Occasion Cookbook*. Nashville: Broadman Press, 1983.

Bryson, J. M. *Strategic Planning for Public and Nonprofit Organizations*. San Francisco: Jossey-Bass, 1988.

Buzzard, Lynn Robert, and Susan Edwards. *Risky Business!* Ann Arbor: J. W. Edwards, Inc., 1994.

Chandler, Ron R. *Improving Facilities Maintenance*. Ft. Worth: National Association of Church Business Administrators, 1993.

Church Administration, monthly periodical produced by the Sunday School Board, Nashville, TN. 37234.

Cionca, John R. *Red Light-Green Light*. Grand Rapids: Baker Books, 1994.

Couser, Richard. *Ministry and the American Legal System*. Minneapolis: Fortress Press, 1993.

Discover the Joy. A deluxe program of stewardship and budget subscription developed and sold by: Resource Services, Inc., 12770 Merit Drive, Suite 900, Dallas, TX 75251, 214/404-7513, 800/527-6824.

Drucker, Peter F. *The Five Most Important Questions You Will Ever Ask About Your Nonprofit Organization*. San Francisco: Jossey-Bass, 1993.

Eims, Leroy. *Be a Motivational Leader*. Wheaton, Ill.: Victor, 1981.

Foltz, Nancy, ed. *Christian Education in the Small Membership Church*. Birmingham: Religious Education Press, 1990.

Foshee, Howard B. *Broadman Church Manual*. Nashville: Broadman Press, 1973.

Frieze, Rex I. *Administrative Forms Manual for Churches and Other Ministries*. Orlando: Frieze and Company, 1993.

Hadaway, C. Kirk, and David A. Roozen. *Rerouting the Protestant Mainstream: Sources of Growth and Opportunities for Change*. Nashville: Abingdon, 1994.

Haller, Leon. *Financial Resource Management for Nonprofit Organizations*. Englewood Cliffs: Spectrum Books, 1982.

Hammar, Richard R. *The Church Guide to Copyright Law*. Matthews, N.C.: Christian Ministry Resources, 1988.

————. *Pastor, Church and Law*. Matthews, N.C.: Christian Ministry Resources, 1991.

————, ed. *Church Law and Tax Report*, a newsletter. Matthews, N.C.: Christian Ministry Resources.

Hansen, David. *The Art of Pastoring*. Downers Grove, Ill.: InterVarsity Press, 1995.

Henry, Jack A. *Basic Accounting for Churches*. Nashville: Broadman and Holman, 1994.

————. *Basic Budgeting for Churches*. Nashville: Broadman and Holman, 1995.

Hitchcock, Mary J. *Foodservice Systems Administration*. New York: Macmillan Publishing Co., 1980.

Holcomb, Tim J., comp. *Church Administration from A to Z*. Nashville: Convention Press, 1994.

————. *A Maintenance Management Manual*. Nashville: Convention Press, 1990.

————. *Personnel Administration Guide*. Nashville: Convention Press, 1988.

Kniskern, J. Warren. *Courting Disaster*. Nashville: Broadman and Holman, 1995.

Keogh, James E. *The Small Business Security Handbook*. Englewood Cliffs: Prentice-Hall, Inc., 1981.

MacMillan, Pat. *Hiring Excellence: Six Steps to Making Good People Decisions*. Colorado Springs: NavPress Publishing Group, 1992.

McCormick, Gwenn E. *Planning and Building Church Facilities*. Nashville: Convention Press, 1992.

Means, James. *Effective Pastors for a New Century*. Grand Rapids: Baker, 1993.

Mintzberg, Henry. *The Rise and Fall of Strategic Planning*. New York and Toronto: The Free Press, 1994.

National Association of Church Food Service, 76 Ivy Parkway, N.E., Atlanta, GA 30342, 1-404-261-1794 (produces a quarterly newsletter and conducts an annual meeting).

Pappas, Anthony G. *Entering the World of the Small Church*. Washington, D.C.: Alban, 1988.

Peterson, Craig. *Risk Management*. Ft. Worth: National Association of Church Business Administrators, 1992.

Pollock, David R. *Business Management in the Local Church*. Chicago: Moody Press, 1992.

Powers, Bruce P., ed. *Christian Education Handbook, Revised*. Nashville: Broadman and Holman, 1996.

Ray, David. *The Big Small Church Book*. Cleveland: The Pilgrim Press, 1992.

Schaller, Lyle E. *Innovations in Ministry: Models for the 21st Century*. Nashville: Abingdon, 1994.

————. *The Small Church Is Different*. Nashville: Abingdon, 1982.

————. *Strategies for Change*. Nashville: Abingdon Press, 1993.

Schmidt, Richard F. *Legal Aspects of Church Management*. Los Angeles: Financial Executives of Christian Organizations, 1980.

Stacker, Joe R., and Bruce Grubbs. *Shared Ministry*. Nashville: Convention Press, 1985.

Stanton, Erwin W. *Reality-Centered People Management*. New York: AMACOM, 1982.

Stevens, R. Paul, and Phil Collins. *The Equipping Pastor*. Washington D.C.: Alban, 1993.

Stewart, Carlyle Fielding, III. *African American Church Growth*. Nashville: Abingdon Press, 1994.

Tidwell, Charles A. *Church Administration*. Nashville: Broadman Press, 1985.

Wagner, C. Peter. *Church Planting for a Greater Harvest*. Ventura, Calif.: Regal Books, 1990.

Warren, Rick. *Saddleback Church Growth Lectures*. The Encouraging Word, 24194 Alicia, Suite M, Mission Viejo, CA 92691.

Wedel, Leonard E. *Church Staff Administration*. Nashville: Broadman Press, 1978.

Welch, Robert H. *The Church Organization Manual*. Ft. Worth: National Association of Church Business Administrators, 1993.

Williamson, Gerald M. *Pastor Search Committee Primer*. Nashville: Broadman Press, 1981.

SECTION THREE:
HOW A MINISTER DEVELOPS
LEADERSHIP AND MINISTRY SKILLS.

Brown, Joe B. *Battle Fatigue*. Nashville: Broadman and Holman, 1995.

Buzzard, Lynn Robert, and Susan Edwards. *Risky Business!* Ann Arbor, Mich.: J. W. Edwards, Inc., 1994.

Dale, Robert D. *Leading Edge: Leadership Strategies from the New Testament*. Nashville: Abingdon, 1996.

————. *Ministers as Leaders*. Nashville: Broadman Press, 1984.

————. *Sharing Ministry with Volunteer Leaders*. Nashville: Convention Press, 1986.

————. *Surviving Difficult Church Members*. Nashville: Abingdon Press, 1984.

Davis, Ann, and Wade Rowatt Jr., eds. *Formation for Christian Ministry*. Brentwood, Tenn.: J. M. Productions, 1981.

Drucker, Peter F. *Managing in a Time of Great Change*. Truman Talley/Dutton, 1995.

Fisher, Roger, and Scott Brown. *Getting Together: Building a Relationship That Gets to Yes*. Boston: Houghton-Mifflin, 1988.

Gangel, Kenneth O. *Feeding and Leading*. Wheaton, Ill.: Victor Books, 1989.

Goodman, Thomas. *The Intentional Minister*. Nashville: Broadman and Holman, 1994.

Holcomb, Tim J., comp. *Personnel Administration Guide*. Nashville: Convention Press, 1988.

Kouzes, James M., and Barry Z. Posner. *The Leadership Challenge*. San Francisco: Jossey-Bass, 1995.

Lawyer, John W., and Neil H. Katz. *Communication Skills for Ministry*. Dubuque: Kendall/Hunt Publishing Co., 1985.

Lee, Harris W. *Effective Church Leadership*. Minneapolis: Augsburg Fortress, 1989.

Lundin, William, and Kathleen Lundin. *The Healing Manager*. San Francisco: Berrett-Koehler Publishers, 1993.

MacKenzie, Marilyn. *Dealing With Difficult People*. Downers Grove, Ill.: Heritage Arts Publishing, 1990.

McCarty, Doran C. *Working with People*. Nashville: Broadman Press, 1986.

McCurley, Steve. *Volunteer Management Policies*. Downers Grove, Ill.: Heritage Arts Publishing, 1990.

Malony, H. Newton, Jr. *Win-Win Relationships*. Nashville: Broadman and Holman, 1995.

Martin, Glen and Gary McIntosh. *The Issachar Factor*. Nashville: Broadman and Holman, 1994.

Morris, Margie. *Volunteer Ministries*. Cincinnati: Standard Publishing, 1994.

Review and Expositor, vol. 78, No. 1 (Winter 1981) Southern Baptist Theological Seminary (issue on "Church Staff Relations").

Senter, Mark. *Recruiting Volunteers in the Church*. Wheaton, Ill.: Victor Books, 1990.

Smith, Donald P. *Empowering Ministry: Ways to Grow in Effectiveness*. Nashville: Cokesbury, 1996.

Stephens, Paul. *Liberating the Laity*. Downers Grove, Ill.: InterVarsity Press, 1985.

Weems, Marion Lee. *Staff Leadership and Teamwork*. Ft. Worth: Southwestern Baptist Theological Seminary, 1990.

White, Ernest O. *Becoming a Christian Leader*. Nashville: Convention Press, 1985.

Williams, Dennis E., and Kenneth O. Gangel. *Volunteers for Today's Church*. Grand Rapids: Baker Books, 1993.

Wilson, Marlene. *How to Mobilize Church Volunteers*. Minneapolis: Augsburg Publishing House, 1983.

Wright, H. Norman. *How to Get Along with Almost Anyone*. Dallas: Word Publishing, 1989.

Endnotes

CHAPTER ONE

1. The differences between a "call" and an "appointment" system of ministerial placement require some adjustments in a minister's start-up work. Adapt these suggestions based on your situation.

2. For help crafting ministry strategy, see items in the appendix. Also see Robert D. Dale, *Leading Edge* (Nashville: Abingdon Press, 1996) for a biblical perspective on ministry strategies.

3. Robert D. Dale, *To Dream Again* (Nashville: Broadman Press, 1981).

4. For more information, see chapter 7.

5. For more information, see chapter 3.

CHAPTER TWO

1. This is an assumption that frequently exists only as an ideal. Church leaders are prone to become positioned as either job- or person-oriented. This author views the ideal as workable and practical in churches in which evaluation and adjustment are normal parts of educational administration.

2. For assistance with specialized church activities, see "Administering Specialized Educational Activities," by Jerry M. Stubblefield, in *Christian Education Handbook, Revised Edition,* Bruce P. Powers, ed. (Nashville: Broadman and Holman Publishers, 1996).

3. Most denominations provide guidance regarding committees and officers. Usually a manual or annual issue of a periodical provides descriptions of duties and suggestions for work. Request information at your denominational office or bookstore. The editor wishes to express appreciation to J. Ralph Hardee, author of some of the material on this topic in the first edition, for his insights related to material in the figures.

4. Information concerning a church council is given later in the chapter.

5. Additional information and guidance in all areas related to educational ministry is available in the companion volume to this edition: *Christian Education Handbook, Revised Edition.* For information related to a *specific* program or organization, consult your denominational office or religious publisher for recommended resources.

CHAPTER THREE

1. See chapter 2 for organizational details.

2. For a good source on working productively with volunteers, see Marlene Wilson, *How to Mobilize Church Volunteers* (Minneapolis: Augsburg Publishing, 1983), 28–36.

3. For more information on meeting management, see Robert D. Dale, *Ministers as Leaders* (Nashville: Broadman Press, 1984), especially chapter 4.

4. The number of relational bonds among people on a staff can be calculated by multiplying the total number of persons in the staff group by the total number minus one, and then dividing by two. For example, a staff of two contains only one relational bond, a staff of four has six bonds, a staff of ten has forty-five bonds, and a staff of fifty has 1,225 bonds.

5. For a profile of controlling members and how to cope with them, see Robert D. Dale, *Surviving Difficult Church Members* (Nashville: Abington Press, 1984).

6. For a discussion of mission as a dimension of congregational climate, see Robert D. Dale, *To Dream Again* (Nashville: Broadman Press, 1981) and, for an exploration of morale as an element of congregational climate, see Robert D. Dale, *Keeping the Dream Alive* (Nashville: Broadman Press, 1988).

7. Edwin L. Baker, "Managing Organizational Culture," *Management Review* (July 1980): 8.

CHAPTER FOUR

1. Legal and ethical issues change rapidly. Current information may be secured from the National Association of Church Business Administrators, from publications recommended by a professor of administration at a divinity school or seminary, or from the director of church relations at your denominational office. Portions of this section have been adapted from the original edition, prepared by Mark Short and compiled by Bruce P. Powers.

2. If you are unsure about the specific procedures for your church, consult the denominational office in your area.

3. This practice varies from denomination to denomination. The focus in this chapter is on churches with a congregational-style polity.

4. Adapted from Leonard E. Wedel, *Church Staff Administration* (Nashville: Broadman Press, 1978), 32.

5. The editor wishes to give credit to Mark Short for this analogy and his ideas related to the characteristics that follow.

6. The most effective tool for team development is a properly developed, properly administered evaluation/analysis system. Any church that desires improvement and skill development for its staff will design and implement such a system. Supervisors will have to be trained to make good use of this tool and workers will need to be led to see how it helps them in becoming more effective in their work. A detailed explanation of this process is found in Tim J. Holcomb, compiler, *Personnel Administration Guide* (Nashville: Convention Press, 1988), chapters 11 & 12.

CHAPTER SIX

1. This chapter is designed to assist church leaders with the specifics of fiscal responsibility, which usually are handled through the church office. The material included supplements the information in chapter 5 and provides background information for planning and budgeting presented in chapter 7. Information in this chapter has been adapted from material in the original edition prepared by Mark Short and compiled by Bruce P. Powers, editor.

2. Request information from your denominational office, religious bookstore, or a theological school.

CHAPTER ELEVEN

1. Chapters 8 and 9 have information and forms related to weddings.

CHAPTER TWELVE

1. It is now possible to pay for an annual license that will provide permission to use most musical works. CCLI is one such source: 1-800-234-2446.

CHAPTER FOURTEEN

1. James L. Sullivan, *Rope of Sand with Strength of Steel* (Nashville: Convention Press, 1974), 119. See also, James L. Sullivan, "Nature and Importance of a Local Church," *Baptist Polity* (Nashville: Broadman Press, 1983), 17–27.

CHAPTER SIXTEEN

1. See chapters 11 and 12 in Tim J. Holcomb, compiler, *Personnel Administration Guide* (Nashville: Convention Press, 1988), for a discussion of this process.

CHAPTER SEVENTEEN

1. Steven Findlay and Gina Rogers-Gould, "The Pressure Is Starting to Get to Our Children," *USA Today*, 8 July 1983, 4D.
2. Charles William Stewart, *Person and Professional* (Nashville: Abingdon Press, 1974), 75–78.
3. A basic and classic perspective on career development, particularly for men, is provided by Daniel J. Levinson, et al. *The Seasons of a Man's Life* (New York: Knopf, 1978).
4. For the original discussion of this model, see Robert D. Dale, "The Minister of Youth: Developing a System of Support" in *The Work of the Minster of Youth*, comp. Bob R. Taylor (Nashville: Convention Press, 1982), 95–107.
5. See Hans Selye's seminal work, *Stress Without Distress* (New York: Signet Books, 1974), 11–51.
6. For an overview of the burnout cycle, see Jerry Edelwich with Archie Brodsky, *Burnout: Stages of Disillusionment in the Helping Professions* (New York: Human Sciences Press, 1980), 28–29.

CHAPTER EIGHTEEN

1. This chapter is designed to help ministers in small churches see how to apply the material presented in the book. Administrative procedures usually are developed for medium and large churches; however, they can be scaled to fit any situation by a knowledgable leader. Consequently, many of the instructions and forms found throughout the book will apply to the material in this chapter.

CHAPTER TWENTY

1. I recall first using this term after reading James D. Glasse, *Putting It Together in the Parish* (Nashville: Abingdon Press, 1972).
2. I was helped in understanding these options when I read the process of vocational guidance presented in Len Sperry, et al., *You Can Make It Happen* (Reading, Mass.: Addison-Wesley Publishing Co., 1977).
3. Bruce P. Powers, ed., *Christian Education Handbook, Revised and Expanded Edition* (Nashville: Broadman & Holman, 1996).